ISLINGTON   Finsbury Library

9.30–5
Fri 9.30–1
Wed closed all day   w.

Library & C uote   r on the
ba   the item.
Item   enewed only once by telephone.

(LIB I)

Finsbury Library
245 St. John Street
London EC1V 4NB
Tel: 020 7527 7960

2

1

ISL/L

SILENT MAGIC

IVAN BUTLER

SILENT MAGIC

Rediscovering the silent film era

FOREWORD BY KEVIN BROWNLOW

Columbus Books
London

First published in Great Britain in 1987
by Columbus Books Limited,
19-23 Ludgate Hill, London EC4

Copyright © Ivan Butler 1987

Designed by Fred Price

British Library Cataloguing in Publication Data
Butler, Ivan
  Silent magic: rediscovering the silent
  film era.
  1. Silent films ——— History and criticism
  Rn: Edward Ivan Oakley Beuttler   I. Title
  791.43   PN1995.75

ISBN 0 86287 315 0

Typeset by Cylinder Typesetting, London
Printed and bound by
R. J. Acford Ltd., Chichester, Sussex

Contents

Foreword

Silent films are no longer the object of derision. Now they are being seen again in good prints, in large theatres, accompanied by live orchestras, people no longer dismiss them as jerky, flickering, ludicrously acted curiosities. Instead, they pack the houses. The revival of silent films with live orchestral accompaniment has spread around the world. Every week, news reaches us of another triumph, another discovery. A new term has entered the vocabulary: 'live cinema'.

All this has happened in an age when films are taken so much for granted that people snooze in front of them on TV. Once, the moving picture came as a miraculous gift to the common people, a burst of light in an existence all too often shrouded in gloom. How can we recapture that feeling, the moment when these films were first seen? One can dig out reviews, but professional critics seldom saw the film with a public audience. The ideal would have been a sort of Marcel Proust of the movies, able to describe it all in minute detail from, if not exactly a bed, at least a *seat* in the stalls. Alas, the movies were far too absorbing for anyone to take voluminous notes, let alone miss the matinée in the cause of writing them up. But all is not lost. Ivan Butler was there on our behalf. He was young and enthusiastic, with a remarkable memory, and sixty years later he demonstrates the impact these films had on him and his generation. He proves an ideal representative for those of us unfortunate enough to have missed that fabulous decade.

His memory has proved helpful to me on several occasions. In 1968, he told me that the 1926 Garbo film *The Temptress* once had a tragic ending instead of the rather banal happy ending with which I was familiar. His description, of Garbo reduced to roaming Paris as a streetwalker, so intrigued me that when I was working on the *Hollywood* television series I made a special request for it from MGM – and got it, to my surprise. Without Ivan Butler's astonishing recall, I might never have known of its existence.

Of course, he has refreshed his memory over the years. But some rare titles, hard to track down, have eluded him. I suspect he might revise his opinions were he to see them again. He would not be so taken with *Beau Brummel* (1924), a costume drama which seems pedestrian today, rather like its 'fifties remake, while he would be far more impressed with Clarence Brown's *Smouldering Fires* (1924), a sophisticated story and one of the most beautifully made films of that era.

But one cannot stress too strongly that the opinions in this book are the opinions *of that time*. They are what makes the book unique. His judgement as a teenager was remarkably prescient; again and again, he forecasts accurately the consensus of film history.

Ivan Butler saw films which have long been lost to us. For the sad truth is that two-thirds of the output of the 1920s have disappeared. This makes his book particularly valuable. And it may even cause some of those films to be rescued – simply by his having mentioned them. Many silent films fell into private hands and survive to this day in secret collections. If you know of old films, perhaps mouldering in an attic, tell us about them, c/o the publishers; you will be saving both a fragment of history, and of an art.

And now, as the lights dim, the curtains part, the conductor raises his baton and the titles fade in on the huge screen, prepare to surrender to the magic of the moving picture . . . the 'silent' film.

Kevin Brownlow

Acknowledgements

First and foremost my grateful thanks to Kevin Brownlow, who painstakingly read through the entire typescript and made numerous notes and constructive comments. Among these not only was he able to identify the first film I ever saw (in 1915) as, almost certainly, *The Pumpkin Race*, directed by Emile Cohl, but he also corrected some popular errors: Josef von Sternberg, for instance, is often credited with having directed certain scenes in *It* (1927), but he informed Brownlow personally that this was not the case and that confusion had been made with *Children of Divorce* (also 1927), in which he *did* participate. Both films starred Clara Bow.

The following books have been particularly useful for checking facts and refreshing memories:

The American Film Institute Catalog, Feature Films 1921-1930 (Bowker, 1971)

American Silent Film, W. K. Everson (Oxford, 1978)

The British Film Catalogue, 1895-1970, Denis Gifford (David & Charles, 1973)

Classics of the Silent Screen, Joe Franklin (Citadel, 1959)

Fifty Great American Silent Films, 1912-1920, Anthony Slide & Edward Wagenknecht (Dover, 1980)

Filmarama, vol. II, John Stewart (Scarecrow Press, 1977)

From Hollywood, DeWitt Bodeen (Barnes/ Tantivy, 1976)

The Griffith Actresses, Anthony Slide (Barnes/ Tantivy, 1973)

The International Film Encyclopedia, Ephraim Katz (MacMillan, 1980)

J. Stuart Blackton, Marian Blackton Trimble (Scarecrow Press, 1985)

London After Midnight, Philip J. Riley (Cornwall Books, 1985)

The Movies, Griffith, Mayer & Bowser (Columbus Books, 1981)

Napoléon, Kevin Brownlow (Cape, 1983)

The Parade's Gone By, Kevin Brownlow (University of California Press, 1968)

A Pictorial History of the Silent Screen, Daniel Blum (G.P. Putnam's Sons, 1953)

Selected Film Criticism, 1921-1930, edited by Anthony Slide (Scarecrow Press, 1982)

The Shattered Silents, Alexander Walker (Elm Tree Books, 1978)

Some Day We'll Laugh, Esther Ralston (Scarecrow Press, 1986)

The Story of Cinema, vol. I, David Shipman (Hodder & Stoughton, 1980)

Who Was Who on Screen, Evelyn Mack Truitt (Bowker, 1983).

In writing on certain films I have also drawn on my *Cinema in Britain*, *Horror in the Cinema* and *Religion in the Cinema*, all published by the Tantivy Press.

Acknowledgements for illustrations are due to the Kobal Collection and the National Film Archive of the British Film Institute, with thanks to Dave King of the former, and the staff in both cases, for their trouble in hunting out some rare stills; and to Allen Eyles for two unique photographs of the old Marble Arch Pavilion from his personal collection.

Finally my warm thanks to Gill Rowley of Columbus Books for her help and encouragement during the making of this book.

I.B.

Introduction

The revival of interest in the silent years has been unprecedented, stimulated largely by the restoration of films that for years have been known only by name and by the enterprise and adventurousness of television companies in backing such notable work. Silent enthusiasts, whose numbers are steadily increasing, owe an incalculable debt to such miracles of reclamation as those achieved by Kevin Brownlow and David Gill, accompanied by the wonderfully evocative scores of Carl Davis; by Raymond Rohauer and others who have rescued disintegrating or long-lost prints; to television screenings of expertly shortened versions of such classics as Griffith's *Orphans of the Storm* and *Blood and Sand* starring Valentino, with an excellent informative commentary.

Much literature is now available on the subject, but for many years it has been written (often superbly) by writers too young to remember in person what 'going to the pictures' in the silent days was like. This book is intended as a first-hand account, mainly of the 1920s, based as far as possible on personal memory, by someone of an age to have 'been there' at the time. Simply by what might be described as natural wastage our numbers are diminishing year by year and soon there will be nobody left to record, from experience, something of a period that is already part of history.

After a brief summary of the earlier period the films of the 'twenties are grouped year by year. Film dating is a notoriously tricky business, not least because copyright dates for these early films are not always available: it may be found, therefore, that a production listed here as, say, 1928 may be found elsewhere as 1927, depending on whether the reference is to copyright year, completion, trade showing, first public screening or general release. Take *Wings* as an example. It had an American première in 1927, a British première in 1928 and a general release (with added sound effects) in 1929. All three dates will be found given preference separately in different reference material. The actual year is not critical in the case of this book but I have tried to be as consistent as possible.

With few exceptions the films were seen during or shortly after the decade of the 1920s. The great majority are from America – foreign and even British productions were fairly few and far between for the average cinemagoer of those years.

Here may be found the story of the initial reception in Britain and America of Abel Gance's *Napoléon* – a far cry from the rapturous admiration that greeted it in the 1980s; the troubled story of the production of Greta Garbo's second American film, *The Temptress*; of Myrna Loy's slow progress through dozens of small-scale Warner Bros. productions (frequently as a slant-eyed Oriental) towards ultimate stardom; of what happened to Louise Brooks after she left Hollywood in disgust (returning after her double triumph with G.W. Pabst in Germany); of the not-always-successful attempts to create the requisite atmosphere of reverence around the production of Cecil B. DeMille's *The King of Kings*; and many others.

Apart from what are generally regarded as 'important' productions I have included many of smaller pretensions but often equal merit as entertainment. Others are of historical interest, have in their cast lists players still well remembered, or were particularly popular at the time.

Even within the limits of personal viewing stringent selection is inevitable. The American Film Institute Catalog alone covers some 6,600 feature films for the decade. Shorts and serials have in general been excluded, or referred to briefly as a class. Few westerns are mentioned; there were plenty of them, but the majority of 'cowboy pictures' were somewhat look-alike and often difficult to remember apart. The *genre* did not really come into its own until the arrival of sound could capture the thunder of hoofbeats (though coconut shells often did not do too badly), the whang of bullets hitting rocks and the thud of falling Indians.

Following the main text for each year I have inserted some details about the world at large to provide a background of events which had some direct or indirect influence on the cinema, followed by listings relating to the movie world, the theatre, literature, music and fashion.

As far as possible I have tried to assess the films as they appeared to us at the time. There is a vogue for re-evaluating films made many years ago according to present-day standards and opinions. This is an entertaining exercise, but in many ways a rather pointless one. A film is made for its time – to reflect the attitudes or present the problems of its own day, to meet the critical judgements of its own audiences, to interest or entertain the public of its own era. It is rooted in the conventions and bound by the technical limitations of the day. Referring to Chaplin, René Clair commented, 'To appreciate the full significance of his work, one has to go back to the period when it was created. That is true of all major contributions to the cinema. Time muffles their power to shock and diminishes their responsibility, because they remain exactly the same while their audiences change.'

The same applies, I would suggest, to minor contributions. Contemporary criticism was often (and often deservedly) severe; but it is surely unreasonable to judge a work loftily from a period of which it could know nothing. Who knows what critical reaction to the cherished, award-laden masterpieces of today will be in sixty years' time?

This, then, is the *raison d'être* of this book – an attempt to describe how the silent films appeared to filmgoers of their period, what it was like to go to the 'pictures', or 'flicks' (if you wished to sound superior), in the 1920s. I hope *Silent Magic* may conjure up memories for former enthusiasts, but even more that it will encourage the interest of younger readers, many of whom have already recognized that before the advent of television the most universally popular and influential of all forms of creative entertainment had a great deal to offer.

'The silent pictures were the purest form of cinema.'
Alfred Hitchcock

The Early Years

I saw my first film in 1915 – from the wrong side of the screen. It was at a private show at a school and my mother had brought me in, aged all of six, by a door at the back of the room. We were probably there for only a few minutes before someone discovered us and found us seats in the proper place. I have no memory of the programme apart from that brief glimpse, through wooden struts holding the makeshift screen in place, of what appeared to be a lot of pumpkins careering down a hill to the accompaniment of raucous laughter of (to me) enormous boys almost drowning a well-thumped piano. It must have been a very primitive production, probably a comedy short made some years previously, but in those pre-television days it was miraculous to a child that a picture could move at all – and I was hooked.

It was perhaps an auspicious year in which to start a lasting relationship – the year of *The Birth of a Nation,* sometimes described as The Birth of the Cinema. In truth, of course, the cinema had been a lusty infant for over a decade, experimenting and stretching its limbs in all directions. In 1893 the first recorded film in America was made when Edison employee Fred Ott sneezed for the camera – in close-up. In the same year Cecil Hepworth in Britain photographed *Alice in Wonderland* in sixteen dissolving scenes, with May Clark posing as Alice, Mr and Mrs Hepworth as some of the creatures she met, and photographer Geoffrey Faithfull as a playing card. Three years later sex reared an early head when May Irwin and John C. Rice performed The Kiss – also in close-up. Despite the fact that they were man and wife enacting a moment from a theatrical production their osculatory activities apparently aroused controversy and threats of censorship.

The American narrative film itself took a step forward with the famous Edwin S. Porter production, *The Great Train Robbery* (1903), the seminal western; two years later Hepworth followed on in Britain with the equally famous *Rescued by Rover,* which might be described as the seminal *Rin-Tin-Tin.* This was very much a family affair, with his wife as author, his baby as victim and his dog as hero.

Companies were being formed and studios opened everywhere. In America, for example, there were Vitagraph (1899), Kalem (1907), Keystone (1912), Universal (1912), Fox (first production 1914), Paramount (formed in 1914 to release Famous Players-Lasky productions) and United Artists (1919). In Britain there were Walturdaw (1905), Merton Park Studios (1912), Bushey Studios (1912), Twickenham Studios (1913), Boreham Wood Studios (1914), Worton Hall Studies, Isleworth (1914), the Stoll Film Company (1918) and the Welsh-Pearson Company (1918). In France 1896 was a key year, that of the formation of Pathé Frères; concurrently, Méliès was making films for his Robert Houdin theatre, Lumière was giving the first public

A matinée queue forming outside the Marble Arch Pavilion, Oxford Street, London, in 1926, when Matheson Lang was a major British star.

performance of his Cinématographe and Leon Gaumont was building his French studio. Gaumont's London branch, Gaumont British, was established two years later. In Germany the great and influential UFA company was formed in 1917.

Experiments with both sound and colour were started almost as soon as pictures moved. Edison and Pathé were trying out methods of sound synchronization in the 1890s, as was a German company in 1900. By 1907 two British systems, Cinematophone at Walturdaw and Vivaphone at Hepworth's, were established. As regards colour, G.A. Smith's Kinemacolour was used to record King George V's Delhi Durbar in 1912. Other processes were the American Prizma and the French Gaumont Chromophone. Experiments began on the most famous of all, Technicolor, in 1915, but it did not come into commercial use until the 1920s. Tinting was widely used through much of the silent period in both major and minor productions, for artistic and dramatic purposes and often to very beautiful effect. It could in fact be said to be the rule rather than the exception, generally taken for granted by the cinema audience.

Buildings were being converted or especially erected for the showing of moving pictures:

1902: the Electric, Los Angeles – the first purpose-built hall in America;
1905: the Bioscope (later known as the Biograph), Wilton Road, Victoria, London, claimed to be the first cinema converted from a row of shops;

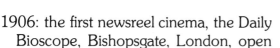
1906: the first newsreel cinema, the Daily Bioscope, Bishopsgate, London, open 12 noon to 9 p.m., admission 2*d* (1p) and 4*d* (2p);

1907: Central Hall, Colne, Lancashire, one of the first buildings in Britain erected exclusively for film shows;

1914: the Marble Arch Pavilion, London, one of the first 'luxury' theatres.

Popular film magazines were already starting to appear in America; among them were the *Motion Picture Story Magazine* (later the *Motion Picture Magazine*), which first came out in February 1911, beating by a narrow margin *Photoplay* (1911), both high-quality publications. *Motion Picture Classic* and *Picture Play* followed in 1915 and *Shadowland* in 1919. The long-lived British *Picture Show* appeared in 1919. It lasted until 1960 but in later years was a mere shadow of its former self.

Most of the major films made during these early years could still be seen in the 'twenties – and in many cases, of course, much later. By 1912 the feature-length movie was gradually becoming established, and astute producers were quick to realize the box-office potential of religious spectacles. The first major Life of Christ appeared that year, Sidney Olcott's *From the Manger to the Cross*, reputedly conceived by scenarist Gene Gauntier while she was in delirium following an attack of sunstroke. The film was shot in Egypt and Palestine, and Miss Gauntier herself played the Virgin Mary. Henderson Bland, dignified and moving as the Prince of Peace, later distinguished himself as a military hero in the First World War.

Judith of Bethulia, the apocryphal story of how Holofernes lost his head, was D. W. Griffith's first entry into large-scale production, already revealing his skill in handling large crowds and vistas without losing individual interest. The cast included most of the later Griffith repertory players – Blanche Sweet, H. B. Walthall, Robert Harron,

Mae Marsh and, in a minor part, Lillian Gish.

Cecil B. DeMille's first feature, *The Squaw Man*, co-directed with Oscar Apfel, appeared in 1914 – the story of a self-sacrificing British army captain who, for love's sake, accepts the blame for embezzling charity funds, leaves England in disgrace for Wyoming, marries an Indian girl with the intriguing name of Nat-U-Rich and (after a hectic time in which the girl commits first murder, then suicide) succeeds to an earldom; he then returns to England with his half-breed son and his first love, thenceforward to live, it may be hoped, a more relaxed life. It went down well with the public and DeMille remade it in 1918.

The first American feature comedy, *Tillie's Punctured Romance* (with Marie Dressler, Mabel Normand, and Charlie Chaplin in a supporting role), appeared in the same year, as did George Pearson's full-length Sherlock Holmes story, *A Study in Scarlet*, though Holmes himself has a lesser share in the action than revenge and murder among the Mormons, with Cheddar Gorge and the Southport (Lancashire) sands representing the Rockies and Salt Lake.

The interior of the Marble Arch Pavilion as it was in 1925: spartan by comparison with the standards of later 'luxury' theatres, but comfortable and attractive in its simplicity.

The Birth of a Nation dwarfed everything in 1915. I remember seeing it in the 'twenties, when its racial and political implications aroused little wrath in the audience; we thrilled to the rescue of Lillian Gish from an American actor in black-face by the galloping white-robed horsemen in the same way as we did to any other heroine in any similar predicament, such as finding herself trapped in an encampment attacked by Red Indians. In the same year Theda Bara worked her wicked wiles on a somewhat starchily upright man in *A Fool There Was* who 'made his prayer to a rag, a bone and a hank of hair', as described in Kipling's poem 'The Vampire', and gave rise to the coinage of a popular diminutive to denote such harpies. And Sessue Hayakawa (years later to rule the roost by the River Kwai) redressed the balance by branding the shoulder of an

The villainous Negro – played by white actor Walter Long in black-face – is captured by the Ku Klux Klan after his attempted rape of 'The Dear One' in *The Birth of a Nation*.

Opposite: dancing (and other) girls in one of the Babylonian sequence from *Intolerance*.

extravagant wife – not his own – in *The Cheat*. According to a contemporary review this revealed 'the beastliness of his Oriental nature'. Theda Bara, incidentally, often ridiculed in later years for her voluptuous vamping and her colourful pseudonym (supposedly an anagram of Death Arab), was apparently, under her true name of Theodosia Goodman, a normal, intelligent and commonsensical young woman.

As *The Birth of a Nation* bestrode 1915, so the equally famous *Intolerance* from the same director bestrode 1916. However, with

the war well under way in Europe and casting its shadow over America, Griffith's great four-in-hand was against the spirit of the times. In addition audiences were confused by the interweaving stories and the quick cutting, and the film lost a fortune.

A film more directly concerned with the subject of war was Thomas Ince's *Civilization* – a spectacular but somewhat artless plea for peace set in a mythical country oddly called *Wredpryd* (Red Pride?), and concerned with a submarine commander whose body is taken over by the spirit of Christ and used as a mouthpiece against war. The aggressive King of Wredpryd is similarly inhabited, and stops fighting. In the real world, alas, the takeover would probably have been less effective. The most distinguished film of the year on the same topic was Herbert Brenon's *War Brides*. Derived from the *Lysistrata* theme, it stars the legendary Russian actress Nazimova as a young wife who, refusing to comply with a decree that women should bear more children solely to carry on the conflict, eventually kills both herself and her unborn baby. The grim story is told with great power and Nazimova gives a performance of tragic intensity.

In contrast, embattled Britain turned from the horrors of the First World War to an old tear-jerker, *Comin' Thro' the Rye* (from Cecil Hepworth, with Alma Taylor and Stewart Rome), *She* (from Will Barker with, of all people, Alice Delysia) and *Ultus, the Man from the Dead*, the opening film of a series made in response to a request for a British partner to Louis Feuillade's notable thriller *Fantômas*. There was also a full-length British documentary, *The Battle of the Somme*, to which all we schoolboys were conscientiously taken, though we would have preferred *Ultus*.

Alla Nazimova, the legendary Russian star (born in Yalta), who gives a performance of tragic intensity in Herbert Brenon's powerful pacifist film *War Brides*.

It was, however, very successful and was quickly followed by *Arras, Ancre* and *St Quentin*. An interesting American production of 1916 that did not concern war was Paramount's *Oliver Twist* (directed by James Young); it featured a girl (Marie Doro) in the title role, and Tully Marshall, a fine character actor whom we shall meet again, as Fagin.

The big one of 1917, at least in production values, was Cecil B. DeMille's *The Little American*, released just after the United States entered the war. In it Mary Pickford, the World's Sweetheart, put up her curls, was nearly drowned in a torpedoed liner (but saved in time), nearly raped in the dark by a former lover, now a German officer (but saved in time), and nearly shot as a spy (but saved in time). Technically much of the film was outstanding for its period. The sinking of the *Lusitania* (thinly disguised as the *Vertania*), with the terrified diners in panic, the table decorations floating higher and higher up the saloon walls, Mary in her party dress in water up to her pretty waist – all this remains in the memory over the years. There is some oddly twisted morality – the German officer (Jack Holt) is regarded as heroic for betraying his country but betrayal the other way round, against England or her Allies, is contemptible – and some crudely blatant symbolism involving a shattered Calvary. But this view is, of course, with benefit of hindsight. It was, in fact, typical wartime propaganda, and we swallowed it wholesale. As DeMille disarmingly remarked, 'The Little American was timely, as I knew it would be.'

Away from the battlefields the enchanting Marguerite Clarke enchanted us with a 'real-life' version of *Snow White and the Seven Dwarfs* (called here simply *Snow White*), with Creighton Hale as her sleep-banishing Prince and some effective trick photography, anticipating Disney by some twenty years. She enchanted us again the following year in Maurice Tourneur's *Prunella*, from the pierrot play by Laurence Housman and Granville Barker.

21

Mary Pickford (centre) and other passengers enjoying a somewhat static final dance before disaster strikes in *The Little American.*

Mary Pickford carried off a remarkably successful double in Marshall Neilan's *Stella Maris,* portraying with equal sympathy the pretty, ringleted little invalid and the poor, ugly slut who sacrifices herself for the other's happiness. The film was notable for some remarkable examples of early double photography. In contrast, Mabel Normand's *Mickey,* possibly her masterpiece and long delayed in release, was a rollicking comedy-drama with action thrills almost worthy of a female Douglas Fairbanks. Sadly, by the time the film was released Mabel Normand's career was in decline. She had already broken her

long association, professional and personal, with Mack Sennett and signed up with Goldwyn. Her private life was hectic and she was suspected of taking drugs. In 1922 her name was linked with the mysterious circumstances surrounding the murder of director William Desmond Taylor; and not long afterwards her chauffeur was found standing over the wounded body of millionaire Cortland S. Dines holding a pistol which belonged to her. Dines recovered and the chauffeur was acquitted, but this second scandal virtually completed the ruin of her career. In 1926 she married actor Lew Cody, who had played the 'heavy' in *Mickey,* and in 1930 she died.

Hearts of the World (1918) was D. W. Griffith's war propaganda effort, originally made partly to help persuade America to join the Allies, but by the time it was completed they had already done so. Though portraying the enemy as rather extravagant monsters of infamy, and glorying in such titles as 'Month after month piled up with its legend of Hunnish crimes in the book of God', it contained some reasonably realistic front-line sequences (Griffith researched by visiting the battlefields in France) and sensitive performances from Lillian Gish and Robert Harron. The scene where the distraught girl wanders around the ruined countryside trailing her wedding dress is a classic. Noël Coward made his film début in this film, playing a tiny part as a farm lad.

Of the plot of *The Claw* (also 1918) I can remember little, but it must have been a harrowing experience. It starred such stalwarts of the period as Jack Holt and Milton Sills, together with the equally admired Clara Kimball Young, and their tragic predicaments worked so violently upon the sensibilities of my sister (then about seven years old) that she startled the audience in the old Polytechnic Hall, Upper Regent Street, by suddenly screaming, 'Take me out! It's too sad! It's too sad!' Parental comforting failed to stop the flood of tears and we all (myself, no doubt, protesting volubly) had to leave the theatre. It is an interesting illustration of the fact that television has nothing on the old silent cinema in its power to affect the sensitive young mind!

In 1919 Griffith once again dominated the screen with his most moving – and in many opinions his greatest – achievement, the exquisite *Broken Blossoms,* starring Lillian Gish and Richard Barthelmess and based on one of Thomas Burke's unique Limehouse stories, *The Chink and the Child.* In its original form, with the original tinting, it was an experience of unforgettable beauty. The second Griffith feature of the year was *True Heart Susie,* overshadowed by *Broken Blossoms,* which had appeared just a short time before, but a rural romance of considerable charm. Playing the 'other girl' in the love triangle was Clarine Seymour, near the end of a tragically short career; shortly after

Lillian Gish as Lucy, 'The Child', and Donald Crisp as the brutal Battling Burroughs in *Broken Blossoms,* D. W. Griffith's adaptation of Thomas Burke's Limehouse tale *The Chink and The Child.*

making *The Idol Dancer* later in the year, also for Griffith, she died following an operation for strangulated intestines, at the age of twenty.

From Cecil B. DeMille came his version of J. M. Barrie's *The Admirable Crichton,* renamed with an eye on the box-office *Male and Female.* Barrie's caustic comment on class distinctions is softened, and he must have been astonished to find his wealthy socialite heroine (played by Gloria Swanson) suddenly if briefly transmogrified into a Christian slave in Babylon – courtesy of

W. E. Henley. However, it is an entertaining romp and noteworthy for the appearance of the famous DeMille bath-tub. In a busy year he also made the first two of his moralistic social comedy-dramas (often regarded as his best work), *Don't Change Your Wife*, and *For Better, For Worse*, both starring Miss Swanson.

Last but not least in this period leading up to the 'twenties was the first appearance as director of Erich von Stroheim, with *Blind Husbands*. Although basically an eternal triangle drama, the film already revealed glimpses of the potential if often wayward genius about to develop in the next decade. Stroheim's original title was *The Pinnacle* (the climax takes place on a mountain summit) but it was changed against his will – the first of many such disagreements. Leading

Gloria Swanson, commendably calm as danger threatens in C. B. DeMille's *Male and Female* – a sequence not found in Barrie's original play.

Opposite: less gorgeously attired and possibly more restful, if not wholly happy: Gloria Swanson on the desert island in *Male and Female*.

players were Sam De Grasse, von Stroheim himself and Francelia Billington – about whom, despite her imposing name, little seems to be known. The film was very successful, though one contemporary critic described it as 'in the end, just an adroitly presented silver-sheet melodrama'.

In other fields Hollywood was humming. Western stars such as Hoot Gibson, William Farnum, Harry Carey and above all William S. Hart – and their horses – flourished. Buck Jones, a popular western actor in the 'twenties

who died tragically in the disastrous fire at the Boston Cocoanut Grove nightclub in 1942, was starting his career. A stream of serial pictures kept patrons returning weekly to see ever-wilder variations on how he (or, just as often, she) achieved freedom from imminent death 'with one bound'. There were *The Adventures of Kathlyn* (Kathlyn Williams), *The Exploits of Elaine* (Pearl White), *The Hazards of Helen* (Helen Holmes, who specialized in dangers on the railway), *The Man Who Disappeared* (Marc MacDermott, who in the next decade was to lose his life twice on account of Greta Garbo), *The Perils of Pauline* (Pearl White, back for more), *The Iron Claw* (and for still more), *The Girl and the Game* (Helen Holmes also seeking further punishment), *The Perils of Thunder Mountain* (Antonio Moreno, also, strangely enough, to suffer at the hands of Garbo) and dozens, even hundreds, of others.

It was high noon for comedy shorts, with Harold Lloyd (known first as Willie Work, then as Lonesome Luke), Max Linder, Buster Keaton, Larry Semon, the undeservedly forgotten Lloyd Hamilton, the underrated Charley Chase (one of the very best light comedians), the ill-fated Roscoe (Fatty) Arbuckle, Chester Conklin, mountainous Mack Swain, swivel-eyed Ben Turpin, Ford Sterling and the Keystone Kops pouring out their miniature masterpieces well into the next decade.

Laurel and Hardy made *Lucky Dog*, their first, quite untypical, appearance together, in 1917, though they were not to form their comedy partnership for several years. In the meantime both were very active on their own, Hardy often as a 'heavy' metaphorically as well as literally. Crowning all, of course, was Chaplin, whose last release before the 'twenties, *A Day's Pleasure*, was among his last short films.

If Britain is but thinly represented in this period immediately preceding the 'twenties it is mainly on account of the devastating effect of the war on the British film industry, which enabled the United States to tighten a grasp on the market which was to remain firm throughout the following decade. However, as we shall see, the contemporary idea that Britain could *never* produce a film of much worth was unjustified.

France and Germany, of course, were even more severely affected by the war. Nevertheless, the former could point to the Louis Feuillade series *Fantômas* (1913), *Les Vampires* (1915) and *Judex* (1916), strange, haunting visions of almost nightmare intensity (who could forget Musidora of *Les Vampires* in her skintight black garb?); and from Germany came macabre hints of future achievements in films such as *The Student of Prague* (1913) and *The Golem* (1914), the first directed by Stellan Rye, the second by Henrik Galeen and Paul Wegener, who also played in both. Directors Ernst Lubitsch and Fritz Lang and players Emil Jannings and Pola Negri were making their mark, and all would establish themselves in America during the coming decade.

Cinema-going in the Silent 'Twenties

During the early part of the 1920s my own cinema-going was restricted by the confinements of boarding-school during term time, and in the holidays (to a lesser extent) by the fact that at least in our neighbourhood 'the pictures', though tolerated and even enjoyed, were still regarded as a poor and slightly dubious relative of the live theatre, the picture gallery and the concert hall. Their passage towards respectability was not helped by scandals in Hollywood such as the 'Fatty Arbuckle Affair'. I can still recollect the atmosphere of something sinister and shuddersome that surrounded the very word 'Arbuckle' long after the trials (and complete acquittal) of the unfortunate comedian, even though my innocent ideas of what actually took place in that San Francisco apartment during the lively party on 5 September 1921 were wholly vague and inaccurate – if tantalizing. In his massive history of American cinema, *The Movies,* Richard Griffith writes, 'During the course of the First World War the middle class, by imperceptible degrees, became a part of the movie audience.' 'Imperceptible' might be regarded as the operative word. However, when it comes to paying surreptitious visits a great many obstacles can be overcome by a little guile and ingenuity, and I don't remember feeling particularly deprived in that respect. I managed to see most of what I wanted to see.

Our 'local' was the cosy little Royal in Kensington High Street, London – a bus journey away. The Royal has been gone for half a century, its demise hastened by the erection of a super-cinema at the corner of Earl's Court Road. To the faithful it was known not as the Royal but as the Little Cinema Under the Big Clock in the High Street. The clock itself is gone now, but on a recent visit I though I could spot its former position by brackets that remain fixed high in the brick wall. The entrance to the cinema was through a passageway between two small shops, discreetly hidden except for two frames of stills and a small poster. A pause at the tiny box-office, a turn to the left, a step through a swing door and a red baize curtain, and one was in the enchanted land – not, however, in sight of the screen, because that was flush with the entrance, so you saw a grossly twisted pulsating picture which gradually formed itself into shape as, glancing backwards so as not to miss anything, you groped your way up to your seat. To the right of the screen was the clock in a dim red glow, an indispensable and friendly feature of nearly all cinemas in those days, and a warning – as one was perhaps watching the continuous programme through for the second run, that time was getting on. Prices were modest: from 8*d* (3p), to 3*s* (15p). This was fairly general in the smaller halls; cheaper seats were available in some, particularly in the provinces, others – slightly more imposing – demanded slightly more for the back rows, possibly with roomier seats and softer upholstery, but such elitism was not, to my memory, practised at the Royal.

Projection was to our unsophisticated eyes generally good, preserving the often marvellously crisp and well graded black-and-white photography. Programmes were changed twice weekly (but the cinemas were closed on Sundays, at any rate during the early years) and continuous from about 2 o'clock. They consisted as a rule of a newsreel such as the *Pathé Gazette* with its proudly crowing cockerel (silent, of course), a two-reel comedy (sometimes the best part of the entertainment), *Eve's Film Review*, a feminine-angled magazine the high spot of which was the appearance of Felix the Cat walking, and, finally, the feature film. This was before the days when the double-feature programme became general. Somewhere between the items there would be a series of slide advertisements – forerunner of Messrs Pearl and Dean – which always seemed to include a glowing picture of Wincarnis among its local and 'forthcoming' attractions. The average moviegoer of those days (much as today, though perhaps to a greater extent) went to see the star of a film rather than the work of its director; Gish rather than Griffith, Bronson more than Brenon, Bow more than Badger, Swanson more than DeMille – though as the years went by the names of the directors became more familiar and their importance more fully recognized. Criticism was often surprisingly informed and uncompromising.

Musical accompaniment at the Royal was provided by a piano during the less frequented hours, supplanted by a trio who arrived at a fixed time regardless of what was happening on the screen. I remember well the curious uplift we felt as the three musicians arrived, switched on their desk lights, tuned up and burst into sound, perhaps at a suitable . moment in the story, perhaps not. Meanwhile the pianist (always, I recollect, a lady) packed up and left for a well deserved rest and cup of tea. The skill of many of these small cinema

groups, even in the most modest conditions, was remarkable; their ability to adapt, week after week, often with two programmes a week and with little or no rehearsal, to events distortedly depicted a few feet before them, was beyond praise. The old joke about *William Tell* for action, 'Hearts and Flowers' for sentiment, the *Coriolan* overture for suspense and that's the lot, was an unfair and unfunny gibe.

I have described the old Kensington Royal in some detail as it was fairly typical of modest cinemas everywhere in Britain at that time. Most were at least reasonably comfortable and gave good value for little money, maintaining decent standards of presentation. Very few deserved the derogatory term 'flea-pit', though 'mouse parlour' might sometimes have been an accurate description. On one occasion the scuttering of mice across the bare boards between the rows of seats rather disturbed my viewing of a W. C. Fields film (*Running Wild*, I think it was), though the print was so villainously cut and chopped about that the story was difficult to follow in any case. But such cases were infrequent. I have forgotten the name of the cinema, and the town shall remain anonymous.

Sometimes, in early days, films would be shown in old disused churches, and it is supposedly through this that the employment of an organ for accompaniment in larger cinemas became general. The first exponent was probably Thomas L. Talley, who in 1905 built a theatre with organ specifically for the screening of movies in Los Angeles. It was soon discovered that such an organ could be made to do many things an orchestra could not: it could fit music instantaneously to changes of action, and simulate doorbells, whistles, sirens and bird-song, as well as many percussive instruments. On one later make of organ an ingenious device of pre-set keys made available no fewer than thirty-nine effects and even emotions, including Love (three different kinds), Anger, Excitement, Storm, Funeral, Gruesome, 'Neutral' (three

A typical, fairly modest but decorative early American cinema – inscribed 'For the Good of the Public'. Judging by the posters for the society drama *Forbidden Fruit* (directed by Cecil B. DeMille), the year is about 1921.

kinds), and FULL ORGAN. This last effect, with presumably all the above, plus Quietude, Chase, China, Oriental, Children, Happiness, March, Fire, etc. all sounding together, must have been awesome indeed.

Prominent among other developers of the cinema organ was Robert Hope-Jones, an Englishman who, already an organ-builder in Britain, emigrated to America in the 1900s for personal reasons. Owing to his later insolvency his patents eventually became the property of the Rudolph Wurlitzer Company, and in time every theatre organ became known by that name (much as every electric vacuum cleaner is apt to be known as a Hoover), though there were in fact other makes. By 1912 the Wurlitzer Company was shipping organs to theatres over a wide area. Remembered as a genius but no business-man, Hope-Jones became increasingly erratic in his behaviour, and in 1914 he committed suicide. Wurlitzer was pioneered in Britain in 1925 by Jack Courtnay, a Scot, formerly organist at the Stoll, in Kingsway, London. Perhaps the most famous of all was Reginald Foort, who made his public début in the Picture House, Edinburgh. Before long the organ interlude became an important part of any programme, as the grandly ornate and gleaming marvel rose majestically from the depths of the pit in a glowing flood of coloured light.

Nothing, however, could equal the effect of a large orchestra in a major cinema, which could be overwhelming. The accompaniment (of Carl Davis conducting the Thames Silents

Orchestra) to the 1983 screening of *The Wind,* for instance, was a revelation that will never be forgotten by those who had never before 'heard' a silent film in all its glory, particularly at the climax of the storm.

Admittedly, at times, particularly from the front seats, the presence of a busy group of players could be distracting; their lights would impinge on the screen, their busy fiddle bows and occasionally bobbing heads would make concentration on what the shadows behind them were up to a little difficult. In general, however, their mere presence, apart from the music, added immeasurably to the sense of occasion and until one got used to it the cold vacancy below the screen in the early days of sound had a chilling effect. Those cinema musicians are surely remembered with warm affection and regard by all of us who were fortunate enough to have heard them.

My own cinema-going problems eased considerably as the years passed. During the latter part of the decade I was touring the provincial theatres with the travelling repertory company run by Hamilton Deane, author of the dramatized version of Bram Stoker's *Dracula* which led to the Bela Lugosi film and all that followed from it. During my years with him he also launched Peggy Webling's play of Mary Shelley's *Frankenstein,* the first time, I think, that the Monster was portrayed on the stage – though not, of course, the first on screen. Being a junior member of the company I was not cast in all the numerous plays he produced, in equally numerous towns, and therefore often had evenings as well as afternoons free in which to indulge my obsession to the fullest extent.

As members of a visiting theatrical company we were frequently granted free admission to a town's picture houses – not always, however: the Provincial Cinematograph Theatres' circuit became notorious for its unfriendliness in that respect, despite the fact that the freedom was generally made reciprocal for cinema staff. On the whole, however, we were made welcome. This could, very occasionally, lead to embarrassment. On a hot, sleepy afternoon in Nottingham I was in the circle of an almost empty cinema watching *Silk Stockings,* a forgettable film but starring that most delightful of light comedy actresses Laura la Plante. The manager greeted me kindly, then came to sit beside me and, more in sorrow than in anger, spent some fifteen minutes pointing out what a disastrous effect our season at the Theatre Royal was having on his business – for Hamilton Deane was extremely popular in Nottingham. By the time he had sighed into silence my conscience was so stricken, realizing that I, one of his few customers, had got in for nothing, that I could not concentrate even on the predicaments of Miss la Plante, and consequently there is a gap in my memory of that film which is never likely to be filled.

It was during this period that the great 'Should cinemas open on Sundays?' debate was raging. Rules differed from town to town and on arrival in each one I and my fellow enthusiasts would be looking anxiously to see whether, as an alternative to the inevitable pub crawl, we would find an open picture-house in which to lighten the gloom of a 1920s provincial Sabbath.

One respect in which the way of the enthusiast was easier in those days was in the procuring of stills as a means of preserving enjoyable memories. Often a mere visit to an accommodating manager would result in an offer to take one's pick – without charge. I remember an occasion in Liverpool when after seeing a very entertaining Howard Hawks film, *A Girl in Every Port,* I approached one such gentleman and asked if he could spare me a still or two. 'Ah,' he said perspicaciously, 'I take it you want the lady in the black tights.' Doubtless blushing slightly, I confessed he was right, and I departed with three precious photographs of Louise Brooks which I treasured until Hitler, in one of his more heinous actions, bombed and destroyed my entire – and by then considerably expanded – collection.

In these days of multi-screen conglomerates it is difficult to imagine the awe and excitement that could be aroused by the greatest of the old-style movie palaces; the thick-piled carpets into which our feet sank, the powdered flunkies and scented sirens who took our tickets with a unique mixture of welcoming smile, condescending grace and unwavering dignity, the enormous chandelier-lit entrance halls, the statues, the coloured star portraits, the playing fountains, the rococo kiosks – all

leading through cathedral-dim corridors to the dark, perfumed auditorium itself, the holy of holies where we would catch our first glimpse of Larry Semon plastering Fatty Arbuckle with bags of flour.

Prices, of course, were rather grander than in the smaller, humbler houses, roughly (for variations were wide) from about 1s 3d (6p) or 2s 4d (12p) to 8s 6d (43p) or even 11s 6d (57p); but once you had paid your tribute to the box-office every effort was made to see that you felt you were welcome, were getting your money's worth and were someone of importance – that this whole occasion was especially for *you*.

Werner Krauss as the sinister hypnotist who, according to the finally altered script, turns out to be head of an institute for the insane, in *The Cabinet of Dr Caligari* – a film which has received more different interpretations than most since its first appearance.

1920

It may seem surprising to start a survey which will be largely devoted to the American film with one from Germany, but *The Cabinet of Dr Caligari* (directed by Robert Wiene) has been discussed, argued over and theorized about more than any film of its time. It is claimed to have influenced almost the whole aftermath of cinema, yet in itself to have been a dead end – much as, in the field of the novel, James Joyce's towering masterpiece, *Ulysses*, changed the world of fiction but led only to *Finnegan's Wake*. It has been described as a fine example of Expressionism transferred to the screen, and equally staunchly held up as Surrealist and not Expressionist at all; as the seminal horror film; as a foreshadowing of the Nazi mentality; as an anti-authoritarian plea for pacifism; as a study of insanity – all of which, together with other interpretations, may well be partly true. It was filmed entirely in the studio, in strange, macabre settings designed by artists affiliated with the Berlin *Sturm* group.

The story concerns a sinister hypnotist who displays a somnambulist (Cesare) at a fair in a small, cramped town, and who is afterwards accused of using this figure to commit a number of crimes. This is recounted in a garden to a man by a second man who represents himself as the hero who ultimately unmasks the hypnotist, but an epilogue reveals that the storyteller is himself insane,

the 'hypnotist' is a doctor, head of the Institute to which the garden belongs, and the whole story has been seen through the distorted vision of the madman. The film ends on a note of ambiguous hope – the doctor (whose expression even then does not really convince us of his benevolence) saying that the young man is now exorcized and can be cured. This framing story was not in the original script, but was placed round it by the director, to the anger of the original authors, Carl Mayer and Hans Janowitz. The narrative technique has been criticized as confusing, which may to some extent be true. I remember seeing the film a few years later screened by an eminent film society, when we all sat through it in respectful but slightly puzzled silence as two reels were projected in the wrong order – nobody appeared to notice this at the time.

Another German film of the year, a remake of *The Golem* (directed by Paul Wegener and Carl Boese) was equally fantastic but more straightforward, based on a mediaeval legend of a rabbi who makes a clay statue and brings it to life to protect his people from maltreatment. The figure behaves satisfactorily for a time but later develops its own personality and runs amok. With its sets of strange, twisted buildings and crooked streets filled with steeple-hatted inhabitants the film had a great if slightly sinister visual beauty. The

Lillian Gish unconsciously awaiting the arrival of Richard Barthelmess in what is still one of the most thrilling of all last-minute rescues, in Griffith's *Way Down East.*

child; when the baby dies, she takes refuge with a rich farmer, wins the love of his son (Richard Barthelmess), is turned out when her secret is discovered, flees through the inevitable storm on to the half-frozen river, and is rescued at the last moment by the son. All is forgiven and, to tie up the various sub-plots, a triple wedding ensues. The hardships of the famous ice-floe sequence have been vividly described by Lillian Gish, Barthelmess and others concerned. Most of it was done on location in horribly suitable conditions; some studio shots were cut in later, so expertly as to defy detection. The film follows the basic plot fairly closely; Griffith later released a shorter version, with some of the 'comic relief' scenes mercifully omitted. It was the first film in which I saw Lillian Gish, and even the thrilling climax hardly left a deeper impression than she herself in her quieter and more intimately dramatic moments. That anyone so sweet, gentle and vulnerable should have to put up with what she went through shocked us all to the roots. Burr McIntosh, a delightful, bald-headed, beetle-browed character actor who played the farmer-squire, was apparently so upset at the way he had to treat her that he kept apologizing for his callousness. He can still be seen ordering her out into the storm in one of the most famous (and most theatrically posed) of all silent film stills.

The film was enormously successful and well received, though Griffith was accused of lack of taste in allowing his heroine to 'writhe about a bed' during childbirth, and of some carelessness in his cutting – as when a character is seen to rise from a chair in close-up and then do so again (though the action is supposed to be continuous) in long-shot. Lillian Gish, we were doubtless glad to be assured (by Burns Mantle in *Photoplay* magazine), 'is thoroughly competent' and luckily her director, 'knowing her limitations, is careful not to press her too far'.

Douglas Fairbanks' *The Mark of Zorro* (directed by Fred Niblo) was also the mark of

similarity to the Frankenstein theme is obvious, with the significant difference that the 'figure' receives life by magical means in the former case, by scientific means in the latter. In both a little girl leads to the monster's undoing.

From the macabre gloom of Germany we move to the sunnier skies of America, where once again D. W. Griffith was dominating the screen with his version of *Way Down East,* a hoary old melodrama with the hoariest of old plots: an innocent country girl (Lillian Gish) is betrayed into a mock marriage by a rich cad (Lowell Sherman, doyen of rich cads), deserted by him and in due course bears his

his progression from silly-ass or go-getting American playboy types to later spectacular costume comedy-dramas and he was a little anxious as to what public reaction would be. He need not have worried. It was an enormous success and, though modestly made, was an excellent transition to his later swashbucklers. The story, that of an apparently effete and foolish Don who, disguised (not very efficiently, one would have thought) in black clothing and mask, fights corruption and rescues the maiden (Marguerite de la Motte) in the California of the early nineteenth century, has been so copied and travestied in sequels as to become stale, but when I first saw it in the early 'twenties there were some splendidly thrilling moments when the slashed 'Z' appeared as if by magic from his sword point, and when, at

John Barrymore at his most sinister in *Dr Jekyll and Mr Hyde* (based on the novel by Robert Louis Stevenson), preparing to club Brandon Hurst to death. Though in his later scenes Barrymore made use of facial make-up, his first 'change' from Jekyll to Hyde was done straight, in a single take.

the climax, that same sword flew quivering into the wooden beam – to be withdrawn later in *Don Q, Son of Zorro*. I remember too the beautifully timed moment of business when the fop dropped his broad-brimmed hat, recovering it unexpectedly and neatly by its long ribbon before it touched the floor.

John Barrymore's *Dr Jekyll and Mr Hyde* (directed by John S. Robertson) was a *tour de force* as he accomplished the famous 'change' with a minimum of make-up in the early stages, relying on his extraordinary powers of instant facial distortion. He made the first transformation in one cut. George Folsey, second cameraman on the film, had no idea what was to happen and nearly fainted when Barrymore reappeared with his face transformed and distorted.

As usual, liberties were freely taken with Stevenson's well-known morality thriller. Not only was Nita Naldi (a famous silent vamp) brought in as a seductive dancer, but Lord Henry Wotton, together with some of his witticisms, was filched from Oscar Wilde's *The Picture of Dorian Gray*, played by Brandon Hurst, an expert in the silkily sinister and soon to reappear in superb form as Lon Chaney's evil master in *The Hunchback of Notre Dame*. Barrymore was particularly successful as the Jekyll character, so much harder to make interesting than the enjoyably wicked and grotesque Hyde. Louis Wolheim, memorable as the coarse but kindly Katczinsky in *All Quiet on the Western Front* (1930), was brutishly impressive as one of Hyde's cronies.

Of 1920's two Mary Pickford films I saw only one, *Pollyanna* (directed by Paul Powell) – with curls – and wish I had seen the other, *Suds* (directed by Jack Dillon) – without them. In *Pollyanna* she extracts what fun she can out of the syrupy story (based on a novel by Eleanor H. Porter) of the little girl who is always Glad, and is never cast down even when knocked down by a car and crippled while rescuing a child. Probably, however much she behaved otherwise, she was as sure as everyone watching her that she would walk again in time for the final fade-out. *Suds*, by contrast, set in a laundry and based on a one-act play, *'Op o' Me Thumb* by Frederick Fenn and Richard Bryce, is a taut little story of love and sacrifice among the lowly, a gentle but sharp mixture of comedy and pathos. In 'opening it out' for the screen the makers seem to have let in a certain amount of whimsy, with dreams of a perfect lover arising from the soapsuds as the little laundress slaves away at her work. They also provided an alternative 'happy ending' – an unhappy (but far from rare) example of bowing to the box-office. The young workman who, as she washes his shirts, she tells the other girls is her fiancé, is played by Albert Austin, the long, lean actor who played important parts in many of Chaplin's famous shorts.

Lon Chaney's *The Penalty* (directed by Wallace Worsley) was a big step forward in his career, and the first in which he demonstrated his skill in letting his acting ability shine through grotesque physical deformity. As an underworld king whose legs have been amputated below the knee owing to a surgeon's mistaken diagnosis, he plays the entire film with them strapped to his thighs. The story is a fairly improbable one involving macabre plans of revenge, a somewhat optimistic demand that the surgeon replace the missing limbs with those of the fiancé of a girl who has fallen in love with the cripple, and an equally unlikely brain operation (performed on the unknowing Chaney) which completely changes his nature. Even all this, however, is rendered plausible – at least while the film lasts – by the actor's spellbinding presence.

Other American films included *Treasure Island* (directed by Maurice Tourneur), in which, following the example of Marie Doro in *Oliver Twist*, Jim Hawkins was played by a girl, Shirley Mason, sister of Viola Dana. It was a fairly faithful adaptation, lively and very attractive to look at. Lon Chaney played the blind Pew in a make-up less painful than that he wore for *The Penalty* but equally effective. Miss Mason was brave and boisterous enough to resign us completely to Jim's change of casting.

Huckleberry Finn was another very good adaptation, with Lewis Sargent as Huckleberry, Gordon Griffith as Tom Sawyer and two reliable character actresses, Edythe Chapman and Martha Mattox. It was directed

Mary Pickford as the little London laundress in *Suds*, with Albert Austin as the young lover who leaves a shirt to be washed and becomes her dream lover. One of her most charming, and underrated, films.

by William Desmond Taylor two years before his unsolved murder gave Hollywood a shaking of seismic proportions.

The Little Shepherd of Kingdom Come (directed by George Holt) was based on the book by John William Fox. A story with an American Civil War background, it starred Mary Pickford's brother Jack, with the 17-year-old Clara Horton, and was remade in 1928 with Richard Barthelmess.

The Last of the Mohicans (directed by Maurice Tourneur) was notable in particular for the scenes of the Fort William Henry massacre, with a cast that included Wallace Beery, Barbara Bedford and, as a marauding Indian, Boris Karloff.

Polly with a Past, an enjoyable version of the well-known stage comedy, featured rare appearances in silent films by Ina Claire and Clifton Webb.

While New York Sleeps (directed by Charles Brabin) was a three-story compilation note-worth for striking performances by Marc MacDermott, particularly in the episode in which, as a totally paralysed invalid able to use only his eyes, he is responsible for the capture of a murderer. Estelle Taylor, one-time wife of boxer Jack Dempsey, appears with him.

In *The Copperhead* (directed by Charles Maigne) a young Lionel Barrymore repeated his highly praised stage performance as a falsely accused Confederate spy – inevitably only a pale shadow of the original, but impressive in its own right.

From Britain not much of interest emerged. Cecil Hepworth described *Alf's Button* as the most successful film he ever made, and it can certainly be remembered with pleasure. The story, of an unusual type for Hepworth, was taken from W. A. Darlington's comic novel about a private soldier who finds that one of his uniform buttons was made from the metal of Aladdin's lamp and controls a genie who works wonders for him. The obvious possibilities for trick camera effects are fully exploited, and Leslie Henson – though apparently kept firmly in check by the director – obviously enjoys himself in the part of Alf.

Alma Taylor provides the female interest. A sequel, *Alf's Carpet,* was made in 1929 with two Danish comedians, known as both Pat and Patachon and Long and Short, in the parts of two busmen, Alf and Bill, who find a magic carpet. The British music-hall type of humour which worked so well in the first film was, however, missing from the second, which was far less successful.

George Pearson's *Nothing Else Matters* is a pleasantly sentimental little film about an old music-hall comic (Hugh E. Wright) who is brought to realize that Love Matters Most. It marks the first appearance of two leading stars of the decade: Betty Balfour (as a comic servant) and Mabel Poulton. The film cost £7,000 to make.

Most of the other productions were film versions of well-known novels such as *Bleak House* (directed by Maurice Elvey) with Constance Collier, *Wuthering Heights* (directed by A. V. Bramble) with Milton Rosmer, *Lorna Doone* (directed by H. Lisle Lucoque) and a current Regency best-seller, *The Amateur Gentleman* (directed by Maurice Elvey), with Langhorne Burton, Madge Stuart, and Alfred Paumier as the Prince Regent.

1920

The World at Large

Warren Harding elected President of the United States on the slogan 'Back to Normalcy'

Volstead Act (Prohibition) comes into force throughout the USA

Gandhi emerges as India's leader in the struggle for independence

First broadcasting stations open in Britain and America

Rapid growth of the Ku Klux Klan

'Black-and-Tans' introduced into Ireland by the British government

Woodrow Wilson awarded the Nobel Peace Prize

Joan of Arc canonized

Sacco and Vanzetti charged with murder in Massachusetts

Cinema

United Artists formed

Mary Pickford marries Douglas Fairbanks

Bruce Woolf forms British Instructional Films at Elstree

British Board of Film Censors established

Alfred Hitchcock at Islington, writing and art-designing for Famous Players

Michael Balcon enters films as a renter

Births: Dirk Bogarde, Montgomery Clift, Federico Fellini, Walter Matthau, Martin Ritt, Mickey Rooney

Theatre

Eugene O'Neill, *The Emperor Jones*
John Galsworthy, *The Skin Game*
J. M. Barrie, *Mary Rose*
Mary Roberts Rinehart and Avery Hopwood, *The Bat*
Jerome Kern, *Sally*

Fiction

Sinclair Lewis, *Main Street*
F. Scott Fitzgerald, *This Side of Paradise* (first novel)
D. H. Lawrence, *Women in Love*
Edith Wharton, *The Age of Innocence*
Agatha Christie, *The Mysterious Affair at Styles* (her first detective novel)
Zane Grey, *The Man of the Forest* (best-seller)

Music

Stravinsky, *Pulcinella* (ballet)
Ravel, *La Valse*
Villa-Lobos, *Chôros* no. 1
Vaughan Williams, *The Lark Ascending*

Popular Songs

'Japanese Sandman'
'Margie'
'Whispering'

Fashion Note

Skirts were now just above the ankles

The orgy scene from *The Four Horsemen of the Apocalypse*, in which German soldiers in war-torn France loot the treasures and abuse the occupants of a château. After the war the sequence was deleted for a time in order not to offend the former enemy. Josef Swickard as the venerably white-haired and distinctly unhappy owner can be seen to the left of the still.

Although *The Four Horsemen of the Apocalypse* is nowadays rarely afforded much space in histories of the silent period, there is little doubt that to the average filmgoer it was the Picture of the Year. In part this was, of course, because it heralded the arrival of Rudolph Valentino, though he had already appeared in some thirty pictures. In none of them, however, had he danced the famous tango. Even so, the scene that impressed us most at the time did not feature Valentino at all, nor the visionary Horsemen galloping across the sky, nor the capture of the town by the victorious Germans, nor even the quite impressive close with the Stranger, Tchernoff, intoning above a field of crosses, 'I knew them all', but the quiet, unspectacular sequence as Alice tends her husband, blinded and in a wheelchair, among similar victims of the war, and decides to fight her growing affection for the handsome Julio (Valentino). On the occasion when I saw it, a soulful soprano in the orchestra pit sang:

> I think of all you are to me,
> I think of all you cannot be . . .

I remember the tune to this day, but have no idea where the song came from.

The Four Horsemen, pre-dating King Vidor's *The Big Parade* by several years, is a key production in the history of the war film. The intentions of the makers were evidently to produce an anti-war picture. Wild coincidences are contrived to point the tragic irony of former friends meeting at the front on opposing sides and being blown up together (the basic story concerns the breaking up of an Argentinian family and their dispersal, one part to Germany, another to Paris), and the grief and waste of the conflict are emphasized. Against this are ranged the usual clichés of patriotic propaganda: villainous Germans or wooden-headed comic ones, the former pacifist (played with great dignity by Josef Swickard, a graduate from custard-pie Sennett comedies) who is brought to view his beliefs with shame, a feckless young man who is regenerated and meets death on the field of glory. So vilely do the 'licentious soldiery' behave in the French château they conquer – taking baths in the beautiful golden tub then carrying it away, insulting the helpless girls they force to wait on them, dressing up in women's under-clothing they filch from wardrobes and dancing on the table – that a whole sequence was cut from later versions to avoid upsetting the now forgiven enemy and replaced by a tantalizing title saying something to the effect of 'After a night of shame and terror . . . .'

Nevertheless the effect of the film when originally screened was overwhelming. Without doubt it caught the mood of the moment, bridging the gap between satiety and nostalgia. The apocalyptic visions, which may seem crude and flat when accompanied merely by a piano or trio, were tremendously effective sixty or more years ago with a full-

Dorothy Gish as Louise (left) and Lillian Gish as Henriette (right), her adopted sister, who become caught up in the French Revolution when they journey to Paris to seek a cure for the former's blindness, in *Orphans of the Storm*.

size orchestra thundering doom. The film brought deserved success not only to Valentino but to Rex Ingram, to his beautiful and accomplished wife, Alice Terry, and a fine supporting cast which included Wallace Beery as one of the villainous Huns, Stuart Holmes, Jean Hersholt and to Nigel de Brulier (soon to be seen as John the Baptist, among other less eminent religious persons).

Valentino's second release of the year, *The Sheik*, was a bit of a let-down. The story, from the famous 'romantic novel' by Mrs E. M. Hull, is of a British girl who goes into the desert dressed as a slave girl for fun and is seized by a 'sheik' who turns out not to be

one after all. Contemporary criticism was not always kind, in one instance declaring that 'the cheap banality of the novel shines out of the screen version – a shocker designed to set flappers blushing'. They may have blushed, but they flocked to be shocked, and the popular Valentino image is still generally clad in Arab robes. It was enjoyable hokum in its day, with Agnes Ayres emoting wildly as an attractive if improbable heroine. Adolphe Menjou plays the Sheik's novelist friend, glorying in the name of Raoul de Saint Hubert.

Douglas Fairbanks disappointed us, if only slightly. Perhaps he was awed by his august author, but after the gaiety of *The Mark of Zorro*, *The Three Musketeers* (directed by Fred Niblo) seemed to give too much attention to getting the period details right and too little to the acrobatic fun and games.

The Gish sisters appeared together in D.

W. Griffith's *Orphans of the Storm,* from a famous old French melodrama of 1874 originally entitled *The Orphans,* about two young girls, Louise and her adopted sister Henriette, who go to Paris for the former to be cured of blindness and become caught up in the French Revolution. They become separated; Louise falls into the clutches of an old harridan and is forced to beg in the streets, Henriette is abducted by a lecherous aristocrat but rescued by another one with more honourable intentions. Various events result in Henriette and her lover being sentenced to death by the usual Reign of Terror method, but they are saved, in one of Griffith's most thrilling last-minute rescues, by none other than Danton, who owes her a debt of gratitude and takes time off from weightier matters of state to repay it. Both Dickens and Carlyle are drawn on for additional material, fictional or historical.

Mary Pickford, in the title role of *Little Lord Fauntleroy,* faces the formidable Earl of Dorrincourt (Claude Gillingwater) in his grim family castle, and proceeds to melt his hard old heart with her charm and vivacity.

Apart from the climax the most famous scene is that in which Henriette, from an upper room, hears her blind sister begging in the street but is prevented from going to her. I happened to see a spectacular stage production of the play at the Lyceum Theatre, London, and would not care to say which was the most thrilling. Lucille la Verne, incidentally, the formidable character actress who plays the old harridan in the film, was later heard but not seen as the wicked Witch in Disney's *Snow White and the Seven Dwarfs.*

Mary Pickford pulled off another double in *Little Lord Fauntleroy* (directed by Alfred E.

Richard Barthelmess forgoes vengeance on his brother's attacker and risks being branded a coward when his mother (Marion Abbott) desperately pleads with him, in *Tol'able David*.

Green and her brother Jack Pickford), playing both Cedric and Mother Dearest. The story is too well-known to need elaboration, and the movie follows it fairly closely. It is visually attractive, with much charm and humour, if a little slow, and generally considered to be her best to date at the time. The important part of the Earl of Dorrincourt was played by Claude Gillingwater; coming to the theatre from a successful stage career, he was one of the most memorable of all silent character actors, specializing in long, lean, grumpy but lovable elderly men, with a face that could convey an inimitable pained, indignant disgust. His death was tragic; towards the end of the 'thirties, while rehearsing in the studio, he fell from a platform and received injuries that would not heal. Soon afterwards his wife died, and in 1939, at the age of 69, he shot

himself. The characters he created live on in his films, and it is always a pleasure to see his name in the opening cast list.

Already well-known for his appearance in Griffith's *Broken Blossoms* and *Way Down East*, Richard Barthelmess increased his following with a remarkable performance in *Tol'able David* (directed by Henry King), from a novel by Joseph Hergesheimer. Described as a 'rural drama', it tells of the development into manhood of a youth forced to accept responsibilities as head of his family when his father dies and his adored elder brother is crippled in a fight with a criminal neighbour. Barthelmess's ability to portray quiet courage and youthful integrity were well served by the script and (together, of course, with appealing good looks) helped to make this a personal as well as a corporate success. Watching Barthelmess as the young boy, it is difficult to believe he was over 26 when he played the rôle.

Charlie Chaplin's *The Kid*, familiar to many today through the small screen, was looked on at the time as *the* film for children – to weep at and laugh with the adorable 5-year-old Jackie Coogan without in any way wondering about the reason for his abandonment or the meaning of the title 'Her Only Sin – Motherhood'. Yet, as David Robinson points out in his definitive biography of Chaplin, there was in those days no little courage in his 'unqualified defence of the unmarried mother'. It is also strange to remember now that he was criticized for the bad taste of his portrayal of a crude but lively Heaven – until, arousing a sudden moment of sharp, childish fear, SIN creeps in. The truth is, of course, that it is exactly the sort of

Probably one of the most famous screen partnerships of all time: the inimitable Charlie Chaplin and the irresistible Jackie Coogan working out their next window-breaking and repairing foray in *The Kid*.

heaven that a humble, uneducated, literal-minded tramp *would* dream of: familiar people transformed into angels complete with white surplices, wings and harps, flying uncertainly around among equally familiar but flower-garlanded buildings.

An enthusiastic critic of the period claimed, in *Theatre World* magazine, that 'Charlie Chaplin has done more to popularize the qualities of Christ than all the Cardinals and Canons of the Christian churches. There is more of Courage, Cheerfulness and Kindness, more of Modesty, Service and Self-respect in *The Kid* than in any sermon I have heard preached.'

Apart from *The Kid* the best comedy films both starred Max Linder, who also directed them and wrote the scripts. The first, *Seven Years' Bad Luck*, concerns the adventures and misadventures of a man returning from a last fling as a bachelor somewhat the worse for drink, and contains the famous gag, repeated later in the Marx Brothers' *Duck Soup*, in which his valet, in an effort to conceal the fact that he has broken his master's cheval glass, attempts to copy all the latter's movements behind the empty frame. Later, when the glass is replaced, Max is confused, throws his shoe at the glass and shatters it, thus triggering the seven years of bad luck. The second film, *Be My Wife*, released a few months later, deals with his eventually successful attempts to defeat a rival in love and (a more difficult job) win the respect of his fiancée's formidable aunt. This is perhaps the lesser of the two comedies, but both are prime examples of Linder's work, to which Chaplin always admitted he owed so much. He invariably wore the smartest of clothes, generally a dress suit or morning coat, top hat and cane, and was inevitably referred to as 'dapper'. During the First World War he was badly gassed and later had a nervous breakdown. Owing perhaps to this, and perhaps to a sense that his career might be declining, he became depressed and increasingly unbalanced. In 1925 he and

his wife, whom he had married only two years before, entered into a suicide pact and died together in a Paris hotel. He was only 42 years old. Although he made many shorts (mainly in France but also a few in America), he attempted only a handful of feature-length productions, and it is more than regrettable that these are so rarely revived. Despite this small output Linder's work is worthy to stand beside that of the Big Four – Chaplin, Lloyd, Keaton and Langdon.

Other American films of 1921 included *Disraeli* (directed by Henry Kolker), with George Arliss in one of his best-known look-alike impersonations, and his wife as his wife, repeated eight years later with sound. There were also two J. M. Barrie adaptations, *Sentimental Tommy* (directed by John S. Robertson, fresh from *Dr Jekyll and Mr Hyde*) with Gareth Hughes and pretty May McAvoy, a reasonably accurate translation; and *What Every Woman Knows* (directed by William C. DeMille), with Conrad Nagel, Lois Wilson and Charles Ogle, the original Frankenstein monster from 1910.

A Connecticut Yankee at King Arthur's Court (directed by Emmett J. Flynn), a lively adaptation of Mark Twain's novel, starred Harry Myers and Pauline Starke, formerly a harem girl in *Intolerance*. Myers has been undeservedly forgotten, a light comedian who could at times be as funny as any of the Big Four, though his style was very different. He was later to play the drunken millionaire in Chaplin's *City Lights*.

The Lotus Eater (directed by Marshall Neilan) was a wrecked-on-a-desert-island melodrama, interesting for the casting of John Barrymore opposite a pre-jazz age, wholly charming, long-haired Colleen Moore.

The always dapper Max Linder, to whom Chaplin paid warm tribute as an influence on his own work. Linder's confident sunny smile is sadly at variance with the tragic events to come in his later years.

Richard Barthelmess, again playing a young man considerably below his real age, in *Experience* – and looking likely to get it from Nita Naldi (cast as 'Temptation'). An extraordinary offering that in recent years might have become known as a 'cult movie'.

Camille (directed by Ray C. Smallwood), a splendidly over-the-top version, starred Rudolph Valentino at his most flashing-eyed and Nazimova at her most emotional. It all seemed excitingly 'adult' to us at the time – almost forbidden fruit. The remake of 1929 with Norma Talmadge had less excess but less excitement.

Peck's Bad Boy (directed by Sam Wood) was one of Jackie Coogan's most popular and enjoyable post-*Kid* films, based on the well-known stories by George Wilbur Peck, dealing with a naughty boy's escapades. His dog, Queenie, is as delightful as her young owner.

Experience (directed by George Fitzmaurice) is chiefly memorable as one of those hilariously solemn and admonitory parables in which Hollywood liked to indulge from time to time, of the type where none of the characters has a name – only a 'personification'. 'Youth' is played by Richard Barthelmess, and that – together with the title

48

– more or less explains everything. Samples from the rest of the cast list include 'Love' (Marjorie Daw), 'Ambition' (E. J. Radcliffe), 'Intoxication' (Helen Ray), 'Temptation' (Nita Naldi: who else?), 'Degradation' (Mrs Gallagher: one would like to know more about her) and, perhaps best of all, 'Gloom' (Leslie King). Viewing was severely restricted to Adults Only. Not having quite reached that pinnacle at the time the film was first screened, a friend and I sneaked in, hoping to learn something. Alas, we came out not much the wiser.

*

The death of Little Nell from Dickens' *The Old Curiosity Shop*, with the popular British silent star Mabel Poulton as Nell, William Lugg hiding his head as Grandfather, and A. Harding Steerman as Mr Marton.

The best news from Britain was the arrival of Betty Balfour in the first of the *Squibs* series (directed by George Pearson), which was to brighten British screens over the next few years. Little remains even in this first film of the original music-hall sketch on which it was founded, except the nickname and character of the chirpy little Cockney girl – now appearing as a Piccadilly flower-seller with a police-constable boyfriend. The films were modest, unadventurous in treatment and tailored to fit their star, who was lively and endearing enough to delight all but the most sophisticated audiences of the time.

A pleasant production of *Kipps* (directed by Harold Shaw), from the novel by H. G. Wells, starred the British ex-Shakespearean actor George K. Arthur. Its success enabled the Stoll company to follow it up with another Wells story, *The Wheels of Chance*, the following year, also with Arthur. Shortly

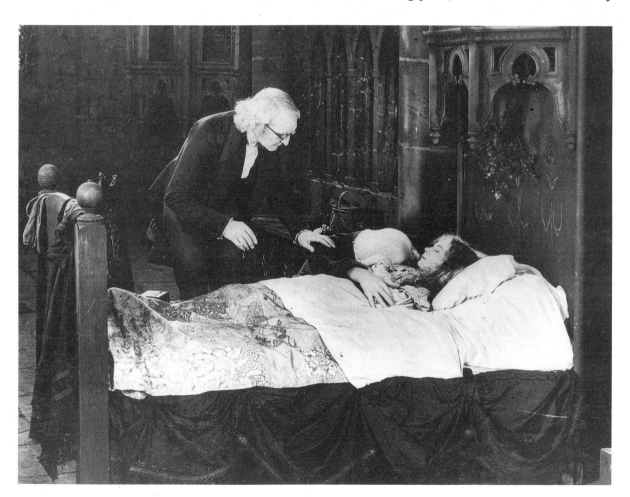

Milton Rosner grimly holding on in an atmospheric still from *A Romance of Wastdale*, A. E. W. Mason's tense drama set in Britain's Lake District.

afterwards he went to America to start a movie career which lasted until he turned to the business side of the cinema in the mid-'thirties.

Kipps was to be remade later with Michael Redgrave, and most recently of all was blown up into a musical, *Half a Sixpence,* starring Tommy Steele.

In her second film Mabel Poulton, former typist and rival to Betty Balfour as top silent star of the decade (she fell victim to the sound débâcle), tackled Little Nell in *The Old Curiosity Shop* (directed by Thomas Bentley), with William Lugg as Grandfather. It was, as far as I remember, a modest but reasonably faithful rendering of the book, and certainly Miss Poulton won our hearts as Nell – who

was much less schmaltzy than she is often made out to be by those who scoff at Dickens for his sentimentality because it does not fit in with present-day attitudes.

Another adaptation from a well-known author, A. E. W. Mason's *A Romance of Wastdale* (directed by Maurice Elvey), a grim tale of jealousy and revenge among the Lakeland mountains, was weakened by having the events turned into a dream; but it generated enough tension between the small group of characters to make certain scenes stick in the memory. The photography has a grey, gritty quality which admirably suits the circumstances, preserved in a fine still featuring Milton Rosmer.

An important event of the year was the appearance of Eille Norwood as Sherlock Holmes, both in a feature film, *The Hound of the Baskervilles* (directed by Maurice Elvey), and in three series of the short stories over the next few years. The period is hazy, but the films themselves, especially the two-reelers, were conscientiously made and thoroughly enjoyable. To many people Eille Norwood, though not greatly resembling the Sidney Paget drawings, remains the finest Holmes of all, and I was fortunate enough to see him on stage (in *The Return of Sherlock Holmes,* 1923) as well as on screen. He died in 1948, at the age of 87.

The only 1921 German film I recollect seeing was Fritz Lang's *Der Müde Tod,* Literally *Weary Death* but more generally known in Britain as *Destiny,* in which he dealt with one of his favourite themes, Man's (or in this case Woman's) struggle against Fate. In impressively – not to say oppressively – elaborate settings in Baghdad, Venice and China, Death offers a woman her lover's life if she can prevent three other deaths. It is slow, ponderous and at times not easy to follow, though lightened by some ingenious trickery with the camera. In those possibly simpler days we were, in general I think, respectful but cool towards the slightly pretentious.

The World at Large

Start of inflation in Germany
Sacco and Vanzetti found guilty of murder in Massachusetts
Severe famine in Russia
Greece declares war on Turkey
Britain signs peace with Ireland
Mackenzie King becomes Premier of Canada

Cinema

Tour of India by HRH The Prince of Wales filmed in Cinecolour
Michael Balcon makes his first film, a documentary on oil-drilling
Screenland magazine launched
William Friese-Greene, pioneer film inventor, dies during a meeting of the British film industry
Births: Jack Clayton, Deanna Durbin, Satyajit Ray, Jane Russell, Simone Signoret, Peter Ustinov, Esther Williams

Theatre

G. Bernard Shaw, *Back to Methuselah*
Eugene O'Neill, *Anna Christie*
Clemence Dane, *A Bill of Divorcement*
William Archer, *The Green Goddess*
Avery Hopwood, *The Gold Diggers*
Sapper/Gerald Du Maurier, *Bulldog Drummond*

Fiction

John Dos Passos, *Three Soldiers*
Sheila Kaye-Smith, *Joanna Godden*
Karel Capek, *The Insect Play*
Rafael Sabatini, *Scaramouche* (best-seller)
A. S. M. Hutchinson, *If Winter Comes* (best-seller)

Music

Alban Berg, *Wozzeck* (opera)
Prokofiev, *The Love of Three Oranges* (opera)
Stravinsky, *Mavra* (*opéra bouffe*)
Honegger, *King David* (oratorio)
Vaughan Williams, Pastoral Symphony

Popular Songs

'If You Would Care for Me'
'Look for the Silver Lining'
'Kitten on the Keys'
'Blue Moon'

Fashion Note

Plus-fours for men in vogue

1922

In general a minor year, though not without its pleasures, such as the emergence of Harold Lloyd into feature-length films. Towards the end of 1921 he completed *A Sailor-Made Man* (directed by Fred Newmeyer), episodic in construction and just on the borderline in length; but it is with *Grandma's Boy* that he is generally regarded as having leapt into major productions and at a bound established himself as one of the great silent comedians. He has described it as a 'psychological study of a boy, cowardly both physically and morally, transformed by a fable invented on the spur of the moment by his despairing grandmother'. The simple moral, that strength will come even to the weakest if they believe in themselves, may seem today naïvely optimistic – if not nonsensical – in a cynical and ungenerous world, but I doubt if any of us questioned the underlying truth of the story then as we laughed our heads off at the surface action.

The plot – though full of incident – is as simple as the moral. The meek, shrinking Harold (in most of his feature films Harold is called 'Harold'), bullied as a boy and scorned as a young man, is the despair of his tough, devoted old Grandma. One day she gives him what she declares is a magic charm by means of which – she tells him – his grandfather, also a coward, overcame his weakness and carried off a great deed of daring during the American Civil War. In a hilarious flashback (with Lloyd in *square* tortoiseshell glasses) he enacts his grandfather's victory as she relates it to him. Back in the present he is filled to bursting with courage, captures a menacing tramp wanted for robbery and defeats the aggressive rival who is making a play for his girl. Finally Grandma reveals the trick she has played on him – the magic charm is nothing more than her old umbrella handle – and duly points the moral.

Lloyd's ingenuity with visual gags, and with tricks played on the expectations of the audience, is already in evidence. In this film, for instance, he is seen turning a crank, photographed in such a way that it appears he is in trouble with a handsome car, whereas in reality it is merely an old ice-cream freezer. Lloyd has said that of all his films *Grandma's Boy* was his favourite. Not all will agree with him now, nor, I think, did those of us who followed him from film to film as they came out – in fact each one was apt to seem the best until the next one arrived – but it is certainly a picture that revives affectionate memories whenever it appears on the small screen today.

Lloyd's other release, *Doctor Jack*, made

Alice Terry, regal and beautiful as Princess Flavia, and a romantically young Lewis Stone as Rudolph Rassendyll (and, of course, as the King) in *The Prisoner of Zenda*, a silent version overshadowed but by no means obliterated by the famous Ronald Colman remake of 1937.

less stir, but is an enjoyable film, revealing the *alter ego* of his screen personality – a bright, cheerful doctor anxious to find a remedy for everybody's ills. It contains some amusing comic mystery-thriller moments.

Valentino returned to Blasco-Ibáñez (author of *The Four Horsemen of the Apocalypse*) for *Blood and Sand* (directed by Fred Niblo), a romantic but surprisingly uncompromising story of a young matador who marries his childhood sweetheart (Lila Lee), achieves success, is vamped by and succumbs to a passionate and unscrupulous Dona (Nita Naldi), refuses to give up bull-fighting even though he is less able to carry on efficiently after being gored, is nursed back to health by his faithful wife in spite of his Naldi-dallying, and eventually receives his deserts from the horns of one of the noble animals on which he has wreaked so much damage. In the original the 'hero's' death is unflinchingly faced, but a 'happy ending' was supplied as an alternative. In its original tinted version it was at least a handsome film.

Pride of place in the histories is rightly given to the 1937 version of *The Prisoner of Zenda*, but it cannot entirely obliterate the memory of the silent one directed by Rex Ingram. For Ronald Colman we had Lewis Stone, that fine and long-lasting actor; for Madeleine Carroll, Alice Terry, looking more regal and beautiful than ever; for Raymond Massey a splendidly villainous Stuart Holmes; for Douglas Fairbanks Jr, as Rupert of Hentzau, a dashingly handsome young man who a couple of years previously had appeared in a bit part as 'An Officer' (anonymous) in *The Four Horsemen of the Apocalypse*, Ramon Samaniegos – soon to become better known as Ramon Novarro. This silent version may have been surpassed, but should not be forgotten. It would be pleasant to see it again.

Smilin' Through is, I suppose, rather in the class of *The Sound of Music*, complete corn and pre-eminently popular. It is one of the two films (directed by Sidney A. Franklin) by whom its star, Norma Talmadge, is best remembered – the other being *Secrets*, which we shall meet later. *Smilin' Through* was remade as a sound film in 1932, with Norma Shearer, but it is perhaps a film in which silence is an advantage, overcoming the necessity for the dialogue to be heard in all its luscious sentimentality. At any rate the queues went round the buildings everywhere to see 'John quietly dying' and joining up with the twenty-year-dead Moonyeen in the Great Beyond. Norma Talmadge, one of the most beautiful and well-loved stars of the period, retired, willingly or not, with the arrival of the talkies, and is famous for her distinctly un-Moonyeen remark to an autograph hunter, 'Go away, dear, I don't need you any more.'

Cecil B. DeMille turned up with *Manslaughter*, a picture somewhere in scope between his grandiose spectacles and his smaller-scale comments on modern (i.e. 'twenties) modes and manners. A wealthy, reckless, thrill-mad girl is taught a lesson by a District Attorney who sends her to prison ('for her own good') when her careless car-driving causes the death of a traffic cop. She reforms, but by now (not wholly to our surprise) he has fallen in love with her, and when she turns him down it is he who – all drink and dissipation – needs reforming. In the end he sacrifices his chance of promotion in order to marry her. DeMille again seizes the opportunity to use the past as an allegory for the present, perhaps straining things a little when the lawyer equates the behaviour of the girl and her friends with an orgy presaging the Fall of Rome. The modern story is rather too predictable, but the orgy is good fun. Thomas Meighan, a popular 'twenties star and an intelligent and reliable actor, plays the District Attorney and Leatrice Joy (the very attractive wife of John Gilbert) the girl. An early sound remake in 1930, directed by George Abbott, starred Fredric March and Claudette Colbert, minus, I think, the orgy.

Another C. B. DeMille throwback in time, on this occasion to a Fall of Rome orgy shown as a warning to a thrill-mad 1920s girl that she should change her ways, in *Manslaughter*.

It was strange in those days how one could be dogged by a particular film. At one time it seemed that every cinema I visited on the off-chance was showing *Under Two Flags* (directed by Tod Browning). However, Priscilla Dean was one of the liveliest and most engaging silent actresses, and it was always pleasant to see her as Cigarette (a 'French-Arab' girl), continually sacrificing herself to save an Englishman in the Foreign Legion from a wicked sheik. The original novel was written by the renowned Ouida, and the film was an early example of the work of Tod Browning, famed later as a

director of horror films. Disaster struck the company when, after the shooting was completed, both negative and positive prints caught fire in the cutting room and all had to be done again. Production values were restricted, as the budget had already been used up – but it looked acceptable enough to us at the time, even on repeat viewings!

D. W. Griffith has often been slated for his excursion into the comedy-thriller, but except for some really dreadful comic relief from a white actor blacked up to play a Negro servant I remember *One Exciting Night* as being rather enjoyable, and with some moments of quite considerable tension. There are two murders, a gang of bootleggers trying to find a large sum of money hidden in an eerie old house, and the usual groping hands, secret panels and other appurtenances of thrillers of the period such as *The Bat* and

Priscilla Dean, one of the liveliest stars of the period, entertains the Foreign Legion as Cigarette, the French-Arab girl in Ouida's *Under Two Flags*.

The Cat and the Canary. It appears that Griffith had already tried unsuccessfully to obtain the rights to the former. Perhaps it was because he was not, to the 'ordinary filmgoer' of the time, the great father figure of the cinema he has since become, that we could happily enter into the spirit of his little joke. The leading parts were played by Henry Hull, who had been in the stage production of the rather similar *Cat and the Canary,* Carol Dempster, and Porter Strong as the comic servant – also a genuine hurricane which arrived just on cue to provide a violent climax.

Sherlock Holmes (directed by Albert Parker) is a mish-mash of various stories derived from the play by the great Holmes actor William Gillette. In it, to every true devotee's horror, Holmes falls in love.

Conan Doyle, however, did not care a jot and willingly gave permission for the sacrilege. The cast was a good one. John Barrymore has a distinct resemblance to generally held ideas of Holmes' appearance (though too handsome for either Doyle's description or Paget's illustrations) and Roland Young is an acceptable, if rather surprising, choice for Dr Watson. The evil genius Moriarty is played by the resoundingly named Gustav von Seyffertitz, surely the most intriguing surname in pictures – changed temporarily, and surely in a spirit of fun, to C. Butler Clonebough during the First World War. He was another of the fine character actors of the period, generally but by no means always a villain, whom we shall meet again. His resemblance to Barrymore on occasion could be striking; many people were convinced that the latter played both Holmes and Moriarty. It was a resemblance which was to be put to good use in a dramatic moment when von Seyffertitz appeared briefly as the evil torturer in Barrymore's *Don Juan* a few years later.

Frank Lloyd, later to make a sound version of *Under Two Flags* with Claudette Colbert as Cigarette, directed *Oliver Twist*. The combination of Jackie Coogan (Oliver) and Lon Chaney (Fagin) ensured box-office success, but critical opinion was lukewarm. 'We fear Jackie's Oliver Twist will fall somewhere between the Dickens lovers and his own fans, missing both of them,' said *Photoplay*.

It was reported that when Jackie Coogan caught sight for the first time of Lon Chaney in his fearsome make-up as Fagin, the trainer of a band of young pickpockets, he was so frightened that he screamed and ran off the set.

Max Linder produced a joyful skit, *The Three Must-Get-Theres*, a good deal more entertaining than the recent Fairbanks film, with some brilliant visual gags. Linder was

John Barrymore as a very acceptable, if slightly too handsome, *Sherlock Holmes* in the film of that title based on William Gillette's play, with Roland Young as Dr Watson. The period is hazy.

'Dart-in-again', while heavyweight Bull Montana played 'Rich Lou'.

Down to the Sea in Ships (directed by Elmer Clifton) requires mention not so much for the film itself (though it was a very respectable, indeed outstanding, picture of life in the whaling industry), but because it has often been regarded as the first appearance of Clara Bow. In fact, she had previously been in a small-scale melodrama called *Beyond the Rainbow* (directed by William Christy Cabanne), playing the tiny part of a young girl, forbidden to attend a ball, who sends anonymous letters to the guests revealing various awkward secrets. *Down to the Sea*, however, is the picture in which she first attracted attention, leading to her eventually becoming the IT Girl (courtesy of Elinor Glyn) and a key figure of the 'twenties and early 'thirties.

Other American films included *Foolish Wives* (directed by Erich von Stroheim), a cynical, sardonic exploration into the violence, lechery and corruption underlying the glitter of high life in Monte Carlo. There are wonderful sets and costumes, some rather heavy symbolism and plenty of action (in fact, as the *American Film Catalog* neatly summarizes, 'Diplomats. Gambling. Suicide. Murder . . . Fires. Duels').

Beyond the Rocks (directed by Sam Wood) starred Rudolph Valentino and Gloria Swanson emoting together both in the present and in the past (a flashback to the Regency period enabling both to look their best), in a steamy romance by Elinor Glyn.

The Young Rajah (directed by Philip Rosen) starred Rudolph again, improbably a descendant of the mortal brother of Krishna who becomes a popular student at Harvard. He falls in love (understandably) with Wanda Hawley, but it does not come to anything. Probability never mattered much, however, where Valentino was concerned.

Over the Hill (to the poorhouse), an old tear-jerker, was directed by Harry Millarde, and Mary Carr plays the super-self-sacrificing mother who ends up, in a famous still, bent double scrubbing floors in an effectively soft grey wig. She went on to a long career in films – often playing similarly devoted mothers and grandmothers – until the mid-'fifties (she died in 1973), but it was when she went over the hill that we all wept with her.

The Man from Hell's River (directed by Irving Cummings), was notable for making the advent of 'The Saviour of Warner's', Rin-Tin-Tin, whose popularity reputedly rescued the studio from bankruptcy. He was first 'starred' in *Where the North Begins* (directed

by Chester M. Franklin) the following year. Records give the date of birth of the German shepherd dog as 1916, his death as 1932. Rumours that he was actually more than one dog are firmly denied. (He had a successor, Rin-Tin-Tin Jr, in the mid-'thirties.) From 1922 until his death Rin-Tin-Tin rescued humans, recovered valuables and revenged wrongs with unruffled determination, ingenuity and good humour, and the advent of sound presented him with no problems requiring voice training.

Finally, 1922 heralded the first appearance of *Our Gang*, a series of comedy shorts which appeared weekly, particularly in the small cinemas, for no fewer than 22 years. The 'gang', a group of lively children who got in and out of scrapes of all kinds in a wild variety of situations, was immensely popular. The cast obviously had to change quite often as the members grew up, but among the longest-lasting were Billy 'Buckwheat' Thomas, 'Stymie' Beard, 'Spanky' McFarland, 'Chubby' Chaney and – perhaps most famous of all – 'Farina' Hoskins.

The most ambitious British film of the year was *The Glorious Adventure*. The director, J. Stuart Blackton, then vice-president of the important American Vitagraph company, came to England to make a large-scale spectacular and to launch the Prizma Color process in which he had an interest. It is a massive, heavily costumed piece set in London during the Plague and Great Fire of 1665-6. The renowned and beautiful Lady Diana Manners – a society leader rather than an actress – was engaged, with a fanfare of publicity trumpets, to play the lead, aptly

Lady Diana Manners as the suitably named Lady Beatrice Fair, attractively posed against an olde Englysshe garden – 1666, to be exact. Despite some exciting set pieces and a general aura of high quality *The Glorious Adventure* turned out to be rather heavy-going for some of us.

named Lady Beatrice Fair, and the Hon. Lois Sturt was a livelier if less glamorous Nell Gwyn. Stage matinée idol Gerald Lawrence played the hero, and Victor McLaglen, in his fifth film, added to his growing reputation as the ruffianly Bullfinch, a condemned criminal whom Lady Beatrice marries for reasons of financial expediency. William Luff takes on Charles II and Lennox Pawle Samuel Pepys.

In her delightful biography of her father Marion Blackton Trimble reports that the 'cream of British society' turned out for the opening (at the Royal Opera House, Covent Garden, no less), and, perhaps awed by the presence of so much nobility on and off screen, critics were mainly kind. Some of us, I confess, found it rather a bore, very slow in parts, at times confusing and with a basic story – two young lovers in the clutches of a wicked lawyer – that was not particularly involving. There are some exciting sequences, however, such as the one in which the hero rescues his lady from Old St Paul's as the Cathedral melts around them. An aura of Harrison Ainsworth surrounds the whole film, though the story is Blackton's original. One bright spot stands out in the memory: Tom Haslewood as the mad, ragged Solomon Eagle striding among the crowds, brazier on head, crying the Wrath to Come.

Betty Balfour made a welcome reappearance in Squibs Wins the Calcutta Sweep (directed by George Pearson), which was unusual in that it both opens and closes in an atmosphere of tragedy: Squibs' sister is married to a cat-burglar who kills a house-holder and finally commits suicide. In between these dismal events, however, there is much simple comedy as Squibs wins the Sweep through a ticket bought for her by her

Betty Balfour was one of the brightest stars in the British cinematic firmament during the silent period, best known for her Squibs series (loosely based on a music-hall sketch). She is seen here berating Hugh E. Wright, her feckless father.

father and arrives in a chauffeur-driven limousine, all airs and graces, to visit her prospective in-laws, the parents of her faithful police constable. A hidden camera sequence, not very common at that time, showing Squibs upsetting the peace of Piccadilly with her rejoicings, adds to the entertainment of this enjoyable if minor movie.

The Wonderful Story, the first from Herbert Wilcox as producer and second from Graham Cutts as director, was also the first to offer Lilian Hall-Davis the chance to rise to the prominent position she held during the silent period. Her death by suicide in 1933, after failing to make the transition to sound, was a sad end to a successful career. The film itself is a quiet, simple tale of the reformation of an over-demanding cripple, set in an English countryside now gone for ever.

To most people nowadays Alec Guinness is synonymous with The Card, following his brilliant performance as the cocky clerk who becomes mayor of a Potteries town and marries the daughter of the man who sacked him. The fact that an earlier, silent version of Arnold Bennett's novel was made in 1922 (directed by A. V. Bramble) with Laddie Cliff – generally regarded as a musical-comedy star – in the part is largely forgotten. Also in the cast are Joan Barry (later to be heard as Anny Ondra's voice in Hitchcock's first talking picture, Blackmail) and Arthur McLaglen, one of the six brothers of whom Victor remains the best-known.

A version of Clemence Dane's A Bill of Divorcement (directed by Denison Clift) features Constance Binney in the role which was to bring fame to Katharine Hepburn in ten years' time; Matheson Lang, imposing stage star, took the title role of Dick Turpin's Ride to York (directed by Maurice Elvey), an episode firmly founded on fiction (in the case Harrison Ainsworth's Rookwood); and Percy Smith led a group of distinguished photo-graphers and naturalists in an excellent series of brief films entitled Secrets of Nature, featuring an early use of time-lapse, micro-

An eerie composition, full of hints of witchcraft and Satanism, from the Danish director Benjamin Christensen's striking *Haxan*, or *Witchcraft Through the Ages*.

scopic and other specialized cine-cameras to record plant, insect and animal life.

In Germany Fritz Lang, in *Dr Mabuse*, used a macabre super-criminal story to symbolize the growing chaos of the country, and F. W. Murnau made his remarkable *Nosferatu*, loosely based on Bram Stoker's *Dracula*. The latter was for many years an exceedingly rare film owing to copyright problems. An order was made that all copies should be destroyed, but this was fortunately avoided. It is full of camera tricks which, commonplace

today, were then unusual and new. Germanic mystic moralizing is imposed on the story, which follows the book fairly closely. It ends abruptly and weakly, however, at the vampire's first encounter with his prospective victim. At some risk, she agrees to seduce him into remaining with her until he is caught by the rising sun and quickly dissipated into thin air before he has had time to get his teeth into her.

From Sweden came *Haxan* (*Witchcraft Through the Ages*), directed by the Danish filmmaker Benjamin Christensen, an exhilarating, sometimes eerie, sometimes shocking collection of witchcraft lore, part documentary, part dramatization, in which the director, later to work briefly in America, appeared as a rumbustious Satan. According to one critic in the United States the film was 'wonderful' but also 'unfit for publication'.

1922

The World at Large

The British Broadcasting Company (later Corporation) founded

The Teapot Dome Scandal in the USA

Mussolini's March on Rome

King Tutankhamen's tomb opened and disasters foretold

Stock market boom in America

Thompson and Bywaters murder case in Britain

William Armstrong murder case in Britain

Cinema

Michael Balcon, Victor Saville and John Freedman form independent company at Islington

Graham-Wilcox company starts production

Beaconsfield Studios open

CBC, later Columbia, makes first feature film

Unsolved murder of William Desmond Taylor, director, in Hollywood

'Fatty' Arbuckle Scandal

Will Hays appointed Head of Motion Pictures Producers and Distributors of America, to improve the image of the industry

Greta Garbo makes her first film (in Sweden)

Jack Pickford (Mary's brother) marries Marilyn Miller in all-star wedding

Piccadilly Cinema, Manchester, the first large cinema in northern England, opens

Out of 420 British films, shorts and features, offered to the United States, only half-a-dozen find buyers

First Wampas Baby Stars list issued (Western Association of Motion Advertisers select annually a number of young actresses deemed most likely to succeed): Marion Aye, Helen Ferguson, Lila Lee, Jacqueline Logan, Louise Lorraine, Bessie Love, Katherine McGuire, Patsy Ruth Miller, Colleen Moore, Mary Philbin, Pauline Starke, Lois Wilson, Claire Windsor

Births: Blake Edwards, Ava Gardner, Judy Garland, Kathryn Grayson, Christopher Lee, Pier Paolo Pasolini, Arthur Penn, Shelley Winters

Theatre

John Galsworthy, *Loyalties*

Eugene O'Neill, *The Hairy Ape*

Anne Nicholls, *Abie's Irish Rose* (2327 performances in the USA)

Austin Strong, *Seventh Heaven*

Fiction

James Joyce, *Ulysses* (published in Paris; 500 copies destroyed by the Post Office on arrival in the USA)

F. Scott Fitzgerald, *The Beautiful and Damned*

Sinclair Lewis, *Babbitt*

Hugh Walpole, *The Cathedral*

Music

Arthur Bliss, Colour Symphony

William Walton, *Façade*

Carl Nielsen, Symphony no. 5

Howard Hanson, Symphony no. 1

Popular Songs

'April Showers'

'Hot Lips'

'My Man'

'Say It with Music'

Fashion Note

Trousered 'smoking suits' for women

Lon Chaney in what is probably his most famous film, *The Hunchback of Notre Dame*. Esmerelda, the girl who comforts him after he has been publicly whipped, and whom he later carries to safety in the cathedral, is played by Patsy Ruth Miller.

With Lon Chaney's *The Hunchback of Notre Dame*, DeMille's *The Ten Commandments*, Rex Ingram's *Where the Pavement Ends* and *Scaramouche*, James Cruze's *The Covered Wagon*, Fairbanks' *Robin Hood*, Chaplin's *A Woman of Paris* and Lloyd's *Safety Last* and *Why Worry?*, this year signalled the opening of the gates to a flood of large-scale, medium-scale and small-scale movies, which made it difficult for the committed filmgoer to keep up with everything he or she wanted to see. Ultimately it became impossible. But we did our best.

Lon Chaney's *The Hunchback of Notre Dame* (directed by Wallace Worsley) and in particular Chaney's own physical appearance in the title role are so well-known that for an audience seeing it today, even for the first time, the effect must be fairly mild. To anyone unprepared as we were, however, it was both electrifying and horrifying. It is easy to look like a monster today (and even easier, unfortunately, to behave like one). A child making Hallowe'en visits can slip on a rubber mask horrible enough to frighten anyone. In those days Chaney, doing his own make-up, had to build up his nose, blind eye and cheekbones with mortician's wax and combine false teeth with wire to keep his mouth twisted open, apart from the more common greasepaint. In addition to wig and false eyebrows, he distorted his whole body with a special restrictive harness and wore a hair-tufted rubber covering.

The mob scenes at the climax were breathtaking, the milling hordes of extras working up an excitement that has seldom been surpassed; according to Kevin Brownlow every arc lamp in Hollywood was utilized in lighting the scene. The huge façade of the cathedral was in fact half a fake; only the lower storeys were built, the whole upper portion being a hanging miniature placed in relation to the camera so as to form an exact match.

Hunchback is one of the major American films of the decade, yet the director's name is scarcely known today, and indeed – except for the earlier Chaney picture, *The Penalty* – his list includes little more of note. More familiar is the name of an assistant on *Hunchback* – William Wyler.

The Tivoli Cinema in the Strand, London, opened in 1923 (on the site of a famous music-hall which lasted from 1890 until 1914) with Rex Ingram's *Where the Pavement Ends*, a story of romance and tragedy in the South Sea Islands, with his wife Alice Terry as a pastor's daughter and Ramon Novarro as a native chief. It was well received by both critics and the public and certainly did not harm Novarro's career. For some reason, though, despite being awed by the grand new building, I found the movie a disappointment – perhaps in expectation of another glamorous *Zenda,* with Alice Terry again looking regal as only she could. However, *Scaramouche,* from Rafael Sabatini's bestseller, was waiting, and that stirring adventure

Ramon Novarro, Julia Swayne Gordon, Lewis Stone and Alice Terry in *Scaramouche*, the splendidly spectacular and fast-moving film of Rafael Sabatini's still very readable romance of the French Revolution.

of aristocrats, rebellious students, travelling musicians and mob violence during the French Revolution, together with Miss Terry looking her ravishing self in a gorgeous white wig, a fine performance from Lewis Stone – nobility personified even when playing the villain – and Novarro at his best as the law student out to avenge his friend's death, all amidst some magnificent settings, soon wiped out any disappointment in the former film from the same stable. The title, incidentally, is derived from the pseudonym taken by Novarro when, in the course of his quest, he joins a family of strolling musicians.

It is not always remembered that in Cecil B. DeMille's first version of *The Ten Commandments* the biblical sequence (filmed in colour) is merely a comparatively brief prologue to the modern story which takes place in twentieth-century San Francisco, and was made in black and white. Even so, despite the technical improvements and the fact that it was largely filmed in the actual locations and benefited from enormously increased resources, the 1956 remake of the Exodus by no means has all the advantages. The comparative brevity of the earlier one meant that there was no need to pad it out with a fictitious and tedious story involving 'Prince Moses', a hereditary Egyptian princess and Pharaoh's son. DeMille defended such innovations by claiming that at least they *could* have occurred. The point is that the overlong film might have been better if they

Theodore Roberts, hair and beard flowing, as an impressive Moses in *The Ten Commandments*, looking a little surprised, perhaps, at the amount of admonition the Almighty can compress into such a modest amount of writing.

hadn't. The 1923 orgy is more exciting than the comparatively restrained goings-on around the 1956 Golden Calf. The silence itself may have been partly responsible here – chatter is apt to slow down orgiastic revellings. The majestic stature of Theodore Roberts – all wind-swept hair and beard, blazing eyes and flamboyant gestures – convey something of the prophetic fire which is missing in Heston's more modern approach, impressive though this is in its way.

The moment we were all waiting for in 1923 – the parting of the Red Sea (filmed at Guadalupe, California) – was simpler and

less technically accomplished, but it was good enough for us at the time. According to Rod la Rocque (in an interview in *The Real Tinsel*, edited by Rosenberg and Silverstein), special-effects expert Roy Pomeroy used two blocks of Jello on a large table cut in two parts. Water was run over the blocks, which were separated and then closed together again. Double exposure made the whole scene so realistic that the Society for the Prevention of Cruelty to Animals complained about the treatment of the horses which had been 'drowned' – or made to appear so.

The modern story, concerning two brothers, one of whom keeps the Command-ments, while the other does not and thereby brings tragedy on himself and his family, is in itself spectacular. Allowing for a slight sense of strain in getting all ten Commandments into the plot, there is plenty of excitement,

A vivid impression is given of the enormous castle built for Douglas Fairbanks in *Robin Hood*. Technical ingenuity may have made the edifice seem somewhat larger than it actually was, but even so it was one of the showpiece sets of the period.

aided by good performances by Richard Dix (one of the few actors able to make 'goodness' appear neither boring nor smug), Rod la Rocque (the bad one) and Edythe Chapman, their typically Hollywoodian mother. Only Nita Naldi, vamping yet again, remains rather too bad to be true. It is interesting to remember that the disease which the young profligate contracts from her, and on account of which he kills her, is described as 'leprosy'; today such details would doubtless be more straightforwardly and frankly represented. The climax is the collapse of a half-finished cathedral which the bad brother has been constructing with cheap, poor-quality sus-

taining fibres, despite the warnings of good Mr Dix. In its fall the building crushes the old mother to death. This whole sequence, with the percussion section of a large cinema orchestra going all out while on screen blocks of cement crack and crash until all that is left is a large stone tablet (the same shape as that which Moses received on Mount Sinai) bearing the words 'THOU SHALT NOT STEAL' in big Gothic lettering, was great stuff.

Equally spectacular, but in a very different way, was Douglas Fairbanks' *Robin Hood*, directed by Allan Dwan, one of the most prolific and long-lasting of filmmakers – over 400 films in some fifty years. In it Fairbanks almost literally leapt back into the form he had to some extent deserted in *The Three Musketeers*. I well recollect the awe with which we gazed at what must have been the largest castle ever built, either for a film company or for anyone else. We did not realize at the time, of course, that it was not quite as colossal as it looked, owing to the ingenious use of glass shots, which could make the height of a set seem far greater. A glass shot was made by painting, in exact proportion to the camera's perspective, the whole upper elevation of a building on a plate of glass placed close to the camera. Even so, at 450 feet long, the castle hall should have been huge enough to make anyone feel at home. The story follows the legend acceptably, Fairbanks leaps and fights with uninhibited gusto (the film contains the famed – and faked – slide down the tapestry on the castle wall) and if, as one critic implied, he is more Douglas than Robin, who cares? We certainly did not.

The western also went splendidly spectacular with the authentic epic *The Covered Wagon*. The director, James Cruze, once well-known and with a long list of productions to his credit, is little remembered today except for this one movie – which is regrettable to say the least. However, it is an imposing enough memorial, dealing with the adventures of two wagon trains on the Oregon Trail in 1848, about two years after the sufferings of the ill-fated Donner party vividly recounted in George R. Stewart's *Ordeal by Hunger*. A stirring tale, it embraces human courage and human failings, human sacrifice and human greed. The simple love interest, though sensitively played by lovely Lois Wilson and manly J. Warren Kerrigan, is rather eclipsed by the spectacle, such as the thrilling and moving sequence dealing with the crossing of the Platte River, but at least it provides a centre around which such events occur. Two magnificent character actors, Ernest Torrence and Tully Marshall (the latter as the real-life scout Bridger), are at their very best. The film, dedicated to the memory of Theodore Roosevelt, broke box-office records, even those of *The Birth of a Nation*, on its first run in New York.

Charlie Chaplin's *The Pilgrim* is generally regarded as a minor work, but it is full of felicities, such as the famous David-and-Goliath sermon he performs, as the fake minister, before a somewhat bemused con-

Charlie Chaplin as the escaped convict in parson's clothing in *The Pilgrim* – a minor Chaplin, perhaps, but with some memorable comedy sequences.

gregation. The story, of an escaping convict who seizes an opportunity to change his prison garb for a clergyman's clothes and finds himself compelled to impersonate a minister expected on a visit to a Texan chapel, develops into a series of not unfamiliar but always amusing Chaplinesque dilemmas. The film ends with the celebrated scene in which a kindly sheriff takes the unmasked convict to the Mexican border in order to allow him to escape. Chaplin, however, cannot understand such generosity. Eventually the sheriff boots him over the border to freedom. Immediately some Mexican bandits appear

and start firing at each other. The small figure disappears into the distance, running with one foot in one country, one in the other — safe in neither. The film aroused criticism in some righteous circles for alleged irreverence — in those days it was not always wise to laugh at even a fake clergyman. Playing the Deacon is the enormous Mack Swain, stalwart of dozens of early short comedies and soon to partner Chaplin in *The Gold Rush*: it is interesting to note how, in *The Pilgrim*, he seems to symbolize the gradual transformation in Chaplin's supporting casts from the early grotesques to more recognizable human types. Gone are the absurd moustache, black-circled eyes and ridiculous hairstyle; in their place is an ordinary, if somewhat overweight, middle-aged man.

As well as performing in front of the camera in *The Pilgrim* Chaplin moved behind it for his sole completed project as director only, *A Woman of Paris*. (In 1926 he worked in what appears to have been rather an uncertain way with Josef von Sternberg on an idea entitled *A Woman of the Sea*; apparently it was screened only once, then withdrawn.) *A Woman of Paris* stars Edna Purviance, leading lady of many short Chaplin comedies, and Adolphe Menjou as the wealthy man-about-town whose mistress she becomes; Chaplin himself makes a brief, unlisted appearance as a clumsy railway porter. This very ordinary society drama is handled with unusual subtlety and restraint, and was highly regarded by many critics. To the general, however, it was caviar: if the name Charlie (or even Charles) Chaplin was seen on a poster outside a cinema he himself was expected to be seen inside.

Both Harold Lloyd's 1923 films show him

Harold Lloyd in *Why Worry?*, one of his lesser-known but most diverting comedies, full of ingenious Lloydian gags. Towering over him is Johan Aasen, looking doubtful about the prospect of having an aching tooth extracted.

at his best, and one of them, *Safety Last*, is his most widely known. Think of Lloyd and at once you see a bespectacled figure halfway up a tall building's outer wall, clinging for dear life to the minute-hand of a large clock which threatens at any moment to become detached from its face. (If you look carefully you can spot the specially made glove that conceals the device worn on his right hand to replace his thumb and forefinger, both torn off several years earlier when a supposedly property bomb he was holding blew up.) *Safety Last* was the final film he made with Mildred Davis, the girl who became his wife. In the next picture, *Why Worry?*, and the following five his girl would be pretty Jobyna Ralston with her charming long curls (real or false).

Why Worry? (directed by Fred Newmeyer), about a young hypochondriac who goes to a South American 'island of Paradise' and gets involved in a revolution which eventually cures him of his imagined ailments, contains one of the most brilliant and elaborate of all Lloyd's gags. In quite a lengthy sequence he strolls unknowingly and unconcernedly through the town with frantic revolutionaries in action all round him, being shot, pushed from buildings, signalling wildly, marching violently from one place to another. By an astonishingly ingenious series of misunderstandings he mistakes all these frantic activities for perfectly innocent happenings. Another asset to the film is a huge, hairy hermit called Colosso (played by Johan Aasen, a Norwegian from Minneapolis who was well over eight feet tall). The giant becomes his devoted companion when Lloyd extracts his outsize aching tooth after a succession of Herculean efforts.

In more serious mould, *The White Sister* (directed by Henry King) is notable not only for the performance of Lillian Gish but as the picture that brought Ronald Colman into prominence. He had previously made one or two minor British films and one American, *Handcuffs or Kisses*, which he was probably willing to forget. *The White Sister*, described as 'a romantic drama', is the story of an heiress who is cheated out of her inheritance and left penniless; when she hears that her fiancé, a young Italian officer (Colman), has been killed in battle she enters a convent. However, the report of his death is false – he has merely been taken prisoner. He escapes, meets her, and tries to persuade her to renounce her vows: the old and well-worn (but nearly always effective) theme of the tussle between duty and desire, or in this case faith and love. Ultimately, as one might guess for those more highly principled days, faith wins. Rather conveniently, Vesuvius then takes a hand and erupts (they are both in the district), so that Colman can die trying to save the townspeople. Henry King's sensitive

Lillian Gish in the title role of *The White Sister*, in which she delicately and triumphantly avoids the mawkish in a potentially embarrassing story of a nun who resists the temptation to renounce her vows for love for Ronald Colman.

direction, Colman's sympathetic playing and above all Lillian Gish's skilful manifestation of the contrast between her fragile beauty and her iron determination to follow her conscience turn what could have been a somewhat naïve and mawkish tale into a sincere and genuine tear-jerker. I remember well that it jerked quite a few out of us when we saw it many years ago.

Rosita, the film Ernst Lubitsch made on arrival in America, was heartily disliked by its star, Mary Pickford. She had originally asked him over to direct *Dorothy Vernon of Haddon Hall* (see 1924), which he had turned down. *Rosita* was quite well received by the critics, less so by the public, and has seldom surfaced since, having been seemingly tucked well away in the Pickford vaults. It is a costume piece (1844) in which the King of Spain falls for a street singer (Rosita) who loves a penniless nobleman, Don Diego. Owing to the cunning of the Queen, the susceptible King is thwarted and all ends well, at least for Rosita and her Don. Apparently glimpses of what became known as the 'Lubitsch touch' were already in evidence. Whether the Spanish royal archives have any record of the events is not disclosed. Perhaps one day the film will be disinterred and a potentially interesting sideline of history revealed for study.

Admirers of Charles Laughton's performance as the valet in *Ruggles of Red Gap* may not all be aware of the fact that the part was played some eleven years previously by Edward Everett Horton, early in his long career, and played very entertainingly too, even though he had not the advantage of being able to recite the Gettysburg Address. It was, in fact, his first important role, and he was well supported by old stalwart Ernest Torrence, Lois Wilson and William Austin. Austin, with his height, long lean face and slightly vacuous smile, looks the typical British 'silly ass'. In fact, he was born in British Guiana, educated at Reading, and made his American stage début in either

Percy Marmont, perfectly cast as the muddled, idealistic Mark Sabre in *If Winter Comes,* enjoys a few rare lighthearted moments with two loyal servants, christened by him High Jinks (Dorothy Allen) and Low Jinks (Eleanor Daniels).

1919 or 1923 before going on to a steady career in supporting parts in silent and early sound films. In 1932 he came to England and played in *High Society* with Florence Desmond, starring the following year as Harris in Basil Dean's production of *Three Men in a Boat,* for which he must have been ideal. Since then I can find no trace of him. As is the case with a number of supporting actors and actresses whose faces over the years become as familiar as those of any of the stars (and their performances as memorable), he appears in few reference books.

A. S. M. Hutchinson's novel *If Winter Comes* won the contempt of the literary pundits and the approval of the vast reading public. In truth it captures much of the spirit of its time, and once the reader has become accustomed to some odd tricks of style it is an immensely readable and often very amusing picture of British village and small-town life just before and during the First World War. This atmosphere was well preserved in the film (directed by Harry Millarde), with Percy Marmont as Mark Sabre. The fairly melo-dramatic story concerns a muddled but idealistic and very likeable man tied to a cold and snobbish wife who engages a young girl to keep her company when he goes off to war. He later suffers what seems to be an unfair amount of trouble as a result of a well-meant action. The film is lightened by sympathetic handling and some entertaining side issues. We are all happy when, after a nervous breakdown (and no wonder), he eventually finds happiness in the arms of a

Nazimova as a bubble-haired Salomé and Nigel de Brulier as a suitably wasted (if surprisingly well-scrubbed) John the Baptist in the remarkable *art nouveau* version of Oscar Wilde's notorious verse drama.

former sweetheart. Percy Marmont, a most engaging actor, is the ideal Hutchinson hero, and was to appear in a film based on another of his novels in the following year.

The most extraordinary film to come out of America (or probably anywhere else) during the year was undoubtedly Nazimova's *art-nouveau* version of Oscar Wilde's French poem *Salomé* (directed by Charles Bryant), designed by Valentino's wife, Natasha Rambova, under the influence of the drawings of Aubrey Beardsley. It was considered highly scandalous, and I was unable to see it when it appeared (decadent stuff!) but caught up with it later. It is one of those maverick, dead-end movies that cropped up from time to time to enliven the general run. Nazimova produced the picture herself, and lost heavily on it, which is regrettable because it was most certainly a brave venture. With her boyish figure and fantastically bewigged head (everything from huge flaxen bob to multitudinous pearly bubbles) she miraculously suggests the youthfulness of the daughter of Herodias, yet she was forty at the time. Nigel de Brulier, though somewhat clean for a long-imprisoned prophet, looks suitably wasted by the fire of fanaticism. As might have been expected, contemporary criticism varied considerably. Highly artificial, sometimes ludicrous, the film is both unique and astonishing, and a constant visual pleasure.

Other films from America included *The Sin Flood* (directed by Frank Lloyd), in which a mixed group of normally selfish people living in a town on the banks of the Mississippi take refuge, when the river overflows, in a café, the owner of which has installed flood-proof doors against such a contingency. When threatened with suffocation they decide to open the doors and drown in preference. Accepting that extinction is inevitable, they overcome their self-centred-ness and unite to help one another to face the prospect. On opening the doors they find the waters have receded, and, now they are safe again, repentance goes by the board — except, of course, in the cases of the hero and heroine. A case, in fact, of 'The Devil was sick, the Devil a monk would be: the Devil grew well – the devil a monk was he!' This brief summary of a play that originated in Scandinavia does not do justice to the small-scale film, which invests a trite moral allegory with considerable tension and involvement, helped by first-class playing by Richard Dix, James Kirkwood, Helene Chadwick and the rest of a competent cast; and by the direction of Frank Lloyd and camera-work of Norbert Brodin, who create a notable sense of claustrophobia. The climactic moments leading to the opening of the heavy doors and a view of water-washed streets and bedraggled but unconcerned passers-by were vivid enough to make it hard to remember that all this was done without any sound of voices raised in anguish and fear.

Under the Red Robe (directed by Alan Crosland) is a well-made and reasonably accurate adaptation of Stanley J. Weyman's costume novel, with an impressive Cardinal Richelieu by Robert B. Mantell, a stage actor who seems to have made only a small handful of films, and Alma Rubens graciously lovely as Renée du Cocheforet. Also in the cast is William Powell, at this stage still a villain. Tragically, Alma Rubens became a victim of heroin addiction and died at the age of 33.

The Courtship of Miles Standish (directed by Frederick Sullivan) represents a gallant but foredoomed attempt to screen Long-fellow's narrative poem about the Pilgrim Fathers. Charles Ray, who both produced it and played the lead, invested all the money he had accumulated as a popular 'country boy' juvenile, and lost the lot. The film was criticized as slow, dull, heavy-going, etc., but it was a brave venture, none the less.

Bella Donna (directed by George Fitzmaurice), Pola Negri's first American film, is an adaptation of the Robert Hichens novel in which an adventuress (with the rather un-adventurous name of Mrs Ruby Chepstow), after falling in love with an Egyptian sheik, tries to poison her husband. She is discovered and turned out by her intended victim, goes to the sheik, finds him with another woman, and exits, tottering, into a desert sandstorm. These sensational events were filmed by Paramount, and rumours were rife about the rivalry raging between Pola and the reigning Paramount star, Gloria Swanson – rumours denied later by Miss Negri as publicity falsifications. Whatever the truth, they undoubtedly helped to keep both ladies in the spotlight.

The comedy-drama *Grumpy* (directed by William DeMille) was based on a popular

May McAvoy, petite and charming silent star, who plays opposite Theodore Roberts in *Grumpy*.

play about a grouchy old lawyer who foils some jewel thieves. A modest, minor picture, it is remembered with pleasure because of the delightful performance by Theodore Roberts, fresh from the more serious business of carrying the Ten Commandments down from Mount Sinai as Moses. It is remembered with pleasure also, of course, because of the presence of May McAvoy.

Trilby (directed by James Young) is notable for Arthur Edmund Carewe's finely menacing Svengali, which even John Barrymore's later portrayal was not to obliterate. The film is a good example of how even a story so dependent on music and singing could be told

Colleen Moore, later to be regarded as the typical 1920s 'flapper', in one of her earlier films, *Flaming Youth*. The ardent young man is Ben Lyon, in one of his first screen appearances.

Clive Brook (already marked out as an officer type), Betty Compson (centre) and Marie Ault (left) in *Woman to Woman*, one of the most successful British productions of the period.

effectively on a silent screen. An alternative (happy) ending was available on request.

Bluebeard's Eighth Wife (directed by Sam Wood) stars Gloria Swanson, glamorous as ever as the daughter of a French nobleman who marries a wealthy American (Huntley Gordon, a pleasant if rather stolid leading man of the period) for his money, only to find he has also had seven wives. This was typical lightweight standard film fare of the time, competently made, amusing, well acted and directed, for passing a pleasant evening at the pictures.

The most interesting product of a dull British year was *Woman to Woman* (directed by

Graham Cutts), which brought together three eventually well-known filmmakers at the beginning of their careers – Michael Balcon and Victor Saville as producers, Alfred Hitchcock as art director. It was one of the most commercially successful films of the decade, partly because of the presence, as female star, of Betty Compson, then at the height of her popularity in America. The story, as Balcon himself said, is naïve and melodramatic, but at the time was generally looked on as highly sophisticated. Set in 1914, it deals with a British officer who has an affair with a French girl, is wounded in the head during the war and as a result loses his memory, returns to England when peace is declared and marries an Englishwoman. The Frenchwoman, now a famous ballerina, arrives in Britain to perform, accompanied by a child. After the confrontation indicated in the title the ballerina – in convenient cinematic fashion – dies, and the child is adopted by the father. In Boston, Balcon says, the film was banned until a compromise was reached whereby 'we arranged for our hero and heroine to be married for Sunday showings only'. The film led to Hollywood stardom for Clive Brook, who played the officer; its editor, Alma Reville, later became Hitchcock's wife.

The two stars appeared together again in *Royal Oak* (directed by Maurice Elvey), a costume drama built round Charles II's escape from Cromwell after the battle of Worcester and his concealment in the oak tree at Boscobel. It is romanticized history, but enjoyable in a simple fashion, and made effective use of period English locations and countryside.

Fires of Fate (directed by Tom Terriss, brother of Ellaline Terriss), from Conan Doyle's novel *The Tragedy of the Korosko*, also had an American star, blonde and pretty Wanda Hawley. The director himself being American too, it seemed natural to enter the picture for British Films Week 1924. Nigel Barrie, a handsome leading man of the British cinema, is the gallant Colonel who saves a white girl from the libidinous desires of an Arab prince during a boat-trip down the Nile – despite the fact that, with only a year to live, he cannot have expected to get much out of it. The film is memorable for an early instance of sex rearing a not-so-ugly head: the raging but concealed lust with which the villain gazes down at Miss Hawley as she sits chatting with her back to him is indicated by a brief dissolve of her gauze shawl to reveal her bare skin beneath, shoulder-blade and all. It was thought pretty daring.

Matheson Lang transferred his most famous theatrical portrayal, *The Wandering Jew,* to the screen (directed by Maurice Elvey), but despite the increased advantages for spectacle offered to the story of the Jew who cursed Christ and was hence doomed to live through the Crusades and mediaeval Italy and to die under the Spanish Inquisition, the restricted stage version was the more effective. It is one of those not very frequent occasions when the loss of a sonorous voice uttering purple-prose dialogue was noticeable.

Cecil Hepworth's revival of his favourite *Comin' Thro' the Rye* (another British Film Week entry) was, sadly, a failure, despite the presence in the cast of the popular Alma Taylor. Little more than a year after its release he was forced to close his business down – the end of a chapter in the history of British cinema.

1923

The World at Large

Hitler's Munich Beer Putsch fails
US President Warren Harding dies, succeeded by
Calvin Coolidge
Stanley Baldwin is British Prime Minister
Dock strike in London
About 15,000,000 cars registered in the USA

Cinema

Irving Thalberg joins Louis B. Mayer
Metro and Goldwyn studios combine
Lee de Forest Phonofilms registered (sound on
side of film)
Cecil B. DeMille voted 'top director' in *Photoplay*
magazine poll
Walt Disney starts work in Hollywood
Warner Bros. founded
Tivoli Cinema, Strand, London, opens
Death of Wallace Reid from morphine and
alcoholism, aged 31
Wampas Baby Stars: Eleanor Boardman, Evelyn
Brent, Dorothy Devore, Virginia Brown Faire,
Betty Francisco, Pauline Garon, Kathleen Key,
Laura la Plante, Margaret Leahy, Helen Lynch,
Derelys Perdue, Jobyna Ralston, Ethel Shannon
Births: Richard Attenborough, Lindsay Anderson,
Charlton Heston, Marcello Mastroianni, Melina
Mercouri, Franco Zeffirelli

Theatre

Elmer Rice, *The Adding Machine*
Karel Capek, *R.U.R.*

Somerset Maughan, *Our Betters*
Sutton Vane, *Outward Bound*
James Elroy Flecker, *Hassan*
Owen Davis, *The Nervous Wreck* (*Whoopee*)

Fiction

Aldous Huxley, *Antic Hay*
Arnold Bennett, *Riceyman Steps*
Felis Salter, *Bambi*
P. G. Wodehouse, *Leave It to Psmith*

Music

Poulenc, *Les Biches*
Sibelius, Symphony no. 6
Gustav Holst, *The Perfect Fool* (ballet)
'Bix' Beiderbecke organizes Chicago jazz band

Popular Songs

'Yes, We Have No Bananas'
'Tea for Two'
'I Want to Be Happy'
'Barney Google'
'Kiss in the Dark'

Fashion Note

Shingled haircuts for women
Short-lived fashion of little panniers on hips
Brief fad for 'Egyptian' fashions following the
opening of King Tutankhamen's tomb

1924

There can be little doubt that Lon Chaney's *He Who Gets Slapped* (directed by Victor Seastrom, or Sjöström) is a landmark in the silent period – indeed, in the history of the cinema. It was the first production to come entirely under the MGM trademark, launching the company to fame and fortune; it contains what many people consider to be Chaney's greatest performance; it greatly furthered the careers of Norma Shearer and John Gilbert; it featured two of the best character actors of the time, Marc MacDermott and Tully Marshall; and it made Seastrom (as his name was spelt in Britain and the USA) widely known throughout the American film world. (His first film in America, *Name the Man,* seems to have made little stir.)

The plot, from a play by Leonid Andreyev, is melodramatic in outline and dependent on coincidence for its development, having as its central character a masochistic figure dripping with self-pity, but is transformed by its direction, playing and camera-work (by Milton Moore) into a brilliant combination of tragedy and strange beauty. A shy, with-drawn scientist loses both his wife and, though her connivance, the papers containing secrets of his work, to the bullying and unscrupulous Baron Regnard. At a meeting of fellow scientists the Baron first presents the work as his own, then, when the scientist (known in the film only as 'He') protests, slaps his face and laughs at him, while the others join in. When his wife also jeers and calls him a clown, He, shattered, takes her literally and joins a circus as a buffoon whose act is one long sequence of being slapped

Tully Marshall, noted for his foxy villains, gives a notable performance in a sympathetic part as a poor nameless worker in a London pub who accepts the blame for another man's murder. The film, entitled *The Stranger,* was adapted from John Galsworthy's short story and play *The First and the Last.*

Lon Chaney in the first of his two famous clown-with-a-broken-heart characterizations, the unique and unforgettable *He Who Gets Slapped,* a landmark of the silent period.

and humiliated by his associates. He becomes famous, and later falls in love with a pretty bareback rider (Norma Shearer) who is herself in love with her partner (John Gilbert).

Pola Negri, tempestuous star from Poland, with Rod la Rocque (Roderick la Rocque de la Rour) from Chicago, as the Czarina and the young officer who wins her love in Lubitsch's sparkling piece of romantic hokum, *Forbidden Paradise*.

Later, hearing that her father plans to marry her to the Baron, He engineers the death of both men by releasing the circus lion. Fatally stabbed by the Baron, He staggers into the circus ring and dies in the girl's arms, while the audience, thinking it part of the show, laughs heartily.

The film made an indelible impression on all of us who saw it on its first release. Later it seemed to vanish for years until, at a recent screening in London, it proved to have lost none of its power to affect an audience. Perhaps one day it will find its way on to the small screen so that millions can experience at least some idea of the brilliance of this haunting film.

After the somewhat abortive *Rosita* the 'Lubitsch touch' was firmly in evidence in two films he directed in 1924, *The Marriage Circle* and *Forbidden Paradise*. The former was the first of a series of 'sophisticated comedies', set preferably in Vienna or Paris, designed to make us all feel that we were truly men or women of the world in that we could so readily appreciate such visual wit, innuendo and light sexual by-play among people more handsome or beautiful than our everyday selves. Florence Vidor, Monte Blue, Marie Prevost and Adolphe Menjou form a quartet soon to become, singly or together, familiar in such featherweight varieties of intrigue. *Forbidden Paradise* moves into higher social circles – no less than the love of a czarina – but also somewhat away from the lightness of the 'Lubitsch touch'. It marked a reunion with Pola Negri, whom he had directed in several films in Germany, and is a handsome, elegant-looking piece of mythical kingdom hokum, updated from a play by Lajos Biro and original only in the treatment the director brings to it. Pola Negri even reminds us at times of a subdued Nita Naldi. Rod la Rocque is handsome, Adolphe Menjou is suave, Pauline Starke has a fresh, sharp beauty, and Clark Gable appears as an extra.

The famous 'Lubitsch touch' is easier to recognize than to describe. Essentially it

The hungry queuing for food in inflation-ridden post-war Germany – a scene from one of D. W. Griffith's most moving films, *Isn't Life Wonderful?*

might be defined as a subtle use of objects, or unconscious movements and attitudes of characters, to make points about personal relationships and intentions, or to reveal thoughts and situations otherwise concealed. In a long and perceptive analysis of the Lubitsch Manner in his book *Hollywood Destinies* Graham Petrie singles out instances such as a drawer full of undarned socks and celluloid collars to indicate neglect in a failing marriage (*The Marriage Circle*) or the use of a decoration or star (*Forbidden Paradise*) to suggest that the wearer has been one of the Czarina's lovers. In a later film, *The Student Prince of Old Heidelberg*, the movements of a small dog accompanying a young couple through a series of arches is cunningly used to signal their growing mutual attraction.

D. W. Griffith turned again to the epic in *America,* a patriotic Revolutionary War chronicle using a simple romance as a peg on which to hang a tapestry of the struggle, from the causes of the revolution to the battle of Yorktown. Criticism was mixed, one source comparing it only slightly to its detriment with *The Birth of a Nation,* another describing it as pretty trickery, with sticky love interest and heavy propaganda. Griffith's genius for handling battle scenes seems to be unimpaired, and in general it would appear that it is the individual touches, surprisingly, which let the picture down, partly owing to the ineffectiveness of the lovers, Neil Hamilton and Carol Dempster. I have no recollection of its reception in Britain, but it appears to have been tepid.

Griffith's next film, however, *Isn't Life Wonderful?*, is one of his most moving: a simple account of the sufferings of ordinary people – a group of Polish refugees living on the outskirts of Berlin during the inflationary years that followed the First World War.

Originally the group was German, but Griffith changed it to Polish because of the continuing antipathy to Germany after the 1914-18 war. The story of these individuals' quietly desperate attempts to brighten their lives, or even to survive at all, is told with a restraint that makes the film all the more heartrending. One of the men, married to a refugee living with the family, returns from the war miserably weakened, but the couple work together on a plot of land to secure some sort of future. When their precious crop of potatoes is grabbed from them by a gang of equally hungry and desperate men, it seems there is nothing left for them to live for – but in fact there is: they have each other. Neil Hamilton and Carol Dempster, in contrast to their work in *America*, give most sensitive and touching performances, in particular Carol Dempster, often regarded as 'Griffith's obsession'. Despite all this, the film never achieved the success it deserved. Perhaps, in America, it came at an awkward time, half a dozen years after the war, but for some of us in Britain – a good many miles nearer the conflict – it was a haunting experience.

I saw Mary Pickford in *Dorothy Vernon of Haddon Hall* (directed by Marshall Neilan) with stern condemnatory warnings from the critics ringing in my ears – and (not for the first or last time in years of filmgoing) thoroughly enjoyed it. It was a rousing story of treachery, intrigue, treason, forbidden love, stern fathers, rebellious daughters, all set in Good Queen Bess's glorious days – and glorious they must have been in these beautiful settings. It had a radiant Miss Pickford (without curls), a splendidly overbearing father in Anders Randolf, an almost acceptable hero in Allan Forrest, an impressive villain in Marc MacDermott, and as realistic and believable a Queen Elizabeth as any in Claire Eames. Estelle Taylor's Mary, Queen of Scots, I must confess, has faded from my memory. If she turned up at Haddon Hall while the Queen was there she was out of place, for according to the history books

the two royal ladies never met. However, the matter is really not of great importance. This is one of those movies, quite a rarity, which it is possible to enjoy without for a moment accepting it as truth. Despite its merits and the abiding impression it leaves – swords clashing as strong men duel in the Great Hall, masculine legs magnificent in tights, feminine necks beautiful in ruffs – the film is rarely mentioned now except derogatorily, was disliked by Mary Pickford herself, and is generally accounted a failure. A pity – quite a lot of people enjoyed it at the time.

Two of Buster Keaton's best enlivened the 1924 screens: *Sherlock Jr.* (directed by Keaton himself), and *The Navigator* (directed by Keaton with Donald Crisp, famous as Battling Burrows in Griffith's *Broken Blossoms*). The invention and ingenuity of parts of *Sherlock Jr.* are unsurpassed by anything in Keaton's work, not excluding *The General*, which is regarded as his masterpiece. He appears as a small-town cinema projectionist who, unlucky in love and suspected of theft, falls asleep in the projection booth, becomes involved in the story unfolding on the screen, and wakes to regain both his reputation and his girl. The start of his dream finds him walking down the cinema aisle, over the orchestra pit and literally *into* the screen: there follows an incredible series of marvellously contrived cuts as the background keeps changing while he remains in the same position and tries to adjust himself from shot to shot as he finds he is most embarrassingly or dangerously out of place. This extraordinary, almost surreal sequence leads to a constant succession of gags, chases and fantastic gymnastic feats.

The Navigator is less complex, with one particularly brilliant gag situation. Circumstances cause Buster and his girl to become marooned in a giant ocean liner which is adrift. Endless comic sequences are extracted from the idea of two small people coping with enormous surroundings – searching for each other wildly through endless corridors and

The start of one of the most ingenious of all Buster Keaton's gag sequences, as he is about to 'enter' the screen in *Sherlock Jr.* The still also provides an interesting glimpse of the musical accompaniment to films in a small cinema of the time.

decks, chasing up and down numerous ship's stairs, attempting to boil a couple of breakfast eggs in a cauldron gigantic enough for several hundred – a sort of *'parvum in multo'*, in fact. It all ends with Keaton in a diving-suit keeping cannibals at bay until a submarine arrives.

One of Harold Lloyd's two 1924 films is also built mainly on one central idea – his battle with, and eventual victory over, his gorgonian mother-in-law. The film, *Hot Water* (directed by Sam Taylor), has three hilarious

highlights: Harold's journey home in a crowded trolley laden with parcels plus a live turkey he has won in a raffle; the appalling first trip in a new car he has proudly bought for his wife, which is ultimately wrecked; and the final routing of the mother-in-law who, through a series of fortuitous (and fortunate) events, becomes convinced his house is haunted. She is played with ferocious skill by Josephine Crowell, memorable as both the mother in *The Birth of a Nation* and Catherine de Medici in *Intolerance*. Lloyd's other production, *Girl Shy* (directed by Fred Newmeyer and Sam Taylor), sees him as a bashful young man writing a book, *The Secret of Making Love*, to help other bashful young men, which affords opportunities for a couple of amusing parodies on vamp and flapper movies. It is chiefly memorable, however, for the tremen-

Harold Lloyd in *Hot Water* is turned off the trolley after a disastrous journey coping with a large collection of assorted parcels and a lively Thanksgiving turkey.

dous race against time to halt the wedding of the girl he loves to a man who, he has discovered, is already married. This climactic sequence involves Harold making frenzied use of cars, horses, motor-cycles, a fire engine, even a trolley-car, to achieve his object and must still be one of the most exciting comic chases ever screened. The girl is Jobyna Ralston, in curls again after putting them up as a young married woman in *Hot Water*.

John Ford had been making films since 1917, but *The Iron Horse* is generally regarded as his first epic western – though it is

a western without cowboys, being the story of the construction of a transcontinental railroad, with a climax in which two competing companies, Union Pacific and Central Pacific, race to meet each other and celebrate the occasion by driving in the famous golden spike. Ford personalizes the meeting by combining it with the reunion of two lovers who have been through various not wildly unusual vicissitudes during the fairly long run of the picture. Westerns were plentiful, if often indistinguishable, during these years, and to have one with locomotives rather than quadrupeds was a change – even though it foreshadowed the eventual shrinking of the legendary West.

John Barrymore's performance as *Beau Brummel* (directed by Harry Beaumont) has always seemed to me one of the best in his career, and it is a pity it has not been revived.

The exciting climax to John Ford's *The Iron Horse*, where the rival railway companies finally meet after their race towards each other across the American continent and the event is duly photographed for posterity.

As the insolent, reckless arbiter of fashion who wins and loses the friendship of the Prince Regent, ending up destitute and accompanied only by a faithful servant, he leads a fine cast in a film of restraint and integrity. In that cast are two more of those superb silent character actors, both at their best: Willard Louis, excellent as the Prince and memorable also as Friar Tuck in Fairbanks' *Robin Hood* and Pedrillo in Barrymore's *Don Juan*; and Alec B. Francis, tall, gentle, kindly – the perfect friend-in-need in dozens of unhappy cinematic situations.

Rex Ingram's *The Arab*, shot in North Africa, was a minor effort, with Ramon Novarro as a sort of stand-in Valentino sheik and Alice Terry not up to her usual style – perhaps because she abandoned her blonde wig. Altogether it was a disappointment.

The Sea Hawk, on the other hand, was not. Directed by Frank Lloyd in his most dashing manner, it starred Milton Sills as Sir Oliver Tressilian, a wealthy baronet who is shanghai'd, blamed by his half-brother for the death of his own fiancée's brother (in a rather confusing manner), captured by Spaniards and condemned to be a galley slave, escapes to the Moors and decides (perhaps not surprisingly) to become the Curse of Christendom under the title of Sakr-el-Bahr. After even more strenuous activities he – even less surprisingly – marries his beloved and presumably settles down. It scarcely seems possible that the 1924 version of *The Sea Hawk* and the 1940 remake (directed by Michael Curtiz) with Errol Flynn can have been derived from the same Rafael Sabatini best-seller, so widely do their events differ, but both claim the same parentage. Whatever their respective merits, however, Flynn certainly lost out in his character's name. 'Geoffrey Thorpe' is a poor substitute for 'Sir Oliver Tressilian *alias* Sakr-el-Bahr'.

The later film, it appears, was shot in black-

Betty Bronson as Peter Pan and Mary Brian as Wendy in Herbert Brenon's delightful version of Barrie's play. Barrie himself agreed to the choice of Betty Bronson for the part, and surely never regretted it.

and-white rather than Technicolor in order that stock footage from the earlier one could be included, but an increased budget rendered this economy unnecessary.

An always immensely watchable actor, Sills made something like seventy films during the decade, and his death in 1930 at the age of only 42 was a loss to the American screen. According to one lurid report he committed suicide by deliberately crashing his car – presumably unable to face the transition to sound – but most accounts, including the official obituary, confirm that he suffered a heart attack while playing tennis with his wife, the charming actress Doris Kenyon.

Sills also starred in *Madonna of the Streets* (directed by Edwin Carewe), a heavy drama set in London in which, showing his versatility, he appears as an ardent priest who inherits a large sum of money and marries a woman who is infuriated when he spends it on charitable work instead of herself. When he finds out that she used to be his uncle's mistress and only wed him for the said inheritance he becomes infuriated himself and (understandably, though perhaps not in the true spirit of Christian charity) sends her about her business. Later, regretting his lapse, he seeks

her out, and discovers what her 'business' has become when he finds her in a home for fallen women. All ends well with reconciliation on both sides. It is one of those films in which the acting transcends the material and impresses itself on the memory, willing or not. Nazimova emotes as only Nazimova could, and Claude Gillingwater and Wallace Beery lend support in the contrasting roles of Lord Partington and Bill Smythe respectively.

Colleen Moore, who during the past year or two had been advancing towards becoming the leading exponent of the Jazz Age, takes a step sideways in *So Big* (directed by Charles Brabin) to prove she is a capable and versatile actress, ageing convincingly in Edna Ferber's best-seller (and winner of the Pulitzer Prize) about a woman's struggle to bring up her son on a farm in end-of-century America, and playing throughout with great sensitivity and skill.

Herbert Brenon has been faulted for not taking sufficient advantage of the added scope the screen offered for spectacular scenes and camera trickery in his production of *Peter Pan*, but so enchanting and high-spirited is the whole film that none of us noticed, or would have cared much if we had noticed, that much of the action was still stage-bound. J. M. Barrie himself approved the choice of Betty Bronson as Peter, and must have been pleased with himself for doing so. She is, quite simply, perfection – for once a Peter looking the right age, with no hint of whimsy. She is well supported by Mary Brian as a sweet but never sickly Wendy, and Esther Ralston as surely the most gracious and beautiful Mrs Darling of all Mrs Darlings. In her delightful autobiography, *Some Day We'll Laugh*, Esther Ralston describes her horror when her agent told her he was putting her up for a 'mother' part at Paramount. 'A *mother* part?' she yelled. (She was about 24 at the time.) He explained that the director – an interesting idea – wanted to cast Mrs Darling as every child sees his or her mother – as a young girl. The film was the making of Betty Bronson, and quite right too, though except perhaps in another Barrie play, *A Kiss for Cinderella*, she never rose to quite such heights again.

Together with *Smilin' Through, Secrets* (directed by Frank Borzage) was probably Norma Talmadge's most popular movie – though I knew at least one devotee who put *Graustark* (1925) before either. Watching by the bedside of her sick husband, Mary Carlton dreams of her English girlhood, her elopement to America, her adventurous – not to say dangerous – life on a Wyoming ranch, her misery when her husband strayed from her, though her love for him never wavered. When she wakes up he is – to our pleasure but not our surprise – better. The original play (produced in London in 1922 with Fay Compton) was transferred to the screen with all its pleasant sentimentality and quiet humour intact, and cinema audiences duly, when called upon, dabbed their eyes.

Percy Marmont portrayed another of A. S. M. Hutchinson's self-tormenting heroes in *The Clean Heart* (directed by Stuart Blackton). There has always been a warm spot in my memory for this film, little known today though critically acclaimed at the time, about a successful novelist's nervous breakdown through overwork and the necessity of his bringing up two young nephews, his wandering away into the country to escape from his responsibilities and from himself, his narrow escape from drowning and rescue by a 'philosophical tramp' – who gives his own life to save him – and his eventual return to health and happiness through the love of a young girl. Marmont, as always, gives an excellent and most sympathetic performance, but in this case it is Otis Harlan who remains clearest in the memory. Harlan, a delightful little round figure of a man, with a gently suppliant face and an endearing habit of twiddling the fingers of one hand, is not much like the tall, fleshy, 'pear-shaped' tramp of Hutchinson's book, but he is wholly appealing, and deeply moving in his final moments

Percy Marmont portrays another A. S. M. Hutchinson hero in *The Clean Heart*, and is superbly supported by Otis Harlan as the tramp who both restores his confidence and saves his life.

when he drowns to save his friend. I was delighted to read recently in the biography of Blackton by his daughter (who also wrote the filmscript of *The Clean Heart*) that she felt the same way as I did about Otis Harlan. He had a long and busy career in the silent period, survived the transition to sound by some ten years and died in 1938 at the age of 74.

Jackie Coogan, always sure to draw audiences in at the little Royal, Kensington High Street, appeared in one of his most likeable films, *A Boy of Flanders* (directed by Victor Schertzinger) from a novel by – of all people – the notorious Ouida. The book was called *A Dog of Flanders*: put the two titles together and the basic story is revealed. A homeless boy saves the life of a dog, lives with him under a haystack, is blamed for a fire and about to be sent away when he attracts attention of a visiting artist by winning a drawing competition; boy and dog are adopted by the artist. In the film Jackie is

Jackie Coogan, slightly older than the Kid, with the tearful, pleading expression that melted the hardest hearts in *A Boy of Flanders*.

An equally winsome waif, Baby Peggy, makes sure that a young (and unwilling) Edward Everett Horton takes his medicine in *Helen's Babies*.

given prominence over the dog, but both are lovable; result, bonanza for box-office. In the supporting cast are two familiar names, Nigel de Brulier and, as the artist, Josef Swickard. Both are frequently found in films set in the European continent; Swickard was in fact born in Coblenz, de Brulier in Britain.

The Coogan film was popular, but the young persons' year really belonged to Baby Peggy (Montgomery), who made no fewer than seven films in her seventh year. A chubby, cheery, appealing rather than pretty little girl, she had an immense following for the new few years, and could almost be dubbed the Shirley Temple of the Silents. One film of her 1924 batch was in fact an early version of Miss Temple's *Captain January* (directed by Edward F. Cline). In another she was 'supported' by Clara Bow, steadily making her way to 'IT'. This was *Helen's Babies* (directed by William A. Seiter), from the then famous stories by John Habberton of two bad children who thought up various ingenious ways of tormenting their uncle – played by Edward Everett Horton. Her films were doubtless fondly remembered by those who saw them, but they were often hard to distinguish from each other.

Other American films included *Dante's Inferno* (directed by Henry Otto), in which a miserly millionaire landlord refuses to repair his tenement properties or lend money to a needy friend, so the latter gives him a copy of the *Inferno* for bedside reading. This shakes him up so badly that he repents at once. This not excessively exciting story merely serves as an excuse for some sensational visions of Hell, with hundreds of figures, fairly discreetly but tantalizingly clad in skintight clothing or with conveniently long, flowing hair, writhing and waving frantic limbs as brawny devils torment them. Probably neither tights nor hair would be considered necessary today. The settings, based as usual on Gustav Doré illustrations, are remarkable. Lawson Butt appears as Dante, Howard Gaye (the

Dante (Lawson Butt) and Virgil (Howard Gaye), surrounded by some discreetly writhing figures in *Dante's Inferno,* a film in which the modern story serves mainly as an excuse for a sensational visit to Hell.

Nazarene in *Intolerance*) as Virgil, Josef Swickard as the man who lends the book, and Robert Klein as chief fiend.

Tess of the d'Urbervilles (directed by Marshal Neilan), starring Blanche Sweet as Tess, Conrad Nagel as Angel Clare and Stuart Holmes as Alec d'Urberville, is reported to be a 'lost film', i.e. no trace of a print can be found anywhere. Copies of films classified as lost have, however, turned up most unexpectedly – for example, *The Mystery of the Wax Museum* (1933) – and it

is always possible that the same might happen here. As I remember, Tess is a reasonably faithful adaptation of Hardy's novel, well acted by the three principals, though Stuart Holmes, professional silent villain, may have been a little bit over the top.

Monsieur Beaucaire (directed by Sidney Olcott) is second-best Valentino, be-wigged and be-frilled up to the nines (except when showing his shapely torso), but it is an entertaining film in its way, particularly for the chance to watch Bebe Daniels pretending to be Princess Henriette, Lois Wilson Queen Marie of Russia, Paulette Duvall Madame Pompadour, and Lowell Sherman (quite successfully) King Louis XV of France. Other famous personages flitting around to give tone to the proceedings were John Davidson (Richelieu), Flora Finch (Duchesse de

A magnificently ornate Rudolph Valentino and a beautiful Bebe Daniels (far removed from her two-reel comedy days) in *Monsieur Beaucaire*, a decorative if minor movie affording entertaining glimpses of Hollywood's idea of some famous figures during the reign of Louis XV of France.

Montmorency), Downing Clarke (Lord Chesterfield) and Harry Lee (Voltaire).

In *The Sideshow of Life* (directed by Herbert Brenon), from a novel by W. J. Locke, one of the best-selling authors of the early twentieth century, Ernest Torrence tackles the sorely-beset-clown routine. The clown in this case had formerly been a British general. Lon Chaney's competition was formidable, but Torrence's skill and likeable personality here, aided by Brenon's customary sensitivity in direction, results in an often quite moving little film.

*

From England, sadly, there was still little to remember. George Pearson's *Reveille* was probably the best of the year. The idea for the film was given to him by a critic who happened to mention a 'poor old widow who had lost three sons in the war'. From this he constructed an episodic story, following up his belief that to be great a film needed to expound a theme – in this case 'the victory of courage' – rather than merely following a neatly constructed plot. The film's quiet emotionalism matched the mood of the time and it was very successful. Its best-known and most effective scene is that depicting the two minutes' silence, in which he leaves the screen without movement except for the gentle brushing of a lace curtain against the mother's face as she stands looking out of the window. During the first presentation the conductor of the orchestra put down his baton, so that the stillness of sound and vision was complete.

Siegfried (Paul Richter) bathes in the life-protecting blood of the dragon in *Die Nibelungen*, a weighty two-part epic in which the sets and props somewhat dwarfed the humans. The splendid dragon, some 20 yards long, was manipulated by men hidden in or under it. Note the carefully placed leaf on Siegfried's back which was to cause him a good deal of misfortune later on.

Owd Bob (directed by Henry Edwards) is a simple country story of shepherds and their dogs, shot mainly on location, with photography of high quality preserving a memory of the Lake District when the voice of the visitor was not so strident. The plot, a sort of canine whodunnit, is taken from a well-known novel by Alfred Oliphant, and the cast is headed by the fine old stage character actor J. Fisher White.

The main interest of *The Passionate Adventure* (directed by Graham Cutts) is that it was the first production to come from the Gainsborough stable. Apart from this it must be admitted that, despite a distinguished cast that included Clive Brook, Victor McLaglen (progressing from glorious adventures to passionate ones) and Alice Joyce, brought over from America to boost business, this improbable story of a rich man posing as an East End coster to escape from marital frustrations is not of intense interest.

Lastly, Matheson Lang turned to costume chronicle again in *Henry of Navarre,* a highly coloured version of history in which – as one might expect from a cast that included the Duc de Guise, Charles IX, Marguerite de Valois *and* Catherine de Medici – a good deal of nastiness goes on, with poison plots looming large. Maurice Elvey directed.

From Germany came Fritz Lang's enormous post-Wagnerian epic *Die Nibelungen*, in two parts. We admired the outsize, character-dwarfing sets, the sheer power of the whole

Emil Jannings reduced from his proud position of hotel head porter to lavatory attendant in *The Last Laugh*.

Greta Garbo in the Swedish film that first brought her wide notice, *The Atonement of Gösta Berling*.

gigantic conception, but wilted at the leaden pace of parts of it and the unrelenting length, even when screened with the relief of an interval. The dragon, however, though phony, is fun.

F. W. Murnau's *The Last Laugh* was hailed as being the first film without titles. Actually, the British *Lily of the Alley* (directed by Henry Edwards, 1923) was also title-less and similar claims have been made for even earlier films. In truth, such 'who was on first?' competitiveness is rather pointless. In the end, it is the quality of the film that counts. *The Last Laugh* impressed us at the time not as an exercise in innovation but as a moving and thought-provoking study of a proud old man, a hotel porter, whose world collapses about him when, because of the increasing incapacities of age, he is deprived of his grand uniform and demoted to the post of lavatory attendant. The film may also be regarded as a symbolic comment on social values, with a deliberately absurd 'happy ending', which infuriated some of those who had their tears so abruptly dried, and amused others as a parody of all such unlikely 'happy endings' whether in fiction or reality.

The Swedish film *The Atonement of Gösta Berling* (directed by Mauritz Stiller) is generally best known now as the film that first brought Greta Garbo to wider notice. It was also her last from her home country and is said to be no longer available in its original two-part form. Taken from a novel by a famous Swedish writer, Selma Lagerlöf, it is basically a fairly conventional love story, embellished with some effective Scandinavian scenery and one or two 'big' sequences, such as the famous, if somewhat irrelevant, chase across the frozen lakes. Berling, an unfrocked priest, is played by Lars Hanson, an actor of some power who was later to have a brief career in America. Garbo, as the girl who loves him, at eighteen years of age is almost (but not quite) unrecognizable as the Hollywood-groomed screen goddess she later became.

1924

The World at Large

'Zinoviev Letter' causes Red scare

First Labour government in Britain (under Ramsay Macdonald) lasts eleven months, followed by Conservative government

Calvin Coolidge elected President of the USA

Germany introduces new Reichsmark to halt inflation

British Empire Exhibition at Wembley

Walter Chrysler produces his first car

J. Edgar Hoover becomes director of Bureau of Investigation (later FBI)

Leopold-Loeb murder case in USA

Hall-Mills murder case in USA

Deaths of Woodrow Wilson and Frances Hodgson Burnett (author of *Little Lord Fauntleroy*)

Cinema

Metro-Goldwyn-Mayer finally formed

Gainsborough Pictures starts production in Britain

Hepworth Company wound up and bought by Archibald Nettlefold

Shepherd's Bush Pavilion, London, opens

Newspaper poll votes Betty Balfour and Alma Taylor favourite British stars

Death of Thomas Ince, American producer, in mysterious circumstances

The following stars voted most popular in *Photoplay* contest: Thomas Meighan, Norma Talmadge, Harold Lloyd, Tom Mix, Mary Pickford, Douglas Fairbanks, Gloria Swanson, Pola Negri, Jackie Coogan, Rudolph Valentino

Wampas Baby Stars: Clara Bow, Elinor Fair, Carmelita Geraghty, Gloria Grey, Ruth Hiatt, Julanne Johnston, Hazel Keener, Dorothy Mackaill, Blanche Mehaffey, Margaret Morris, Marian Nixon, Lucille Rickson, Alberta Vaughn

Births: Lauren Bacall, Marlon Brando, Doris Day, Lee Marvin, Sidney Lumet, Sidney Poitier, Sabu

Theatre

Eugene O'Neill, *Desire under the Elms*

Maxwell Anderson and Laurence Stallings, *What Price Glory?*

Noël Coward, *The Vortex*

Sean O'Casey, *Juno and the Paycock*

Bernard Shaw, *St Joan*

Sidney Howard, *The Knew What They Wanted*

Marc Connelly and George S. Kaufman, *Beggar on Horseback*

Rudolf Friml, *Rose-Marie*

George Gershwin, *Lady, Be Good*

Sigmund Romberg, *The Student Prince*

Fiction

E. M. Forster, *A Passage to India*

John Masefield, *Sard Harker*

Margaret Kennedy, *The Constant Nymph* (bestseller)

Hugh Walpole, *The Old Ladies*

Michael Arlen, *The Green Hat* (filmed as *A Woman of Affairs*)

P. C. Wren, *Beau Geste*

P. G. Wodehouse, *Jeeves* (best-seller)

Music

Arthur Honegger, *Pacific 231* (tone poem)

Janacek, *The Cunning Little Vixen* (opera)

Respighi, *The Pines of Rome* (tone poem)

Gershwin, *Rhapsody in Blue*

Popular Songs

'Yes, Sir, That's My Baby'

'Rose-Marie'

'Indian Love Call'

'Lady, Be Good'

'I'll See You in My Dreams'

Fashion Note

Skirts rise towards the calf

The cloche hat arrives

Silk and artificial silk stockings become fashionable

Russian boots popular as winter arrives

1925

Great mangled masterpiece or gross exhibition of megalomania (according to opinion), Erich von Stroheim's *Greed* must top the list for 1925. (Some sources give its year of release as 1924, but the American Film Catalog fixes the date firmly as 26 January 1925.) For several years previously, while still with Universal, Stroheim had been yearning to bring to the screen Frank Norris's great novel *McTeague* (published in 1899), a grim, relentlessly sordid story on the theme of money as 'the passport to life', the hoarding of gold for its own sake, set in a milieu of lower-middle-class life. As Herman G. Weinberg put it in his reconstruction, *The Complete Greed,* Stroheim 'went beyond this into the darkest recesses of the human psyche: the disintegration of spirit, beyond even the grace of humiliation'. His move to the Goldwyn Company in 1923 gave him the chance to start work on his film, though ironically his move was followed shortly by that of Irving Thalberg, with whom he had already clashed at Universal over the question of his alleged extravagance and wild spending on such inessentials as silken underwear for military extras, embroidered with a coat of arms – all unseen.

ZaSu Pitts gloats over the pieces of gold in Erich von Stroheim's *Greed.* Her shattering portrayal in this film arouses regret that she should have become so associated with fluttery comedy that comparatively few serious parts later came her way.

Stroheim's aim was to film the novel paragraph by paragraph, on location rather than in the studio, if necessary tearing down the inner walls of houses to do so. The completed film ran to about seven hours (there was even, according to some reports, a nine-hour print) but relentless cutting after it was taken out of the director's hands reduced it to a more manageable 2 hours 10 minutes, several characters and complete sub-plots being totally excised.

From the three leading players – Gibson Gowland as the simple, struggling, clumsy but fundamentally good-natured dentist; ZaSu Pitts as Trina, his prim, ineffectual wife who is corrupted by avarice when she wins a lottery; Jean Hersholt as his friend, who can lose his girl with generosity but not the money she now represents – Stroheim extracts performances these players never surpassed. In particular the film reveals ZaSu Pitts, usually associated with daffy comedy roles (she was later cast as the young soldier's mother in *All Quiet on the Western Front* but had to be replaced because no one would take her seriously) as a potentially fine dramatic actress. Grey and gritty throughout, the picture darkens gradually from the crude family junketings at the wedding of McTeague and Trina to the horrific murder and the final confrontation between the erstwhile friends in the blinding heat of Death Valley. In the original print all articles either of gold or related to gold (the brass bedstead, even the

John Gilbert as the American soldier and Renée Adorée as the French farm girl whom he falls in love with and eventually marries; a quiet moment from King Vidor's masterly epic of the First World War, *The Big Parade*.

gold fillings in Trina's teeth) were painstakingly tinted by hand.

Standing out among dozens of extra-

ordinary scenes is that of McTeague kissing Trina as she lies back in his dentist's chair insensible under the influence of ether; of Trina spreading a mass of gold coins over her bed-sheet as if welcoming a lover; and in particular of McTeague and Marcus in the closing sequence, when the dentist kills his former friend then discovers that during their struggle Marcus has handcuffed them together

Crowds massing outside the Astor Theatre in New York City for the opening of *The Big Parade*. Note the almost complete absence of a bare head.

and the blistering desert sun glares down on the two doomed figures.

Contemporary criticism, as might be expected, was wildly mixed, often running on the lines: 'A masterpiece, but . . .' James R. Quirk wrote in the influential *Photoplay* magazine: 'The New York newspaper critics acclaimed it as a masterpiece. *Greed* is sordid. *Greed* is depressing. *Greed* is brutal. *Greed* is shocking. It reeks with good acting and wonderful direction . . . Director von Stroheim has emphasized the detail of a sordid story until it becomes almost repulsive. It is the realism of vulgarity to the nth degree, and if that is art, von Stroheim has produced a masterpiece.'

The Big Parade (directed by King Vidor)

opened the screen to what might be called the nostalgic period of war films. Though apparently it did not start out as a spectacular, it certainly ended up as one, with magnificent set pieces of advancing convoys, of a tense trek through machine-gun-infested woods (timed to a metronome), of troops hurriedly evacuating a French village. Almost as interesting as these actual war scenes is the opening sequence showing ordinary men being caught up in patriotic hysteria, whipped up by bands and flags, and dashing off to participate in something which will alter their whole lives (or deprive them of life) without their really knowing what it is all about – in fact being, in Paul Rotha's expressive phrase, 'howled into war'. In essence the film is neither a pro-war nor an anti-war tract, but a boy-meets-loses-finds-girl story set against massive battle sequences. Nevertheless many of the front-line scenes – though weakened since by imitation in later films – were at the time we first saw it both harrowing and moving. Vidor has freely confessed that he inserted the famous moment when the young French girl runs after the lorry which is taking her American soldier to the front and is left behind clutching his boot as a means of bringing a tear to the spectator's eyes – and in this he undoubtedly succeeded. A grimmer and equally unforgettable scene is the confrontation between the soldier and the dying German in the shell-hole, copied since but never so effectively. The gum-chewing lesson between the soldier and the French girl (played delightfully by Renée Adorée) and above all the final moments of the film where, having had a leg amputated, the soldier hobbles across the screen, first in silhouette across a hill-top and then into her arms, are also memorable, with John Gilbert giving one of his greatest performances. An effort must be made nowadays to appreciate the appallingly overdone 'comic relief' supplied by Tom O'Brien and, in particular, Karl Dane. The latter, after appearing in such major silents as *La Bohème* and *The Scarlet Letter*, and a successful series of popular comedies with the British actor George K. Arthur, found his career blighted by his thick accent after the arrival of sound, and committed suicide in 1934.

Comedy was king this year, with all three leading exponents at the top of their form: Harold Lloyd with *The Freshman* (in the UK, to help the ignorant British, it was called *College Days*), Chaplin with *The Gold Rush* and Keaton with *Seven Chances*.

Lloyd's *The Freshman* (directed by Sam Taylor and Fred Newmeyer) is about an innocent, over-eager young student determined to become, immediately, the most popular man in college; instead he is soon spotted as a greenhorn and made to undergo ridicule and ingenious humiliations. However, in time he redeems himself on the football field in one of the most famous of all Lloyd's comedy sequences, which was to reappear long afterwards as a prologue to his last picture – the very disappointing *Mad Wednesday*, also known as *The Sin of Harold Diddlebock* (directed by Preston Sturges). The Lloyd

character in *The Freshman* is more fully developed than hitherto – a trend which was to continue – and the storyline stronger. The fact that in those days the British knew little or nothing of the rules of the American game in no way lessened our enjoyment of the climactic sequence – it is, after all, just another way of getting a ball over a painted line.

Chaplin's *The Gold Rush*, regarded by many as his best film, has as its basis the epic true story of the Donner party in its calamitous trek to the West, but transforms its sufferings into laughter. The film contains three of Chaplin's best-loved scenes: the 'dance of the rolls' on the dinner table as he awaits the arrival of his guests; the moment when, delirious with hunger, he sees big Mack Swain transmogrified into a succulent chicken; and the dilemma of the two men as their little hut sways perilously over a cliff in a blizzard, held in place only by a knot in a rope. 'Chaplin pathos' also has its place, for instance in the scene where his guests, including the dance-hall girl with whom he has fallen in love, fail to turn up at the little hut where he has prepared Christmas dinner for them with the greatest care. Accompanied by the Tivoli orchestra softly playing 'Auld Lang Syne' it was to us, in those softer-hearted days, a touching moment. Many years later Chaplin reissued the film with a commentary written and spoken by himself – but the result only demonstrated that he was right in his resistance to sound.

Buster Keaton's *Seven Chances*, based on a play about a man who learns he will inherit a fortune if he is married by seven o'clock that same evening, contains two of his most celebrated and bizarre sequences: the arrival of literally hundreds of white-clad prospective

In what many regard as his greatest film, *The Gold Rush*, Charlie Chaplin endeavours to protect himself from his erstwhile companion Big Jim McKay (Mack Swain), who, driven mad by hunger in the Frozen North, sees the Little Man as an appetizing meal.

brides in the church where he has fallen asleep, all answering an advertisement, which, in despair at finding a wife, he has placed in a local newspaper; and his nerve-shattering experience when, running down a hill to escape from the hordes of pursuing women, he dislodges a few small pebbles, which in turn set larger ones rolling, until he is frantically dodging hundreds of enormous boulders which seem to be chasing him down with deliberate, implacable malice. Both sequences are marvellous mixtures of menace and mirth. The Girl (Ruth Dwyer) is of less importance than in most Keaton pictures; Jean Arthur may be spotted in a small part.

The Thief of Bagdad (directed by Raoul Walsh), perhaps Douglas Fairbanks' most inventive – if rather overlong – production, had its New York première in 1924, but was not generally released until 1925. A gorgeous fantasy in an East that never was, it includes trick photography (the magic carpet, the instant raising from dust of an entire army of warriors), which in those days before television's endless display of technical gimmickry thrilled and mystified us. It still looks good today, as anyone who saw the recent 'restored' version will agree. The story – of a rascally and irrepressible thief who wins the love of a beautiful princess, is converted by a holy man, suffers incredible dangers, secures happiness in the symbol of a magic box and returns to save both princess and the city from invading Mongols – is told with splendid panache amid magnificent settings. The Princess is played by the lovely Julanne Johnston, who made one or two talkies then, sadly, seemed to disappear from our ken. The film also brought into prominence captivating Anna May Wong, charming oriental menace in numerous silents, born in China-town, Los Angeles, California.

Fairbanks also made his sequel to *The Mark of Zorro, Don Q, Son of Zorro* (directed by Donald Crisp), playing both parent and offspring. Though a better-made film than its more primitive predecessor it seemed to have less sparkle about it, perhaps because old father Zorro when young had the glamour of a first appearance. Nowadays, of course, the whole Zorro family has been done to death and should be buried.

No fewer than four Lon Chaney characters made their appearance during the year: an old woman (*The Unholy Three*), a monster (*The Phantom of the Opera*), a Swedish farmer (*The Tower of Lies*) and a mad doctor (*The Monster*). *The Unholy Three* (directed by Tod Browning) is a decidedly different crime thriller, the gang consisting of three circus performers – a giant, Hercules (Victor McLaglen), a dwarf, Tweedledee (Harry Earles), and Professor Echo, a ventriloquist (Chaney), whose main occupation is picking pockets disguised as an old woman. Seeking to increase their illegal profits, they open a store stocked with mute parrots which are made to appear to talk by Echo's ventriloquial skill. If a disillusioned purchaser later complains that his bird has gone dumb they go to his house, Echo wheeling Tweedledee disguised as a baby in a pram. While Echo 'ventriloquizes' the parrot into speech again the 'baby' has a good look round, and later they return to rob the place. If not an every-day criminal occupation, it is certainly an ingenious one. Though the ventriloquism was cleverly suggested it would obviously have been improved by the use of sound and the film was remade some five years later by another director (Jack Conway) with Elliott Nugent replacing McLaglen but Chaney and Earles in their original roles. Chaney revealed he could be as adept at changing his voice as his appearance. The climactic moment occurs when, being questioned in court as a suspect, he gives the game away by inadvertently dropping his voice from the old woman's shaky treble to his normal deep tones. For a silent film, sound has an unusually important part in the story – the parrot, Chaney's voice as an old woman, the rattle of jewellery in a toy elephant – yet in the opinion of at least one critic this film works better than Jack Conway's sound version.

Chaney's second film is probably his best-known – except perhaps for *Hunchback of Notre Dame* – and his most popular. No subsequent remake has dimmed its memory despite advanced technical facilities. *The Phantom of the Opera* was directed by Rupert Julian, little remembered today except as the man who replaced Erich von Stroheim on *Merry-Go-Round* after the latter's dispute with Universal Studios. The famous 'unmasking' scene, when Chaney's hideously disfigured face is seen for the first time, remains among the supreme moments of the horror film, sound or silent. He is seated playing the organ to the girl whom he loves and has kidnapped and taken to his secret chamber below the Paris Opera House. His face is covered by a mask of gentle refinement. Unsuspected by him, the girl (Mary Philbin) creeps softly up behind him and, giving way to her curiosity despite repeated warnings, whips off the mask. Instantly Chaney rears up to his full height and the ultimate frightfulness of his appearance is revealed: the fact that this does not occur until well into the film heightens its effect. In his book on Chaney, *Faces, Forms, Figures,* which pays special attention to the actor's make-up, Robert G. Anderson describes in detail how the effect of a 'death's head' was achieved: the artificial forehead and taped-back ears to elongate the face, the nose uptilted, the nostrils widened with pieces of wire and blackened to simulate an *absence* of nose, the cheekbones built up with putty, the jagged guttapercha teeth inserted to keep the mouth open. At the time, the fearsome result was kept secret as long as possible. Nowadays, when the stills are so familiar from books, the effect is much weakened. Other memorable moments include the Phantom gliding along the sewers beneath the building, visible only as a breathing tube projecting from the murky waters until his hand rises to drag down his victim; the swinging chandelier about to descend upon the crowded auditorium; and the final flight of the monster. The story is ludicrous and the performances of Norman Kerry and Mary Philbin were wooden, but Chaney managed to make us believe in quite a lot of it.

The film's appearance in Britain was delayed for some time – to our intense frustration – supposedly as the result of an absurd scandal. By some means it seems that Universal's publicity department contrived to have the cans containing the reels met at the British dock and escorted by a contingent of the army. This so shocked government and army officials that they lost any sense of humour they possessed and, instead of laughing the whole thing off as an impertinent but ingenious hoax, confiscated the film and avenged the 'insult' by depriving the innocent filmgoer of seeing it until a considerable period had elapsed. Doubts have sometimes been expressed as to whether such a farcical situation could have arisen, but it was certainly widely accepted at the time. If it had indeed been untrue, then maybe by inventing it and whetting our appetites the Universal geniuses excelled themselves still further.

In his third film, *The Tower of Lies* (directed by Victor Seastrom), Chaney further showed his versatility, playing a serious, hardworking Swedish farmer who becomes grief-stricken and crazy when his daughter leaves him to look for work in the city and thus save them from eviction, but fails to return. Gloomy and with a somewhat unconvincing story (despite being derived from a work by Selma Lagerlöf, the distinguished Swedish author of *The Atonement of Gösta Berling*), the film was unsuccessful and is today listed as 'lost'. Being one of Seastrom's few American productions, and with Chaney's powerful performance supported by Norma Shearer, Ian Keith and David Torrence, its disappearance is to be regretted.

In the last of the year's pictures, *The Monster*, which is an enjoyable out-and-out horror comic, Chaney, almost devoid of

Pretty and talented Vera Reynolds as a Jacobean girl in the flashback sequence from C. B. DeMille's *The Road to Yesterday*.

make-up, could be seen obviously enjoying himself as a mad surgeon practising bizarre experiments on unfortunate motorists whom he lures by means of false headlights down a chute into a dark dungeon. The original play (by Crane Wilbur) acquired some notoriety later through its connection with the American actor Philip Yale Drew, who was playing in it at the County Theatre, Reading, Berkshire when he was under suspicion of murdering a local tobacconist; he was however cleared at the inquest.

To this year belongs Erich von Stroheim's famous – or notorious – production of *The Merry Widow*, in which he turned a light-hearted Viennese operetta (by Victor Léon and Leo Stein) into an excoriating exposé of the vulgarity and decadence of contemporary high life. A notable cast includes John Gilbert, Tully Marshall, Roy D'Arcy (a splendid eye-and-teeth-flashing villain of the 'twenties)

and Josephine Crowell, moving effortlessly from Harold Lloyd's awful mother-in-law to Queen of a mythical kingdom. The Widow herself is played by Mae Murray – famous for her 'bee-stung lips'. Stroheim's clashes with Miss Murray are legendary, but appear not to have affected the quality of the film itself, which to my regret I never managed to track down.

Cecil B. DeMille's *The Road to Yesterday* is one of his lesser-known 'big pictures'. In it he indulges once again in his rather pleasant fancy for transporting his characters into the past in order to teach them a lesson for their future. The story deals with the relationships of two slightly interlinked couples. Kenneth is a man with a deformed arm who on his honeymoon discovers that his wife Malena shrinks from him – because, he thinks, of his infirmity; Beth is a young girl who falls for a younger man, Jack, but turns him down when she discovers his is a minister of the Church. All four are staying in the same hotel. Except for Jack, they belong to what would probably be described today as the jet-set. Also in the hotel is the girl's aunt, a believer in the occult and in reincarnation, in which she tries to interest them. Tension rises between Kenneth and Jack: the minister advises Kenneth to pray to God about his arm, but a specialist says it must be operated on quickly. Later they are all on a train together bound for Chicago when it is involved in a horrific accident. Beth is knocked unconscious, and through her delirium all find themselves back in seventeenth-century England. Kenneth is a knight, Beth a pretty Jacobean girl, Malena a gypsy, Jack her one-time lover. After numerous increasingly hectic adventures a climax is reached when the gypsy is about to be burnt at the stake. Fortunately in the nick of time they are all hurtled back, or forward, to the present. Beth is in Jack's arms, Kenneth rescues Malena from the wreckage in which she is trapped, and all ends satisfactorily. DeMille's flair and some attractive photography (by Peverell Marley) make all this quite convincing while it lasts; the train crash, too, is stupendous. The transition from present to past is effectively contrived, fading finally into a travelling shot with Beth, in charming costume, running along a country road towards a retreating camera. An attractive cast consists of Joseph Schildkraut, Jetta Goudal, William (later to become Hopalong Cassidy) Boyd and Vera Reynolds. A most delightful actress, Vera Reynolds made some 25 silent films and several talkies after starting her career as a dancer. At one time married to actor Robert Ellis, she retired from the screen soon after the arrival of sound and seems to have vanished without trace until her death 30 years later, in 1962.

The tearjerker of the year was undoubtedly *Stella Dallas* (directed by Henry King), a story of mother-love with a difference, in that the devoted parent is not the usual frail, ageing figure in spectacles and white wig but a dowdy slut, 'gaudy but not neat', as a contemporary critic neatly put it. Belle Bennett is outstanding in the role, in no way effaced by Barbara Stanwyck's admirable performance in the 1938 sound remake. A distinguished cast includes Ronald Colman as the man who weds and leaves her, Alice Joyce as the 'other woman' and pretty Lois Moran as the daughter for whose happiness Miss Bennett sacrifices what is left of her own – not much, it would appear. The famous ending shows the mother out in the cold street watching through the window of a fine house the wedding of her child to a highly eligible young member of society (no less than Douglas Fairbanks Jr, in fact). This heartrending moment, derided by a critic as trite, was positively wept over by countless contemporary filmgoers.

William S. Hart made his farewell to the screen in *Tumbleweeds* (directed by King Baggot, probably with Hart's co-operation). It is one of the best of all westerns from the silent period, though Hart's star was fading and it did not have the success it deserved. The final shot of the tumbleweeds symbolically blowing across the dusty ground is a

One of the greatest of early western stars, William S. Hart, in his last film, *Tumbleweeds*. Though known mainly for his westerns, Hart was earlier celebrated as a Shakespearean actor in the theatre and for his performance as Messala in the 1899 Broadway production of *Ben-Hur*.

memorable one. The film was re-issued after the arrival of sound, with Hart speaking a prologue.

Two other westerns this year stand out from the general run: *Riders of the Purple Sage* (directed by Lynn Reynolds), from the novel by the ever-reliable Zane Grey, with Tom Mix at his best and Warner Oland, a fine 'heavy' from Sweden, later to be the philosophizing Charlie Chan, as a villainous lawyer; and James Cruze's *The Pony Express*, not another *Covered Wagon*, but a good film all the same, set during the Civil War. Its cast includes Betty Compson, Ricardo Cortez, and three fine figures of men – Wallace Beery, George Bancroft and Ernest Torrence.

Marie Prevost was sprightly in a lightweight

Ronald Colman (Lord Darlington), Bert Lytell (Lord Windermere) and May McAvoy (Lady Windermere) face one another in somewhat stilted style in Lubitsch's visually witty production of Oscar Wilde's verbally witty comedy-drama, *Lady Windermere's Fan*. Miss McAvoy, it seems, is standing on a box.

'typical Lubitsch' comedy, *Kiss Me Again*, from a Sardou play, but his other film, *Lady Windermere's Fan*, was among his most notable. Tackling Oscar Wilde's play without the dialogue to express his witticisms must have presented problems, but he contrives brilliantly to translate them into what might be called visual epigrams. Even the creaky mechanics of the melodramatic plot are made to run smoothly by the Lubitsch treatment. The cast is a good one: Ronald Colman as Lord Darlington, Irene Rich (a popular and clever leading lady) as Mrs Erlynne, Bert Lytell as Lord Windermere, and petite May McAvoy (who seems in some stills to be standing on a box to bring her up to the level of the others) as Lady Windermere.

James Cruze turned to comedy with *Beggar on Horseback*, deftly transferred by Walter Woods from a well-known George S. Kaufman and Walter Connelly play. Edward Everett Horton, steadily increased his reputation, and Esther Ralston our admiration, in this delightful fantasy about a struggling classical composer forced to write jazz for a living, who is trapped into proposing to the daughter of a family of appalling vulgarity but has his potential future revealed to him in a nightmare of exaggeration, and saves himself in time. Ethel Wales, always reliable as an ill-bred parent, plays the prospective mother-in-law.

Graustark (directed by Dimitri

Buchowetzki) is another of those generally enjoyable love-or-duty romances set in a mythical country. In this case it is Norma Talmadge (as Princess Yetive – the names alone in these films are almost worth the price of admission) who has to face an unhappy marriage with the prince of a neighbouring country, and very appealingly she faces it. Fortunately she meets an attractive American (Eugene O'Brien as Grenfall Lorry, another name worth preserving) while on a train journey in the United States, and after numerous evil machinations – with Marc MacDermott and Roy D'Arcy in the cast we were expecting these – the Princess appeals to her people, who are only too pleased to welcome Mr Lorry as their prince. Graustark, Ruritania, Karlsburg – what colourful pictures even their names conjure up, and what magnificent clothes their more illustrious citizens wore. A pity they are not so often visited nowadays.

Josef von Sternberg's first American film, *The Salvation Hunters*, became of interest, long after it was made, mainly because of the director's later fame. At the time it aroused little general enthusiasm, except perhaps among the most discerning. The simple story, of a penniless young couple's drab existence, first on a steam dredger in a muddy river and later in the seamier parts of a city, seemed sordid and static to the majority of filmgoers, and none of the cast, which included George K. Arthur, Georgia Hale (Chaplin's girl in *The Gold Rush*) and Stuart Holmes, had a sufficiently strong name to bring audiences in. No less a critic than Robert E. Sherwood dismissed it as 'a frightfully artistic picture, with some good acting, some striking composition and almost no action'.

The Eagle (directed by Clarence Brown) is the last but one of Rudolph Valentino's films, and one of the most entertaining, with plenty of humour and less eye-flashing lovemaking. Valentino, in fact, seems to enjoy making kindly fun of his own image. Set in a Russia that never was, ruled by a Catherine the Great who never existed, during a period that looks decidedly confused, it is directed by Clarence Brown with the utmost wit and charm. Valentino is strongly supported by Louise Dresser as the susceptible Czarina, Vilma Banky as the most delightful of his heroines, and in particular Albert Conti, whose resemblance to Adolphe Menjou is more marked than ever and who gives a delicious performance in the Menjou manner. Among other familiar friends are Mack Swain, Russell Simpson, Gustav von Seyffertitz and Eric Mayne – though sharp eyesight is necessary to spot the last two. James Marcus, another reliable character actor of the period, proves a most likeable villain.

Other American films included *The Lost World* (directed by Harry O. Hoyt), early science fiction from the well-known Conan Doyle story about an intrepid band of explorers confronting prehistoric monsters in a hitherto unknown part of South America, with Wallace Beery (excellent as the great Professor Challenger), Lewis Stone and Lloyd Hughes in the cast. Also present is Bessie Love, considered necessary for the box-office, though not in the original book. However, nobody seems to have worried very much about a little romance being added to the pterodactyls and dinosaurs.

Seven Keys to Baldpate (directed by Fred Newmeyer) was the best of several versions of George M. Cohan's ingenious comedy-mystery in which a young man retires to a deserted inn to complete a novel by a strict deadline only to be disturbed by a host of very strange visitors. The twists and double-twists are worthy of Agatha Christie at her best, and the play has been transferred to the silent screen with no loss of tension or mystery, aided by a first-rate performance by Douglas MacLean, another light comedian of the period, undeservedly forgotten today, who turned producer in later years.

Zander the Great (directed by George Hill) was not, as the title might suggest, a spectacular about a powerful exotic ruler but an

exciting and sometimes touching story with a western background concerning an orphaned girl who becomes attached to a small boy and decides to take him in search of his missing father. After various adventures with smugglers and assorted villains all ends well. Marion Davies, whose potential success as a comedy actress was supposedly thwarted by William Randolph Hearst's determination to make her a serious one, gives one of her best performances, starting off with pigtails and freckles but growing out of both and injecting plenty of light relief into this minor but enjoyable picture. Also in the cast are Harrison Ford, Emily Fitzroy and the not-very-good actress who was later to turn viperish gossip-writer, Hedda Hopper.

Smouldering Fires (directed by Clarence Brown) was a rather heavy-going drama about a strong-willed and successful business-woman who unwisely falls in love with a man a good deal younger than herself; trials and tribulations inevitably follow. The film is redeemed by powerful playing from Pauline Frederick, a distinguished Broadway actress who also had a notable film career during the silent and early sound periods. Her most famous part was in the title role of *Madame X*, a courtroom drama, but she was equally at home in smart comedy roles. Daughter of a railway yard-master, she had five husbands and died in 1936 at the age of 55.

Madame Sans-Gêne (directed by Léonce Perret) starred Gloria Swanson as the laundry proprietress who had Napoleon as one of her 'clients'. Described as historical romance, more romance than historical but entertaining, with Swanson at her liveliest and wearing some memorable costumes. A mainly French cast included Emile Drain as Napoleon.

Gloria Swanson finds herself the cynosure of all eyes, and, in that costume, who can wonder at it? A scene from *Madame Sans-Gêne,* in which a one-time laundry proprietress numbers the Emperor Napoleon among her 'clients'.

Sydney Chaplin who, busy managing brother Charlie's business affairs, appeared in too few films but proved himself an admirable comedian in the famous old farce *Charley's Aunt.*

Lord Jim (directed by Victor Fleming), an acceptable adaptation of Conrad's novel, featured Percy Marmont at his tormented best as a ship's first mate whose life is ruined by one moment when his nerve fails him.

In *Charley's Aunt* (directed by Scott Sidney) Sydney Chaplin, Charlie's brother, who appeared in too few films himself, is an excellent Fancourt Babberley – 'Sir' here, 'Lord' in the sound version made five years later with Charles Ruggles.

The Wizard of Oz (directed by Larry Semon) remains interesting both as the fore-runner of Judy Garland's film and as one of Semon's few feature films. Hardly ever seen now, even in compilation movies, the white-faced comic was one of the most popular and prolific actors in silent 'shorts', but his career

Larry Semon, a leading silent comedian now undeservedly overlooked, as the Scarecrow in the early version of *The Wizard of Oz*. Dorothy Dwan, as Dorothy, may not have been a Judy Garland, but she had a lively charm all her own.

faded as he launched out into feature films; though he made a fortune, he was always a big spender and was eventually declared bankrupt; he died of pneumonia following a nervous breakdown in 1928, aged 39. Memories of this silent *Oz* are vague, perhaps wiped out by Judy, but the two versions had little in common. The cast includes Oliver Hardy as the Tin Woodsman, Charles Murray (another comedy stalwart of the period) as the Wizard, Josef Swickard as the Prime Minister, Mary Carr as Dorothy's mother, and Dorothy Dwan, in what appears to have been her first film, as Dorothy. Semon himself, as well as directing and working on the script, plays the Scarecrow.

We Moderns (directed by John Francis Dillon), in which Colleen Moore continues to develop her personification of the jazz-and-flapper age, is a bright version of Israel Zangwill's comedy about what would later be called the generation gap. The viewpoints of both sides of the gap are represented with spirit, and the climax is a jazz party on board a zeppelin, during which Miss Moore escapes the customary fate worse than death by the somewhat excessive intervention of Providence in the shape of an aeroplane which crashes into the zep. Claude Gillingwater is the ideal representative of the older generation, whose views Colleen Moore, understandably sobered by recent events, comes to respect. Two further jazz-age movies were *Bobbed Hair* (directed by Alan Crosland), in which Marie Prevost faces the dilemma of whether to cut it or not, torn by the differing views of two suitors; and *Sally, Irene and Mary* (directed by Edmund Goulding), with Joan Crawford, Constance Bennett and Sally O'Neil as three contrasting types of 1920s chorus girls interlinked in various romantic and dramatic events. These, with *We Moderns*, form a representative trio of popular films depicting adventurous youth in the 'roaring 'twenties'.

The most successful British film at the box-office was in all probability *The Rat* (directed by Graham Cutts), which Ivor Novello transferred to the screen from the stage, where it had already proved extremely popular; it was, in fact, originally written as a film script. Constance Collier had persuaded him to turn it into a play, and following its favourable reception in the theatre he rewrote the movie version. Despite its improbable story of a handsome Parisian apache, a *demi-mondaine* and her wicked protector, who casts a lustful eye on an innocent girl who in turn loves the apache, the film has the benefit of imaginative direction and photography which transcend the material. It marks the first real attempt in Britain to develop the mobility of the camera, even if this meant nothing more than traipsing after the characters and acting as a substitute for cutting from medium to close shots. The film helped to establish Novello's position as a matinée idol, though his film career was mainly confined to the silent period, before his series of spectacular musical plays at the Drury Lane Theatre. Mae Marsh, who had worked with Novello earlier in Griffith's *The White Rose*, came to England to play the girl. It was, in fact, her last silent picture. Afterwards she retired for several years, but returned to re-create Mary Carr's self-sacrificing mother in *Over the Hill* 1931 and continue a modest career in sound films until 1961. She died in 1968, aged 73.

Another transatlantic visitor was Betty Blythe, who, following her success as the Queen of Sheba, came over to star in *She* (directed by Leander de Cordova), though the film was actually made in Berlin. This version of Rider Haggard's tale of whitest Africa and its eternally youthful Queen has since been declared a total disaster, but its critical reception at the time, if not rapturous, was at least respectful. Its imaginative qualities, sense of spectacle, good camera work and the excellence of its softly-lighted interiors were among the attributes mentioned by critics. 'Good for any type of hall' was the Bioscope's somewhat ambiguous recommendation, together with the cautious addition that Miss Blythe (glittering in costumes that apparently caused some unspecified difficulties during production) is 'at her best in scenes which make least demand on her emotions'.

Sir John Martin Harvey, one of the earliest theatrical knights, made a rare screen appearance in the role which is forever linked with his name in the theatre, Sidney Carton in *The Only Way* (directed by Herbert Wilcox), based on the well-known adaptation of Dickens' *A Tale of Two Cities* and filmed on a very spectacular scale (costing all of £24,000) with enormous sets and lots of milling extras. Though inevitably theatrical in conception and performance it was not merely an overweight prestige production.

Wilcox received high praise for his handling of the vast crowds, and Norman Arnold for his impressive sets. A leading critic said of the 'Far, far better thing . . .' climax that 'at this point the film ceased to be great – it became sublime': who could have asked for more?

The major film from the Continent was E. A. Dupont's German production *Variety*, known in Britain at the time as *Vaudeville*. For most of us it was the first time we saw Emil Jannings – *The Last Laugh* came later. From the opening shots of the huge, grey, bent, shuffling figure (a typical Jannings posture) to its return at the film's closing moments we sat motionless and enthralled. In the intervening period we had witnessed the rise to moderate success of a trapeze artist, 'Boss Hüller', who abandons his colourless wife for an attractive young trollop, makes her his partner in the act and later murders the younger and more handsome acrobat who displaces him as her lover. Then, very slowly, he lumbers off to the authorities and gives himself up. The framing prologue and epilogue show him receiving his release after a remission for good conduct, and shambling off to the nothingness that lies ahead. Jannings was later to make rather a habit of humiliation (*The Way of All Flesh*, *The Blue Angel*) but at this time he was unknown to most of us and during the unfolding of the grim, sordid story he held the audience in a vice. The film also introduced Lya de Putti – small, far from conventionally beautiful, but unrelentingly potent as a vamp apart from being a competent actress. Dupont's direction is both subtle and adventurous. The gradual development of the situation is hinted at by a succession of small incidents; Hüller's murder of his rival is done out of sight below the frame; the victim – played with admirable smoothness by the British actor Warwick Ward – slips down as the killer's hands follow him, a restraint a good deal more effective than the fake gouging, writhing and blood-

Emil Jannings as the burly trapeze artist and Lya de Putti as his faithless mistress and partner in the circus act in the grim and gripping *Variety*, also known as *Vaudeville*.

spattering which would have been considered necessary in later years. Karl Freund's swinging and swaying subjective camera in the acrobatic circus scenes is used with remarkable skill, the horrifying climax being reached when one of the acrobats falls, the camera seeming to fall in his place and catching the shock on the faces of the audience, upturned as they watch. As we watched the prison gates, in a cleverly angled shot, close behind the released, bowed old man, over sixty years ago, they closed for us on an unforgettable experience.

G. W. Pabst's *The Joyless Street* was the first film in which Greta Garbo appeared outside Sweden and the last before she left, with Mauritz Stiller, for America. It tells of the hardships of the middle classes in post-war Vienna when food was short, inflation rampant, and a butcher with meat in his shop could rule the roost. Finally the desperate people break down the doors of a brothel (the butcher had been supplying its inmates in preference to his other clientele) and trample the man to death. Garbo's role is secondary to that of the great Danish actress (daughter of a washerwoman) Asta Nielsen. An apparently insoluble mystery surrounds the arrival of Garbo and Stiller in America: did Mayer (and MGM) want Stiller without Garbo ('In America they don't want fat women' – it seems Mayer was referring to her slightly plump appearance in certain early photographs) or Garbo without Stiller? Or both? The question is intriguing, but surely by this time academic. After *The Joyless Street* and a brief return to Sweden she came, she saw, she stayed.

It was at about this time, from 1924 or 1925 on, that the new Russian films began to be screened in Britain – *Battleship Potemkin*, *Strike*, *Mother*, *The General Line*. They were watched, in general, with appreciation of the brilliance of the set pieces such as the Odessa Steps sequence in *Potemkin*, the symbolism, the sometimes remarkable photography and composition, the *montage* – always the *montage* – but watched dutifully rather than enthusiastically. Perhaps the propaganda was rather too overt and strident, as if we were being bellowed at; maybe, in some cases, it was just an allergy to tractors.

1925

The World at Large

Locarno Treaty signed
First transatlantic broadcast
Estimated 1, 654,000 radio sets in Great Britain
Hitler publishes first volume of *Mein Kampf*
The New Yorker founded
The so-called 'Year of the Charleston'
Floyd Collins is pinned down by fall of rock in Kentucky Cave (filmed as *Ace in the Hole*)
John T. Scopes tried for preaching evolution in Tennessee (filmed as *Inherit the Wind*)
Norman Thorne murder case, Crowborough, Sussex
Death of Queen Alexandra

Cinema

Warner Bros. buys Vitagraph Company
Samuel Goldwyn joins United Artists
Oscar Deutsch, later founder of the Odeon circuit, enters the film industry
Cecil B. DeMille leaves Paramount to go independent
Capitol Cinema, Haymarket, London, opens
Rebuilt New Gallery, Regent Street, London, opens
An estimated 95 per cent of British screen time is given to American films
Deaths of Louis Feuillade and Max Linder
Wampas Baby Stars: Betty Arlen, Violet Avon, Olive Borden, Ann Cornwall, Ena Gregory, Madeline Hurlock, Natalie Joyce, June Marlowe, Joan Meredyth, Evelyn Pierce, Dorothy Revier, Duane Thompson, Lola Todd
Births: Richard Burton, Tony Curtis, Rock Hudson, Paul Newman, Jack Lemmon, Rod Steiger, Peter Sellers, Sam Peckinpah

Theatre

Noël Coward, *Hay Fever*
Frederick Lonsdale, *The Last of Mrs Cheyney*
Arnold Ridley, *The Ghost Train*
George Kelly, *Craig's Wife*
Alfred Neumann, *The Patriot*
Rudolf Friml, *The Vagabond King*
Jerome Kern, *Sunny*

Fiction

F. Scott Fitzgerald, *The Great Gatsby*
Theodore Dreiser, *An American Tragedy*
Sinclair Lewis, *Martin Arrowsmith*
Somerset Maugham, *The Painted Veil*
Hugh Walpole, *Portrait of a Man with Red Hair*
Warwick Deeping, *Sorrell and Son*
Franz Kafka, *The Trial*
John Erskine, *The Private Life of Helen of Troy*
Anita Loos, *Gentlemen Prefer Blondes*
Edna Ferber, *So Big* (Pulitzer Prize-winner)

Music

Sibelius, *Tapiola* (tone Poem)
Shostakovich, Symphony no. 1
Aaron Copland, Symphony no. 1
Ravel, *L'Enfant et les sortilèges* (opera)

Popular Songs

'Only a Rose'
'Who?'
'Show Me the Way to Go Home'
'Thanks for the Buggy Ride'
'Don't Bring Lulu'

Fashion Note

Dresses lose their waists
Oxford bags (ultra-wide trousers) in favour for men

1926

Ben-Hur (directed by Fred Niblo) was, by most measurements, the big one of the American year. The tortuous story of its creation has often been told – most fully in Kevin Brownlow's *The Parade's Gone By*. The first film version, a skeletal two-reeler directed by Sidney Olcott, appeared in 1907, two years after the death of the author, Lew Wallace, a Union general in the American Civil War, later Governor of New Mexico and Minister to Turkey. (In 1899, after considerable persuasion, he had allowed a stage version to be produced which achieved enormous success; the villain, Messala, was played by William S. Hart, later doyen of the silent western.) In 1923, largely owing to the unceasing efforts of June Mathis, the powerful scenarist with the Goldwyn Company, a major production was planned and started in Italy, with Charles Brabin as director, George Walsh as Ben-Hur, Francis X. Bushman as Messala and Gertrude Olmstead as Esther. General mismanagement, together with chaos caused by the political upheavals between fascists and anti-fascists in Italy, brought about – after the screening of some disastrous early rushes – a wholesale re-

Ramon Novarro in the magnificently handled chariot race (by Reaves Eason, second unit director) in *Ben-Hur* – silent (if a full orchestral accompaniment at its most tumultuous can be called silent) but evoking as much excitement at the time as that of the later sound version.

shuffle. Fred Niblo took over from Brabin, Bess Meredyth from June Mathis, Ramon Novarro (who had previously been tested for the part) from George Walsh, and May McAvoy from Gertrude Olmstead (who became instead Lon Chaney's potential victim in *The Monster*).

Troubles, however, continued, resulting eventually in the whole production being carted – or shipped – back to America. The huge Circus Maximus set (scene of the great chariot race) was reconstructed in California, but further setbacks occurred, and the site of the construction had to be changed because the authorities decided it was necessary to lay a big storm drain beneath it. Despite all this, and the inevitable accidents befalling any major production, an end – and a beginning – was reached and the film's first public screening took place on the last day but one of 1925.

As we gathered excitedly at the Tivoli, London during its first long run the following year we had of course no knowledge of all that had taken place during the making of what Brownlow describes as the Heroic Fiasco. The facts that the big Circus set was really only half its apparent height (the rest being brilliantly matched with miniatures) and a large part of the cheering and waving crowds consisted of small puppets worried us not at all because the deception was entirely undetectable. The two famous set pieces of the chariot race (shot, incidentally, not by

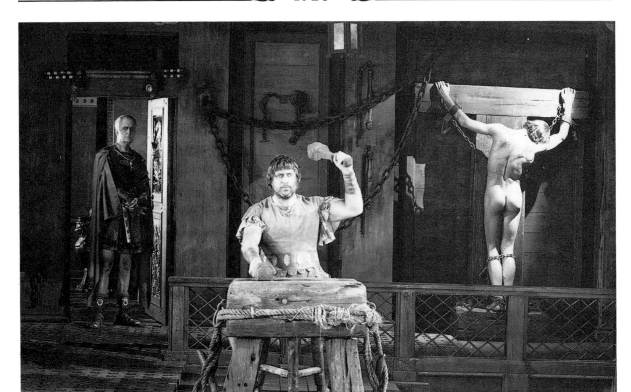

In the galley ship in *Ben-Hur*, with the time-beater in full action and a (commendably clean) slave chained up as an encouragement to the others. Looking on from the entrance is Frank Currier as the ship's commander.

Fred Niblo but by second unit director Reaves Eason) and the sea battle excited us as much as the 1959 version excited a later generation – perhaps more, as they were in many ways the most stupendous examples of film spectacle we had yet seen. We knew nothing at the time of the supposed death of one or more extras during the battle – a mystery never really solved. The somewhat flamboyant style of acting, particularly from the magnificently built Bushman, suited both the subject and the times. The shorter duration of the film, only about two-thirds that of the later version, tightened the action and lessened the *longueurs*. Considered dramatically, the film's two main climaxes occur too early in the story, which causes an inevitable let-down when leprosy and mysticism take over from action and conflict, but this fault may be blamed on the original author, who after all could not foresee what was to happen to his work.

Judah Ben-Hur is a contemporary of Jesus Christ, and their lives run parallel and coincidentally cross on a number of occasions, His presence being indicated generally by a hand, a footprint, a figure with the head out of frame. It is an ingenious and reticent method, but has a sort of jigsaw coyness that becomes irritating, particularly as the hand, white and slim with tapering fingers, suggests that of an *effete* fop or a woman living in comfort. In the original print the Nativity and other religious moments were photographed in Technicolor. Betty Bronson – fresh from *Peter Pan* –

appears as a charming if somewhat youthful and picture-book Virgin Mary. Christy Cabanne, who ran the tests, wanted 19-year-old Myrna Loy for the part, which, considering the sort of films she was appearing in at about this time, would have seemed even less appropriate. She did appear in the film, however, as a 'hedonist', among the crowds in the Circus Maximus.

Seen with a full, and visible, orchestra pounding away full blast, *Ben-Hur* was a great and memorable occasion sixty years ago: so vivid was its effect that strangely, though photographed mainly in black-and-white, the film appears to the eye of memory in the fullest and brightest of colours.

Francis X. Bushman, the definitive Messala, was a classically handsome star of the silents, known inevitably as Francis Sex Bushman. He graduated from the stage in 1911 and appeared in literally dozens of films through

Hero and villain face to face but forcibly restrained, with horror on every countenance: Ramon Novarro and Francis X. Bushman anxious to come to grips in *Ben-Hur*. At a quick glance, one might wonder what a Buster Keaton lookalike is doing in the centre of such a gathering.

the period, frequently with his wife Beverley Bayne. Their house, a centre of Hollywood social life, stood on the site later occupied by Grauman's famous Chinese Theatre. In later years, divorced and with much of his fortune lost in the Wall Street Crash, he worked in radio series. He died in 1966, of a heart attack following a fall, aged 83.

Exhilaration rather than spectacle was the keynote of Douglas Fairbanks' *The Black Pirate* (directed by Albert Parker), which can best be described as a rollicking yarn of pirates and blue water – literally blue, because one of the reasons why audiences

Lillian Gish pilloried with her illegitimate child in her arms and the red letter of adultery emblazoned on her breast, as Hester Prynne in *The Scarlet Letter*, based on Nathaniel Hawthorne's classic novel.

flocked to see it with high expectations was that for the first time they would see a major film in 'superb Technicolor'. And superb it was – as a novelty. We took too much for granted in those days the beautiful quality of the black-and-white pictures then current. Even the most modest ones had a crispness, a subtlety of shade gradations that are a revelation when (far too seldom) a really first-class 'silent' print is screened today, even without the lovely tinting which seemed to enhance the purely black-and-white sections of the film. Apart from this, *The Black Pirate*

has a delightfully cheerful nonchalance about it – and it doesn't really matter that the story stretches credibility to the limit. Billie Dove is lovely enough for any swashbuckler to hold hostage, and the usual reliable character players (in this case Anders Randolf and Donald Crisp) are on hand to lend staunch support. A big moment in the film is the famous slide down the ship's sail on a knife: faked or not, 'doubled' or not, it looked fine, and it never occurred to any of us at the time to doubt its authenticity. The comparative brevity of the film, 8 reels against the 12 or more usually given to Fairbanks spectaculars, meant that the action was brisk and breezy throughout, avoiding the slower and less interesting patches, romantic or otherwise, occasionally found in earlier productions.

Mantrap (directed by Victor Fleming), from a novel by Sinclair Lewis, marked a big step forward in Clara Bow's career. In a more solid role than hitherto, she plays a former manicurist, now the wife of a large, lumbering woodsman named Joe (a sympathetic study by Ernest Torrence); when he brings a disillusioned divorce lawyer (Percy Marmont) to his trading post she almost automatically starts to flirt with him. Eventually she goes back to Joe, but as the film ends he seems to have few illusions as to her future behaviour. All three actors give fine performances in somewhat untypical parts and the result was a considerable success both critically and financially.

The 'best' Lillian Gish film would be a hard choice to make, but *The Scarlet Letter* would surely be near the top of any list. As directed by Victor Seastrom the somewhat stolid Nathaniel Hawthorne classic becomes softer, and even lighter, without losing any of its power. When I first saw it the close of the film was greeted by dead silence followed by rounds of applause – a sound not often heard in the cinema, at any rate in those days, except perhaps at a première. Lillian Gish exhibits to the full her unique power of suggesting iron will under a gentle, even fragile exterior (an attribute, apparently, of her private self as well) and the Swedish actor Lars Hanson, soon to partner her again, gives superb support as the Rev. Arthur Dimmesdale.

Her second picture of the year, *La Bohème*, excited less notice, but is surely remembered with affection by all of us fortunate enough to have seen it at the time. Criticisms varied wildly: 'a pretty dismal entertainment'; 'a triumph for MGM'; '. . . will prove a real joy' – though 'joy' seems an odd word, considering the tragic story. The supporting cast is a fine one – John Gilbert at the height of his fame, Renée Adorée wholly enchanting as Musette, Roy D'Arcy and Edward Everett Horton; and how pleasant, after the customary massively healthy prima donna, to see a Mimi who looks as if she really *might* be dying of consumption. In a way this year

Lillian Gish dying in the arms of John Gilbert in a silent *La Bohème,* and presenting, for once, a Mimi frail enough to convince audiences that death cannot be far away.

was something of a come-back for Lillian Gish, whose 1925 film, *Romola* (which I missed), was apparently something of a turgid failure, beautiful though she looks in the available stills.

In lighter mood Colleen Moore (later to follow Lillian Gish in a sound remake of *The Scarlet Letter*) delighted audiences in one of her best, if not her best, comedies, *Ella Cinders* (directed by Alfred E. Green), in which Harry Langdon makes a brief, slapstick appearance. This enjoyable and gently satirical picture, based on a comic strip, of a

An early example of aquarium symbolism, with the sinister tentacles of the octopus shadowing the meeting between the beautiful German spy (Alice Terry) and the Spanish sea captain (Antonio Moreno) whom she plans to ensnare, in *Mare Nostrum.*

young, downtrodden slavey who wins a 'movie contest' and causes a series of upsets in the studios, shows another side to her jazz-age persona, as does her performance as the little Limehouse street dancer in *Twinkletoes* (directed by Charles Brabin), from the same author as *Broken Blossoms* and set in the same surroundings and similar circumstances. Though not another Griffith masterpiece, this undeservedly neglected film is yet another example of the star's versatility. Tully Marshall, Gladys Brockwell, Lucien Littlefield and Warner Oland provide strong support, with Kenneth Harlan – a pleasant if rather stodgy leading man – on hand as a champion boxer who rescues Twinkletoes from a watery suicide.

Mare Nostrum, Rex Ingram's second film based on novels by Vicente Blasco-Ibáñez set during the First World War, is a story of espionage in and around the Mediterranean. The title refers to the name of a boat but has also a symbolic meaning. The production has a multi-national cast, which was no problem in those happy days free from the dreadful practice of dubbing words of a different language on to an unfortunate actor's lips. Antonio Moreno plays his own nationality, Spanish, Alice Terry is a German spy, André von Engelman a German submarine commander, and the cast list contains various other exotic names. It is, as customary with Ingram, a visually beautiful movie, filmed on location and taking every advantage of it. At least one scene has been much copied since, the playing of a significant meeting (in

this case between lovers) in an aquarium, with an octopus providing the symbolism. Alice Terry, blonde wig restored, is at her most proudly beautiful; her walk to execution at the climax of the film is a model of imperious courage. A major production, *Mare Nostrum* has the integrity not to shrink from its natural ending of double tragedy – Antonio Moreno following Alice Terry swiftly to extinction.

Probably most omnivorous filmgoers have a film or two, or more, which – for no easily definable reason, and whatever critical opinion may be – cast a spell over them which remains immutable over the years. I missed Garbo's first American picture, *The Torrent* (directed by Monta Bell), but later caught the second, *The Temptress* – and was duly spellbound. Contemporary criticism was not wholly severe, indeed some was quite favourable, but even some of the latter implied that the mere presence of Garbo

Greta Garbo in her first American film, *The Torrent*, playing a humble Spanish girl who becomes a famous opera singer. With her is Lucien Littlefield, a character actor who appeared in dozens of films, often unrecognizable in almost as many changes of make-up (though less extreme) as Lon Chaney.

redeemed all faults. The story, from Blasco-Ibáñez once again, is a hot-house drama about a *femme fatale par excellence*; wherever she goes men fight for her, ruin themselves for her, kill for her, even engage in whip duels for her, from Paris to the Argentine. There were two available endings – either she could be reunited with a sorely-tried hero (having been indirectly responsible for the destruction of a big dam which he had been assiduously constructing) or she could give him up and be reduced to walking the streets of Paris for hire. The former was screened during the film's British release.

Antonio Moreno, caught in the clutches of the Temptress (Greta Garbo) on their first meeting in the film of that name.

Roy D'Arcy, a splendidly flashing-eyed villain in numerous silents, seen at his best as the dashing Argentinian Manos Duros in *The Temptress*.

The production was beset with difficulties. Direction was started by Mauritz Stiller, but he departed after ten days (for reasons that remain mysterious) and was replaced by Fred Niblo. The final version was cut – an entire important character, played by H. B. Warner, being omitted, though he continues to appear misleadingly in stills accompanying accounts of the film. Nevertheless the film's spell remains. For many people besides myself it contained a first sight of Garbo. On its first screening at the Capitol, London – one of the most comfortable and attractively decorated of all cinemas at the time – it was accompanied by a superb orchestra playing a fine score, and the print itself was beautifully tinted. The whole supporting cast is excellent – in particular Roy D'Arcy as a dashing Argentinian bandit resplendent in black from head to foot, with gauntlets and broad-brimmed hat to match. Among other Garbo victims are Marc MacDermott, though seen only briefly, Lionel Barrymore and Armand Kaliz. One small imaginative touch which disappeared from later untinted prints was a brilliant red flash which flooded the screen for an almost subliminal moment – a moment of murder.

Apart from the collapsing dam (which was highly effective, the orchestra's percussion section playing at maximum volume), the high spot of the picture is the famous whip duel between D'Arcy and Moreno. When the film was first screened at the Capitol a title 'spoken' by D'Arcy as he chose the weapons to be used in the contest read, 'We will fight – Argentine.' This apparently caused some offence in that country; for later verions it was altered to 'We will fight – with whips.' Such is the tenderness of national susceptibilities. The remarkable and famous travelling shot near the opening of the film – where the camera moves above and along the whole length of a lavish dinner-table between the guests and then reverses *under* the table to point the contrast between the smart, polite social scene and the franker 'comments' and movements

The on-screen romance of Garbo and John Gilbert in *Flesh and the Devil* was enhanced by the off-screen one reputedly taking place at the same time, but here they are interrupted by the lady's lawful husband (Marc MacDermott).

of the diners' feet below — may have been inspired by a somewhat similar but slightly less complicated shot in Valentino's *The Eagle,* directed by Clarence Brown the previous year.

Though far from being a masterpiece, this film has been described at some length because it does seem to explain something of the secret of the cinema — 'the magic of the movies' is no mere catch-phrase. Though individual opinions may vary wildly (what to one viewer is impressive to another is rubbish) films can, and occasionally do, cast a spell, which is, I think, something of which we can be glad.

Garbo made a third film the same year, far more famous, more often discussed, and generally (though not always) more highly regarded. *Flesh and the Devil* (directed by Clarence Brown) is excellently directed, with some stunning scenic effects (such as the duel in silhouette), a splendid supporting cast including Lars Hanson and Marc MacDermott, a choice of endings, and a real-life romance between Garbo and her co-star John Gilbert to bolster up the one taking place on screen and to help the publicity department. It is thoroughly professional, very enjoyable hokum. But put the two films in adjoining cinemas and – provided the Capitol orchestra was there – I known to which box-office I would turn.

Mary Pickford returned from Dorothy Vernon to ringlets in *Little Annie Rooney* (directed by William Beaudine), which I

Mary Pickford in one of the most popular of her later little-girl roles, with the pathetic group of unwanted children whom she rescues from the clutches of the infamous Farmer Grimes (Gustav von Seyffertitz), in *Sparrows*.

missed but do not regret, and in what many regard as the best of all her child performances, *Sparrows*, also known as *Human Sparrows*, by the same director. It concerns her rescue of a group of unwanted children from the infamous Farmer Grimes (Gustav von Seyffertitz at his magnificently villainous best) through miles and miles of crocodile-infested swamps. The climax of many moments of suspense is the thrilling sequence in which the desperate children have to crawl along a rotting bough above a stream full of expectantly open-jawed reptiles.

Herbert Brenon followed up his *Peter Pan* with another Barrie play, *A Kiss for*

Cinderella. It was a welcome return, too, for Betty Bronson, offering her more opportunities than the delightful but somewhat one-way Peter. She won our hearts both as the downtrodden slavey and as the belle of her dream ball. Tom Moore is totally convincing as the London policeman who befriends her and eventually loves her, conveying with subtlety his knowledge that – in the language of the period – 'she is not long for this world'; and Esther Ralston is graciously lovely as the Fairy Godmother. Unfortunately this tender, gossamer-delicate film never had the success it so strongly deserved.

Though minus an eye in *The Road to Mandalay* (directed by Tod Browning), Lon Chaney forsook his extravagant make-ups in his 1926 productions. In both this film and in *Tell It to the Marines* (directed by George Hill) he plays the kind of tough characters he

Betty Bronson as the little slavey and Esther Ralston as the Fairy Godmother in the lovely dream sequence from *A Kiss for Cinderella,* the second of Miss Bronson's Barrie films, which has never had the success it deserves.

evidently enjoyed: a disreputable and shady storekeeper (Singapore Joe) in the first, a formidable sergeant in the second. Both are minor Chaneys, telling of assorted adventures in foreign parts. They neither added to nor detracted from his high reputation and popularity.

John Barrymore's *The Sea Beast* (directed by Millard Webb) is an unhappy mixture of Melville and romance, Moby Dick and marriage. Whether the excrescence was forced on Barrymore by the box-office or was his suggestion is uncertain – probably the former. The film has its moments: Barrymore giving us his mad, glaring look as Ahab, some of the whaling scenes, the horrific amputation sequence; and some allowance may be made for a glimpse of lovely Dolores Costello, soon to become his wife; but on the whole it is a travesty of which the adaptor and whoever pushed her to make it should be

ashamed. Barrymore himself was so frustrated that he remade the film in 1930 under its proper title, *Moby Dick,* though again with a female co-star, Joan Bennett, in a sound (Vitaphone) version. We saw it at the big new Kensington cinema in London, and sat silently watching while Melville was no doubt turning in his grave.

Barrymore's other 1926 film, *Don Juan* (directed by Alan Crosland), is portentous as the first experiment of Warner Bros. with a feature film using their Vitaphone process, being issued as a silent film with musical and sound-effect accompaniment. It is a good-looking, entertaining costume piece (by the

125

Myrna Loy at her slinkiest as a Filipino half-cast who attempts to lure Monte Blue from his sweetheart in *Across the Pacific*. Astonishingly, she fails.

same screenwiter as *The Sea Beast* – 'inspired', at some distance, by Byron), with a fine climactic duel between Barrymore and Montagu Love, an English-born former stage actor who became a leading villain in Hollywood with a vast number of movies to his credit. Warner Oland and Estelle Taylor clearly enjoy themselves immensely as Borgias, Mary Astor is an appealingly innocent long-dark-haired heroine and Myrna Loy can be glimpsed slinking around as a scheming maidservant.

Miss Loy had indeed been slinking in a number of films before this. In *Across the Pacific* (directed by Roy del Ruth), a melodrama of the Spanish-American war,

she slunk in fact quite prominently as a Filipino half-caste with her eyes on Monte Blue, her performance being the most memorable thing in a minor but not unentertaining picture in which Mr Blue leaves his sweetheart (Jane Winton) to enlist in the army, but is able – surprisingly – to resist the half-caste girl and return finally to his true love.

A larger conflict, the First World War, is the background to *What Price Glory?* (directed by Raoul Walsh), from a long-running play by Laurence Stallings and Maxwell Anderson. The film softens the anti-war content down to the story of two tough marines (Victor McLaglen and Edmund Lowe) squabbling over Dolores del Rio. Neither the fairly realistic battle scenes nor the classic 'Stop the blood!' outcry (contemptuously dismissed by one critic as the 'sickly and obvious tragedy of the Mother's Boy') are allowed to outweigh the slapstick. To my knowledge it is the only film in which a silent 'raspberry' is introduced. A theme song written to accompany the picture, 'Charmaine', lived on for a good many years afterwards, and can still have a strong nostalgic effect on those of us who saw the original screening.

The real hero of *Old Ironsides* (directed by James Cruze) is the renowned US frigate *Constitution* for which the film's title was the affectionate nickname, and which was active in the American War of 1812. Once again history has to be embellished with 'human interest' (as if it had none of its own!), but the love story that has been built round the facts is an acceptable one, not entailing too much distortion. British audiences, having in the main to take a certain amount of US history on trust, found no complaint to make when the result was a good part for Esther Ralston and the presence of Wallace Beery and George Bancroft, together with the introduction of Charles Farrell, soon to leap to fame as Janet Gaynor's partner in *Seventh Heaven*. In cinemas equipped with the necessary facilities a new wide-screen

In *What Price Glory?*, from the famous stage play by Laurence Stallings and Maxwell Anderson, Dolores del Rio sits between Victor McLaglen (right) and Edmund Lowe (left) confident that she can have whichever one she chooses.

process was used called Magnascope, which gave spectacular scenes a larger image.

Although both Keaton and Lloyd made good comedy features, Keaton *Battling Butler* (which he also directed), with a boxing background, and Lloyd *For Heaven's Sake* (directed by Sam Taylor) in which he plays a carefree young man who becomes involved with an evangelical mission, the most noteworthy comic event of the year was the appearance of the two first feature films of Harry Langdon. Many attempts have been made to analyse the strange effect this dead-white baby-faced figure with the hesitant movements and queer, twisted smile has on the spectator. He is certainly not a comfort-

able comedian to watch, laugh though we undoubtedly may. Under the innocence and vulnerability there is a decided suggestion of both guile and destructiveness. He may look like, and often behave like, a small child, but any clouds of glory he might have trailed have long ago fallen away. Of all the great silent clowns (even Larry Semon, whom at times he oddly resembles) he is the least 'human' and yet the most disturbing comment on human beings, even though the plots of his few full-length films follow mainly conventional lines – except perhaps for a central situation in the second one, *The Strong Man*.

The story of the first, *Tramp, Tramp, Tramp* (directed by Harry Edwards), is simple. Langdon plays a young hobo who enters a transcontinental walking contest hoping to win a girl he is attracted to ('love' is not a word that seems to fit Langdon), wins, and finds she is already bespoke. It took no fewer than five writers to concoct this not

Harry Langdon in his first feature film, *Tramp, Tramp, Tramp,* as a young hobo who enters a walking contest hoping to win Joan Crawford, seen here regarding him with an ambiguous expression of something less than unalloyed ardour.

very elaborate tale. In the second, *The Strong Man* (directed by Frank Capra), he arrives home in America from the First World War – after a hilarious episode at the front – determined to find a girl with whom he has been exchanging 'pen pal' letters. When he does so, he discovers that she is blind: a risky situation, perhaps, for a comic film, particularly as, despite his efforts to find a cure, she does not regain her sight, but so delicately is this handled by Capra, and so droll are the events in between – his adventures with a professional weight-lifter and others – that by the end we accept the unemphasized suggestion that perhaps, after all, the only possible hope for their future happiness is that she should not see him as he really is.

Reginald Denny, an Englishman with some stage experience behind him, had by 1926 appeared in a number of American films, including a popular boxing series, *The Leather Pushers,* and, in 1925, an amusing if unremarkable light comedy, *Oh Doctor!* (directed by Harry A. Pollard), with Mary Astor and Otis Harlan. In 1926 he came suddenly to the fore with two of the most entertaining movies of the entire decade, *What Happened to Jones* and *Skinner's Dress Suit,* both directed by William A. Seiter and both co-starring the inimitable Otis Harlan mentioned earlier. The first is taken from a wild old farce of 1910 and follows the adventures of a young man suffering from the effects of an unwise pre-wedding poker party; it reaches a frenetic climax when he is forced, with Harlan, to take refuge from the police in a Turkish bath on what turns out to be Ladies' Night. Denny, together with his director and writer (M. W. Brown), transformed the creaky old play into a highly amusing contemporary movie.

Skinner's Dress Suit had a little more body to it – if one may put it that way – and describes the calamitous, but finally fortunate, effects of the gift of an evening dress outfit on a hitherto mild and modest young clerk. In the first picture Denny's leading lady was Marian Nixon (who many years later married Ben Lyon after the death of Bebe Daniels); in the second it was Laura la Plante, delightful both as comedienne and thriller victim, who was to play Magnolia in the first version of *Show Boat* in 1929. It is difficult to decide which of these two comedies is the more enjoyable. Either – or both – would be welcome revivals on television today. Though he appeared in films, at increasingly long

Reginald Denny and Laura la Plante, two wholly delightful comedy stars of the silent era, ideally together in *Skinner's Dress Suit,* giving a demonstration of the charleston.

Princess Vera (Elinor Fair) is rescued in the nick of time from the clutches of the licentious Russian soldiery by Prince Dimitri (Victor Varconi), seen here putting his overcoat to good use in *The Volga Boatman.*

intervals, almost up to his death in 1967, Denny's career received a severe setback with the arrival of sound for an unusual and ironic reason – he spoke English with an English accent. His life and work are fully outlined in a very interesting personal interview with Kevin Brownlow that appears in his book *The Parade's Gone By.*

Two of Raymond Griffith's best comedies appeared in this year, *Hands Up!* (directed by Clarence Badger), a spy story set in the Civil War, and *You'd Be Surprised* (directed by Arthur Rosson), a house-party murder mystery. The cast of the first included Marian Nixon, Mack Swain, and George Billings as Abraham Lincoln; of the second, tall,

dignified Edward Martindel and Dorothy Sebastian, soon to appear with Buster Keaton in his last silent film. Griffith, a dapper little man with a slight resemblance to Max Linder, suffered from a throat affliction which badly affected his voice and more or less ended his career as an actor when the talkies arrived, though he worked for several more years as producer. Ironically he is best remembered not for his enjoyable silent comedies but for his tiny role (in which, admittedly, he was remarkable) as the dying French soldier in the early sound film *All Quiet on the Western Front* – a voiceless part in which his affliction did not matter.

The Volga Boatman was new ground for DeMille – a story of love, death, violence and sacrifice set in the early stages of the Russian Revolution. Unusually for its time it takes no sides, and the characters are not represented as partisan caricatures. The spectacular scenes, not so much in evidence as usual, are handled with DeMille's customary flair,

Left to right, Jewel Carmen as Dale Ogden, Emily Fitzroy as the formidable Cornelia van Gorder, Louise Fazenda as Lizzie and Eddie Gribbon as Detective Anderson in *The Bat*, adapted from the well-known stage comedy-thriller.

notably that in which the aristocrats, joined by a peasant who has fallen in love with a Russian princess, are forced to haul a huge boat along the river under the lash of revolutionaries while the orchestra pounds out the famous song. The film caused some flutterings in the dovecots of the sensitive on account of a sequence in which the Princess is taken to be the peasant's wife, and forced to stand on a table while the drunken royalist officers divest her of her clothing. In fact, it is done with almost excessive discretion (and, ironically, is all the more erotic for that), merely showing delicate garments landing among the molesters after their removal from an invisible Princess. Long before crisis point is reached her rescuer arrives and covers her up in his greatcoat. Even so, it was enough for the picture to be dubbed, with dull wit, 'The Vulgar Boatman'. Elinor Fair, at one time wife of William Boyd who played opposite her as the peasant, is a beautiful and regal Princess, even in often trying circumstances.

Roland West, an unduly neglected director, made a good workman-like job of *The Bat*, from one of the two star comedy-thrillers of the 'twenties (*The Cat and the Canary* being the other), a stage play adapted from the novel by Mary Roberts Rinehart. It is notable for giving Emily Fitzroy a rare chance to show that she could play more than formidable aunts, cruel mothers-in-law and dragon- like schoolmistresses. As Miss Cornelia van Gorder, the wealthy spinster whose house becomes the centre of a jewel-robbery mystery, she easily dominates the film surrounded by a cast of such competent character actors as Andre de Beranger, Louise Fazenda, Tullio Carminati and Sojin. A tall, strongly handsome Englishwoman, born in London in 1861, she entered the American film world in about 1916 after a theatrical career and made her mark, often in quite minor roles, in film after film. She was instantly recognizable, a powerful presence even when appearing as little more than an extra – as in John Barrymore's *Don Juan* ('The Dowager'). Yet very little is known about her, and she is mentioned in few reference books. I remember with pleasure that, at the première of the 1929 *Show Boat* at the Tivoli, London, an ovation was given – not for the stars (who were of course in America) – but for the 68-year-old actress playing Parthenia Hawks. While in Britain Emily Fitzroy made one or two British films, returning to America after a year or two. Her last film was *Forever and a Day* (1943); after a long retirement she died in 1954, aged 93.

D. W. Griffith was considered to have added little to his reputation with *The Sorrows of Satan*, from Marie Corelli's superheated allegorical supernatural melo-drama in which Satan, fed up with finding people so easy to corrupt, pays Earth a visit, calling himself Prince de Rimarez and taking on the semblance of Adolphe Menjou. In that irresistible guise he tries to work his will on a penniless author who has failed to find a publisher for a book attacking God. (He would not, one feels, encounter the same difficulty today.) The film was slated at the time and has not fared much better since, but – to be frank – we rather enjoyed it. It is not vintage Griffith, and the story may be

regarded as tosh, but there were some undeniably effective moments, such as the first entrance of Satan/Rimarez, and a well contrived feeling of darkness and mystery which leaves the atmosphere, if not all the details, alive in the memory. Too much attention, admittedly, is paid to the rather uninteresting young lovers, both struggling writers (Ricardo Cortez and Carol Dempster), particularly in the earlier part of the film, but to compensate we have Lya de Putti – who came to America shortly after starring in *Vaudeville* – as the luscious Princess Olga. Uncredited in a small part is Eric Mayne, a tall, sturdy, bearded Irish actor who came to America after a stage career in Dublin and London and played a wide variety of parts in silent films and early talkies, including Harold Lloyd's *Doctor Jack* and John Ford's *Hangman's House*. In later years he appeared in so many films as an extra that, according to Adam Reilly in his book on Lloyd, he was known to film buffs simply as The Man with the Beard. Mayne died in Hollywood in 1947, aged 81.

Other American films included *Beau Geste* (directed by Herbert Brenon), in which the director shows he is just as much at home with the rigours of the Foreign Legion as with the delicacies of *Peter Pan* and *A Kiss for Cinderella*. With some fine spectacular sequences, and an equally fine cast including Victor McLaglen, Ronald Colman, William Powell, Ralph Forbes and Alice Joyce, this silent black-and-white version can bear comparison with any sound remake in colour.

The Winning of Barbara Worth (directed by Henry King) is a superior western about unscrupulous activities connected with a desert irrigation project, starring Ronald Colman and Vilma Banky but notable for a comparatively brief but screen-stealing per-formance by a young Gary Cooper, and a sensational flood sequence which is itself almost the star of the picture. 'Gary Cooper,' said a contemporary critic, 'is worth watching.'

Rudolph Valentino, with Vilma Banky, in a typically romantic setting from his last picture, *The Son of the Sheik*. He also doubles as his father from *The Sheik* (1921), with Agnes Ayres returning briefly in her original character from the earlier film.

So This Is Paris (directed by Ernst Lubitsch), typical Lubitsch wit extracted from an old French farce, updated, enlarged and considerably altered, concerns a young dancing couple and their flirtations. A spectacular ballroom sequence helps to keep things moving.

The Wanderer (directed by Raoul Walsh), a biblical drama of the Prodigal Son with elaborations, is notable mainly for the ravishing beauty of Greta Nissen, a Swedish actress destined to be beaten by the sound barrier. Ernest Torrence and Wallace Beery sweep around happily in their flowing robes, and William Collier Jr, a sensitive and likeable actor, looks suitably good and bad in turn as the script requires.

The Fire Brigade, known on its first release in Britain as *Fire!* (directed by William Nigh), deals with corruption again, this time among building contractors, with an awesome conflagration as the climax and May McAvoy and Charles Ray in support. Also in the cast is Holmes Herbert, yet another of those unfailingly reliable character actors who deserve, but do not often get, as much recognition as the stars themselves. Born in Nottinghamshire as Edward Sanger, he went to America in about 1918 and played in a vast number of films, first as a 'juvenile lead' and then as a character actor – often as stern fathers, lawyers, doctors and other dignified persons – until the early 1950s. He died in 1956, aged 73.

Bardelys the Magnificent (directed by King Vidor) is a spectacular adapatation of Rafael Sabatini's best-seller about love, treason and general double-dealing in the France of Louis XIII. An excellent cast includes John Gilbert, Eleanor Boardman (Vidor's one-time wife), Roy D'Arcy, Emily Fitzroy, George K. Arthur, Arthur Lubin (Louis XIII) and Edward Connelly (Cardinal Richelieu).

Beverly of Graustark (directed by Sidney Franklin) and *The Red Mill* (directed by William Goodrich – otherwise Roscoe Arbuckle) are two comedy-dramas different

Probably best remembered as an emotional dramatic actress, Norma Talmadge was just as capable of playing light comedy, as evidenced in *Kiki*, the story of a Paris gamine who lives by her wits.

in subject but similar in spirit which may be taken as fairly typical Marion Davies vehicles. In the first she is a girl just out of finishing school, but under a slight shadow (it seems possible she has been expelled). Sent to visit a relative in (mythical) Graustark, she becomes involved in a take-over plot, and, in a situation not unlike that which arises in most mythical countries, notably Ruritania, finds herself impersonating a prince. After numerous adventures the conspirators are overthrown, the Prince is restored to power and Marion marries his handsome aide (Antonio Moreno), who himself turns out to be a prince of the kingdom next door – leaving her in a happier position than Rudolph Rassendyll in *The Prisoner of Zenda. The Red Mill,* an adaptation of a musical comedy by Victor Herbert and Henry Blossom, finds her as a downtrodden Dutch servant girl who dreams of her ideal young man and, after getting herself locked up in a haunted mill by her cruel employer, actually finds him. Both are trifles lighter than air, but prove their star adept in pleasant comedy, and equally fetching whether in make-believe uniform with close-cropped hair or Dutch cap and clogs.

In *It's the Old Army Game* (directed by Edward Sutherland) audiences found W. C. Fields pretty funny even before they heard his famous voice. It consists of more or less the same string of separate, loosely linked episodes, based on various music-hall sketches, that were to make up *It's a Gift.* Even the well-known one in which he tries to get some sleep on an outside balcony during a heat-wave and is disturbed by a succession of noisy interruptions was surprisingly successful, despite the fact that none of the noise could be heard. Louise Brooks – by this time apparently rather fed up with Hollywood – is charming in a fairly small part.

Kiki (directed by Clarence Brown) displays a light touch from the director, a delightful performance from Norma Talmadge –

relieved for once from heavy emotionalism – and a strong supporting cast including Ronald Colman, Marc MacDermott, Gertrude Astor, Mack Swain and George K. Arthur, who make this version of a David Belasco adaptation of a French comedy worth watching and remembering. Mary Pickford made an early sound version in 1931.

The Grand Duchess and the Waiter (directed by Malcolm St Clair), one of Adolphe Menjou's typically enjoyable exercises in suavity, finds him in this case as a wealthy man-about-town who, in order to become acquainted with a refugee Russian grand duchess with whom he has become infatuated, disguises himself as a waiter in the hotel where they are both staying. The name Menjou became more or less synonymous with this sort of part during the decade, but he was capable also of considerably more demanding characterizations.

Irene (directed by Alfred E. Green) and *Lady, Be Good* (directed by Richard Wallace) are two quite successful examples of musical plays being transferred to a silent screen, with Colleen Moore and George K. Arthur in the first; Jack Mulhall, John Miljan and Dorothy Mackaill (a former chorus girl, born in Hull, Yorkshire, who brightened a number of fairly lightweight pictures in the 'twenties and early 'thirties), in the second.

In Britain 1926 was an important year in the career of Alfred Hitchcock. It saw the completion of his first feature film, *The Pleasure Garden,* and the one that he himself described as the 'first true Hitchcock film', *The Lodger.* In between he made a minor picture, *The Mountain Eagle,* starring Nita Naldi and at present presumed lost.

The Lodger is a landmark in the British silent period. The story, from the novel by Mrs Belloc Lowndes, concerns a suspected Jack the Ripper-type murderer who haunts the foggy London streets in search of golden-haired girls to kill. It is weakened by the fact that, after some rather dishonest hints to the contrary, he is proved to be innocent, but it was apparently felt that to have the handsome matinée idol Ivor Novello found guilty of such infamy would kill the box-office stone cold. The atmosphere is heavily Germanic, full of symbolic shadows and chiaroscuro lighting. 'Hitchcock touches' are already in evidence, though of course we did not recognize them as such at the time: a screaming girl's face, filling the screen at the opening; the close-up of a hand descending the banisters; the lodger's feet pacing his floor, photographed through the ceiling of the room below (actually through a thick sheet of plate glass); the martyr-like figure hanging from the railings at the climax. The film also focused on the problems of guilt and innocence which were to interest Hitchcock in his later work.

The Pleasure Garden, taken from a novel by Oliver Sandys, the pseudonym of Countess Barcynska, stars John Stuart and three American actresses, Virginia Valli, Carmelita Geraghty and, again, Nita Naldi. It is set mainly in the tropics and deals with the dilemma of a chorus girl who marries a drunkard with a native mistress. According to Hitchcock, in his famous interview book with François Truffaut, the film was well received, one percipient critic describing him as 'a young man with a master mind'. The film was made in Munich.

Mademoiselle from Armentières was also important both as Maurice Elvey's first production for the Gaumont company and as a big commercial success which marked a major step forward in his busy career. It makes no pretence of investigating the grim realities of modern warfare (the First World War), treating the whole thing as an exciting thriller in which the heroine of the famous song (played by the young Canadian actress Estelle Brodie with great vivacity and charm) uses her wiles to spy on the bad Germans and help the good British. It hit the mood of the moment admirably, providing a sort of incongruous nostalgia for a disaster survived.

Ivor Novello and Isabel Jeans returned together in *The Triumph of the Rat* (directed by Graham Cutts). It was used to open the big new Astoria cinema in Charing Cross Road, London, but never achieved the success of its predecessor.

Dorothy Gish crossed the Atlantic to play *Nell Gwynne* (*sic*) in a production by Herbert

Vivacious Canadian actress Estelle Brody, with British star John Stuart, in the First World War comedy-drama *Mademoiselle from Armentières*.

Below: Dorothy Gish as a glamorous Mistress Nell Gwynne in the British production of that name directed by Herbert Wilcox, based on Marjorie Bowen's novel.

A shocked Gustav Frölich supports a collapsing slave-worker in *Metropolis*, a disturbing portrayal of life in a fantastic city of the future.

Wilcox which opened the Plaza, Lower Regent Street. Though based on Marjorie Bowen's novel *Mistress Nell Gwynne*, the film lacks a true sense of period and Wilcox was to do much better with his later sound version starring Anna Neagle and Cedric Hardwicke. The antics of the Restoration Court are glossed over, and the true relationship between a kittenish Nell and her Sovereign (played with dignity by Randle Ayrton) remains discreetly vague. There is, however, a pioneer nude scene, with Nell teasing the censor – and the audience – in a barrel, and after all we did not go to the Plaza for a history lesson.

Even less history would be learnt from Sinclair Hill's *Boadicea*, anti-Ancient-Roman propaganda depicting the unhappy plight of the oppressed Britons and the rising of the Iceni tribe under their famous queen. The ingenious and frightful tortures and humiliations she reputedly inflicted on the Roman matrons when her own turn came remain unrecorded in the film. Its strong, simple narrative line, however, is effective, despite obviously inadequate resources in the battle and other would-be spectacular scenes. It has a splendidly regal Queen in Phyllis Neilson-Terry, a splendidly bearded King in Humberston Wright, and in Lilian Hall-Davis and Sybil Rhoda two ancient Britons who would grace any Icenian family. Apart from collaborating on the script a young Anthony Asquith – future director of *Tell England, French Without Tears, The Way to the Stars, The Browning Version*, etc. – doubled for Miss Neilson-Terry as Boadicea in a chariot, wearing a long blond wig.

Without any doubt the film from Germany that made the greatest impression was Fritz Lang's *Metropolis*. Its story is too well-known

The hidden phantasms in the subconscious mind of worried chemistry professor Werner Krauss are revealed under psychoanalysis in the remarkable German film *Secrets of a Soul.*

and it has been too often revived since to need more than brief mention here. I saw it first during its original run at the much-lamented Marble Arch Pavilion, a beautiful and comfortable cinema long ago smashed to pieces in the interests of commerce, and its effect on the audience was dramatic. Its theme – 'the Mediator between the Hands and the Brain must be the Heart' – may be trite, even if true, and its solution simplistic, but the brilliance and originality of the sets, the hordes of robot-like workers, the cataclysmic climax when the rebellious crowds destroy both the machines and their own homes, above all the magical beauty of the sequence depicting the creation of the female robot from gleaming metal into the form of Brigitte Helm's evil counterpart – have never been surpassed, though often emulated.

A film of equal originality, though much less well-known, was G. W. Pabst's *Secrets of a Soul,* a literal translation of the film's original German title, in which an attempt is made to present psychoanalysis in visible form on the screen. The subject under treatment is a professor of chemistry (a remarkable performance by Werner Krauss, of *Caligari* fame) who is suffering from a series of phobias following a murder which has taken place near his home. The phantasms of his dreams are reproduced on the screen as we follow the course of the case to a satisfactory conclusion. Much use is made of models and trick photography to try to indicate his state of mind as the underlying meaning of the apparently unconnected visions is made clear. As psychoanalytical theory the film may be outdated, but as a dramatic experience it is remarkably gripping, even if the final solution is a little too neat.

1926

The World at Large

Germany is admitted to the League of Nations
Goebbels becomes Gauleiter of Berlin
French franc is devalued
General Strike in Britain, lasting nine days
Birth of Queen Elizabeth II
J. L. Baird demonstrates television in Soho
Gertrude Ederle first woman to swim English Channel
Aimée Semple MacPherson, evangelist, disappears while bathing off Ocean Park, California
Death of Erich Weiss ('Houdini')

Cinema

British International Pictures formed
Columbia acquires its own studio
Kodak produces the first 16mm film
Plaza Theatre, Regent Street, London, opens
Kensington Cinema, Kensington High Street, London, opens, claiming to be the largest in Britain
Paramount Cinema, Times Square, New York, opens
London Film Society formed
Death of Rudolph Valentino
Wampas Baby Stars: Mary Astor, Mary Brian, Joyce Compton, Dolores Costello, Joan Crawford, Marceline Day, Dolores del Rio, Janet Gaynor, Sally Long, Edna Marion, Sally O'Neil, Vera Reynolds, Fay Wray
Births: Roger Corman, Bryan Forbes, Norman Jewison, Klaus Kinski, Karel Reisz, John Schlesinger, Kenneth Williams

Theatre

Sean O'Casey, *The Plough and the Stars*
Eugene O'Neill, *The Great God Brown*
W. Somerset Maugham, *The Constant Wife*
John Galsworthy, *Escape*
Sidney Howard, *The Silver Cord*
Ben Travers, *Rookery Nook*
Sigmund Romberg, *The Desert Song*

Fiction

D. H. Lawrence, *The Plumed Serpent*
William Faulkner, *Soldier's Pay*
Sylvia Townsend Warner, *Lolly Willowes*
Edna Ferber, *Show Boat*
John Galsworthy, *The Silver Spoon*
DuBose Heywood, *Porgy*
A. A. Milne, *Winnie the Pooh*

Music

Bartok, *The Miraculous Mandarin* (ballet)
Puccini, *Turandot* (opera)
Kodaly, *Hary Janos*
First Duke Ellington recordings

Popular Songs

'One Alone'
'The Blue Room'
'When Day Is Done'
'Bye-Bye, Blackbird'
'In a Little Spanish Town'

Fashion Note

Skirts rise to just below the knee
Eton crop (ultra-short hair for women) arrives

1927

If last year's Big Film in America was *Ben-Hur*, this year's was undoubtedly *Wings* (directed by William Wellman). The triangular love story is no more than a novelette; it is the famous First World War flying scenes that matter, still regarded as a standard against which to measure all flying scenes since. Even so, it is a little ungenerous to denigrate – as certain critics did then, and still do today – the human beings in comparison with the machines, for Buddy Rogers, Richard Arlen and Clara Bow all give very creditable performances, as does Jobyna Ralston in a smaller role, and when all is said and done the flying scenes require some human interest as a framework if the film is not to be regarded as just a fake documentary. *Wings* was chosen to open the Carlton Theatre, Haymarket, as a cinema in May 1928, complete with the Magnascope process for enlarging the screen for the spectacular scenes, as in *Old Ironsides*. This had much the same effect on audiences of the day as the opening out of the triple screens in Cinerama had on a later generation. It also, unfortunately, had exactly the reverse effect when, afterwards, the screen eclipsed as if to say, 'There, you've had the good bit; now back to normal.' Maybe this

A vivid panoramic shot from the amazing battle sequences in *Wings*, made all the more impressive by the large-screen Magnascope process.

was why the 'human interest' earned the contempt of the critics – though not the audience, who were perhaps not so easily overwhelmed by mechanical wonders.

The torrents of praise that were in later years very rightly poured over F. W. Murnau's *Sunrise* (from Hermann Sudermann's *A Trip to Tilsit*) have largely obliterated the fact that when it first appeared its reception was far from universally favourable. In general the superb technical qualities were praised at the expense of the subject matter. The simple story, subtitled 'A Romance of Two Humans', concerns a young married farmer who meets a Woman from the City (none of the characters is given a name), becomes infatuated with her, attempts to drown his plain little wife, finds he cannot bring himself to do so, pursues her in remorse as she flees to the big city, is reconciled with her as they watch a wedding, has the horror of thinking she has been drowned in a storm on the way home but – in a tacked-on happy ending – finds she is safe. Out of this far from strikingly original material Murnau, aided by superb performances from Janet Gaynor and George O'Brien, created a masterpiece of visual beauty, totally unsentimental human warmth and sympathy and potential tragedy that, particularly on a first viewing many years ago, made it almost unbearably moving. It in fact provided one of those experiences in the cinema when one dreads the lights coming up as the curtains close,

George O'Brien trudges through the marshes to meet his Woman from the City in this finely atmospheric still from F. W. Murnau's masterpiece, *Sunrise.*

because of the spectacle one might present — not realizing that most of the audience was feeling the same. Yet according to some contemporary opinions it was 'as cold as the marble that a sculptor uses' and 'the sort of picture that fools highbrows into hollering Art'. 'There is not a heart-throb in *Sunrise,*' said another (he should have been a member of our audience). Even the blonde wig which Janet Gaynor is given, with obviously deliberate intention, was described as 'all wrong'. On many counts, however, the film was highly praised: the farmer's walk through the moonlit marsh to his trysting-place (done in the studio); the long trolley-ride to the city (done without back-projection), and other sequences. The seemingly enormous city set

was skilfully built in false perspective. There are some delightful lighter scenes — and one misjudged moment where 'comic relief' is unintentional, when the Woman from the City suddenly breaks into wild charleston-like cavortings in the swamp. All in all, however, *Sunrise* is a classic not only of the silent film but of all cinema.

Janet Gaynor's other main film of the year 1927 (she also appeared in a minor production, *Two Girls Wanted*) was the one that really gained her the Best Actress award in the first Oscar ceremony, *Seventh Heaven* (directed by Frank Borzage, who won the Best Director award). A most cunningly con-

Love among the rooftops of Paris. Janet Gaynor and Charles Farrell in a tear-jerker *par excellence, Seventh Heaven.*

Jacqueline Logan as surely the most glamorous Mary Magdalene ever envisaged, in the opening scenes of *The King of Kings*.

trived tear-jerker, it had an easier passage than the great but less immediately popular *Sunrise*. We went in our thousands, duly suffered from lumps in our throats, but they dissolved fairly quickly once we left the theatre. The story – of a Paris sewer worker who rescues a maltreated waif named Diane from her unpleasant sister, falls in love with her, is called to fight for his country in the First World War before their marriage can be consummated and returns to her, blinded, for the final fade-out – is milked for all it is worth in Borzage's treatment and the performances of Janet Gaynor and Charles Farrell, but

even in those less cynical days there was a slight feeling of emotions being cleverly manipulated.

One of the most discussed productions of the year, inevitably, was Cecil B. DeMille's *The King of Kings*. The super-cinema in which we first saw it, after being greeted by much quivering organ-playing and then regaled with an elaborate stage prelude of awesome solemnity, seemed actually to smell more like a cathedral than our friendly familiar picture-house. Perhaps, indeed, it did, an astute management having wafted incense around to ensure that we were in the proper frame of mind and would converse, if at all, only in hushed whispers. In the years since the film's appearance much amusement has been derived from and much scorn poured upon the manner of its making: the silent periods in the studio, the prayers before the day's shooting, the code of good conduct imposed upon the players (apparently not too conscientiously observed by H. B. Warner, who played Jesus and was, according to rumour, discovered in rather un-Christ-like conditions at times) – but the question as to how much of all this was mere ballyhoo is irrelevant. What mattered was the film's effect upon the audiences of that time, and there is no doubt that it was considerable. Many who saw it carried away something more than the memory of 'just another DeMille epic', and it is quite certain that DeMille, who was a genuinely and deeply religious man, meant what he was doing to be taken seriously, ballyhoo or no ballyhoo.

The film shows him, as director, at his best and at his worst. It begins appallingly, with Mary Magdalene (Jacqueline Logan at her most glamorous) living in conditions of unbelievable splendour, bejewelled and besilked, surrounded in her marble palace by baths, leopards, zebras, revellers and slaves; this sequence was originally in colour. Judas (played by Joseph Schildkraut), it seems, is her lover but has lately been playing truant. She goes off in a tantrum to see 'this

H. B. Warner as Christ in the da Vinci-inspired Last Supper scene from *The King of Kings*. Joseph Striker (John) is on Warner's left, Ernest Torrence (Peter) is left of Striker; on Warner's right is Joseph Schildkraut as Judas.

carpenter' who has been luring him away. Then, of course, she falls for the 'carpenter' herself, and we wait apprehensively for what will happen next. What does happen is completely unexpected. The story has so far been reduced to the level of a sex triangle, with dubious undertones. From now on, however, as if he had expelled his spectacle complex from his system, DeMille changes course and produces a film of considerable restraint and dignity, even if much of it is rather on a pretty-picture-book level. Hereafter it follows, in episodic form, the main events of the Resurrection, and almost immediately after-

wards – by a concentration of time – the Ascension. Whatever his off-screen performance, Warner's on-screen one had deep sincerity, authority, humility and compassion. Physically he was half-way between the silken-haired, fragile figure of Victorian illustrations and the more realistic portrayals of later years. The first sight of his face on the screen is imaginatively contrived. A young blind girl is among a crowd outside a fisherman's hut listening to a boy's excited description of a man inside who has cured him of lameness. She is taken into the hut. All goes dark as we are placed behind her sightless eyes. Gradually, from all corners of the screen rays of light begin to glow, becoming ever brighter and more concentrated until – at first in a haze, then clearly – she sees the gentle face of her healer smiling down at her. Remembering this moment, it is easy to

Sorrell and Son is illuminated by a sensitive and moving performance from H. B. Warner as Sorrell, the 'gentleman and ex-captain', seen here with Carmel Myers as the coarse beauty who owns the hotel where he works as porter to support his son.

believe the story of the American minister who is said to have told Warner some time later, 'I saw *The King of Kings* when I was a child, and now whenever I speak of Jesus it is your face I see.' The actor's reply to this surely rather embarrassing compliment is not recorded.

H. B. Warner gave another fine and sympathetic performance this same year in *Sorrell and Son,* adapted from the novel by Warwick Deeping which was a runaway best-seller and the only one for which he is remembered. It relates the story of an ex-army captain, awarded the Military Cross, whose wife deserts him when he returns from the war, leaving him to bring up his son – in poverty, ill-health and degradation. He succeeds in the task (the son ultimately becoming a well-known surgeon), but at the cost of his own life. Between them the director (Herbert Brenon) and Warner transform what might seem to be a catalogue of a disproportionate number of woes into an intensively moving story of mutual love and respect between father and son. With considerable courage, the film introduces the subject of mercy-killing, when the father, having found a measure of happiness and peace at last, is dying, asks his son to help him to do so with dignity. The film had a special relevance to the period in which it was made, when many men returning from France after 1918 might have found themselves in a not dissimilar situation: it was a popular success, and deserved to be.

Emil Jannings has his share of suffering in *The Way of All Flesh* (directed by Victor Fleming), his first American film, but it is suffering of a more flamboyant and extrovert kind. As a bank cashier who falls into the hands of an adventuress (Phyllis Haver), with all that not unexpectedly follows, he suffers very convincingly but is unable wholly to conceal a suggestion that he is rather enjoying himself in his misery. Phyllis Haver, an ex-Sennett beauty, later to make a big hit in *Chicago,* is certainly attractive enough to make his downfall appear credible, particularly as behind him looms the shadow of a dull and irritatingly patient wife (Belle Bennett) and no fewer than six children. Masochistic or not, Jannings' performance was powerful enough to secure him an Oscar for Best Actor, taken together with *The Last Command* (1928).

Two of Lon Chaney's 1927 films are listed as 'lost', though one of them, *London After Midnight* (directed by Tod Browning), has been brilliantly reconstructed in book form by Philip J. Riley, who has collected together a vast number of stills, a complete film script

One of Lon Chaney's most horrific appearances, as the supposed vampire in *London After Midnight.* As the film appears to be irretrievably lost his remarkable make-up is preserved only in still photographs.

and much other material. It was remade by the same director about eight years later under the title *The Mark of the Vampire*. In each case the 'vampire' turns out to be a hoax thought up by a detective investigating a several-years-old murder case, who also makes use of hypnotism to ferret out the truth. Examined even with moderate care it turns out to be an engagingly impossible plot, but at least this first version contains the most terrifying of all Chaney's grotesque make-ups. the book version cannot of course reproduce Chaney's eerie, half-gliding, half-creeping progress along the corridor of the old house, nor his crouching figure, visible first only as the black circle of his tall hat, as he rises menacingly out of a mist billowing from a closed door, but it is good to have so satisfactory a substitute available.

The second Chaney film, *Mockery* (directed by Benjamin Christensen, of *Witchcraft Through the Ages*), is set during the Russian Revolution, Chaney playing a destitute, harelipped peasant who is persuaded to guide a countess on a dangerous journey, becomes devoted to her, but is later attracted by revolutionary propaganda and turns against her. Ricardo Cortez and Barbara Bedford head the rest of the cast, which also includes Emily Fitzroy and Mack Swain.

In *The Unknown* (directed by Tod Browning) Chaney plays a fake 'armless wonder' in a circus sideshow who has his arms amputated in reality because (a) he has two thumbs on one hand and (b) the girl he loves (Joan Crawford) dislikes being pawed. There are good grounds for the removal of the double thumb because its discovery by the police might result in his conviction for murder (of which he is guilty), as the fingerprints are on file, but it says something for Chaney's skill that he can make credible the somewhat extreme step of having both arms lopped off completely.

His fourth picture in a busy year was *Mr Wu* (directed by William Nigh), based on a famous 1914 stage play – updated, modern-ized and enlarged. There is a hint of Madam Butterfly in the central situation – a young Chinese girl falling in love with an Englishman – but the development is very different, in that her grandfather, Wu, takes her life to prevent the marriage, then determines to revenge himself on her lover's family. Chaney is seen as Wu at three different stages of his life; in the last, as the aged grandfather, his make-up is truly remarkable, convincing even in the stills, where it is possible to see how a black shawl helps to suggest the cavernous hollow cheeks.

Paul Leni, whose best-known German film was *Waxworks* (1924), came to America this year to direct, sadly, only four films before his sudden death in 1929 from blood poisoning. Of the two released in 1927 the first, *The Cat and the Canary*, is the better-remembered. The widely popular stage thriller by John Willard, first produced in New York with Florence Eldridge and Henry Hull, then in London with Dennis Neilson-Terry and his wife Mary Glynne, has been filmed several times since, but never so effectively as on this first occasion. Leni's German influence is apparent in the heavy shadows, mysterious passages lined with billowing curtains, oddly angled close-ups, a slow tempo and general atmosphere of moody mystery. As long as the action remains in the gloomy old mansion an admirable tension is maintained. Unfortunately a number of wholly irrelevant exterior scenes are introduced involving a 'comic milkman' as the thriller reaches its climax, greatly weakening the atmosphere that has been so carefully built up. The climactic appearance of the 'Cat' is also disappointing, mainly owing to a very inadequate horror make-up, with one staring eyeball apparently

Another fine feat of make-up from Lon Chaney, as the aged grandfather in *Mr Wu*. Tending him is the British actor Claude King.

Laura la Plante, in *The Cat and the Canary*, looks apprehensive, but the face of her assailant is made less terrifying by the band that holds his artificial eye in place. The player behind the mask is Forrest Stanley.

kept in place by a rubber band. Up to this point, however, the story (of which this film is a prototype) of prematurely opened wills, mysterious disappearances, clutching claws emerging from panels, and a heroine whom *someone* is trying either to frighten to death or to prove insane, is told with enjoyable verve and much effective camera work. The cast includes Laura la Plante (as convincing as a terrified victim as she is as a lively comedienne), Creighton Hale (an old hand at 'clutching claws' from the serials), Tully Marshall (as a slightly foxy lawyer whose dead body provides one of the best thrills of the film) and Lucien Littlefield, excellent in a brief appearance as an extremely sinister doctor whose presence is never really explained. Littlefield is to be found in the cast list of dozens of silent films and in almost as many make-ups as Lon Chaney, though less elaborate. His main forte was bumbling old men (though far from old himself), but he could be mild, sinister, obsequious, kindly, mean, humble, ancient or youngish at the drop of a wig. He once conjured up an almost perfect likeness of President Coolidge without any artificial aids at all. For a time it was possible to spot him by a signet ring on his little finger, but even that seemed to disappear later. His film career started in 1913 and he was still working, with a huge list of titles to his credit, in 1958. He died in 1960, aged 65.

Leni's second film, *The Chinese Parrot,* is an Earl Derr Biggers mystery, and the first

Edward Burns and Marian Nixon look questioningly at the Chinese parrot. Though uncredited in the cast list, the bird solves the mystery in the entertaining if unlikely comedy-thriller of that title.

feature picture in which Charlie Chan appeared – though he was to be seen in a 1926 serial. *The Chinese Parrot* is a fairly conventional jewel-robbery jaunt, without the flair of *The Cat and the Canary* but very enjoyable all the same, with Marian Nixon as delightful as ever as the heroine and at least one novel touch: the mystery is solved by a parrot, who tells Chan about it. Chan is played by the Japanese actor Kamiyama Sojin, always known simply as Sojin.

He became famous in America after appearing with Douglas Fairbanks in *The Thief of Bagdad,* and was in constant demand, mainly, but by no means always, as an Oriental villain. It was, in fact, a pity that he was not seen more often in sympathetic roles, for his screen personality, when not darkened by dire deeds, was a most pleasant one. His constant villainy apparently caused him some trouble in his native country as it was felt that he was misrepresenting his people to the rest of the world. Soon after the

A well composed and atmospheric still from *Old San Francisco* showing an attractive though seamy side of the city, as Sojin and Anna May Wong smilingly await the old man's verdict.

arrival of sound he appeared in Japanese films. He died in Tokyo in 1954, aged 63.

Sojin had a minor (and sympathetic) role in *Old San Francisco* (directed by Alan Crosland), one of the year's spectaculars, a story of corruption, murder and revenge in the 'tenderloin' (high-crime-rate) district of the city. Dolores Costello is her usual lovely self and Charles Emmett Mack an acceptable hero, but the film really belongs to the Swedish actor Warner Oland, who revels in a meaty role as an unscrupulous and cruel crime king. He was to become known to thousands later in his Charlie Chan series: thus in *Old San Francisco* we had two Chans together, past and present, in the cast list. Others taking part were Josef Swickard, John Miljan and Anders Randolf. The earthquake of 1906, as might be expected, takes a hand in matters at the climax, obligingly disposing of the villain. The disaster was quite effectively engineered. The film's title sometimes causes confusion among researchers owing to its similarity to the 1936 film *San Francisco*, with Clark Gable, Spencer Tracy, Jeanette MacDonald and Jack Holt.

From villainy Warner Oland turned to decency in *Good Time Charley* (directed by Michael Curtiz). Charley is a song-and-dance man who is losing his sight, and the story of his various family and financial troubles, and his eventual quiet happiness in an actors' home with a little theatrical prop man (Clyde Cook) who helped and befriended him, is told with sympathy and a complete lack of sentimentality. It is one of those modest, thoroughly enjoyable movies, made with confident, unassuming craftsmanship, one might have come across at any time in some small cinema in those days, and I remember it warming a cheerless winter afternoon for me in Lancashire while touring with such cold-blooded monsters as Dracula and Dr Frankenstein's.

Three major comedians each produced major films, Keaton and Langdon two each. Keaton's *The General*, which he directed with Clyde Bruckman, is commonly regarded as his masterpiece; it is certainly his most costly and elaborate, based on a true incident of the Civil War. The story of a theft by the Union army of a Confederate railroad train and its recovery by a young Confederate engineer affords Keaton the opportunity to stage a glorious collection of memorable gags, in which he is greatly helped by the most delightfully foolish of any of his heroines, Marion Mack. Helping him to keep up the supply of engine fuel she first hands him a tiny twig, then throws away a sizeable log because 'it has a hole in it', and starts, like a busy little housewife, energetically sweeping the engine floor clean. The moment when he, in exasperation, first starts to choke her, then kisses her instead, is one of the most charming in his entire output. At the time a number of people felt some discomfort at the realism of the final battle scenes and the wrecking of the train, which were thought to be too convincingly grim for a comedy despite the continuing flow of gags taking place during them. Perhaps audiences were more sensitive in those days.

The second film, *College* (directed by James W. Horne), is minor Keaton, and, though he made the most of the old theme of the studious college boy who becomes a super-athlete when racing to the rescue of his girl, it is one of the more forgettable of his productions. The cast, too, made little lasting impression – unusual with Keaton films.

Harry Langdon's *Long Pants* was the last of his features to be directed by Frank Capra, whom he fired before the editing was completed. The growing tension between them, however, is not apparent in the film. Langdon's 'Boy', imagining himself as a ladykiller while still trying to get his mother to let him wear grown-up trousers instead of childish knee-breeches, seems to embody his essential film character closer than any, and the adventures and misadventures that follow his sartorial emancipation are both hilarious and oddly disturbing. *Three's a Crowd*, which he directed himself, was both the first of his films without Capra and the last of the small body of 'essential Langdon' output. Perhaps a little of the Capra influence remained despite their differences. Seen at about the time of its release, with no foreknowledge of the sad decline to come, it was enjoyed as just another typical Langdon mixture of farce, pathos and, once again, slight unease.

Harold Lloyd's *The Kid Brother* (directed by Ted Wilde) treats its typical Lloyd character – a family weakling who makes good in the end – in more depth than hitherto, with fuller development and more sympathy to offset the knockabout comedy. It contains the usual succession of typical Lloyd gags, including one of the most famous. The villain has pushed him against the side of a ship from which an iron bracket protrudes, unseen by the audience, and of which he also is unaware: it exactly touches the top of his head. The villain then proceeds to bash Harold's head with a heavy belaying-pin without any apparent effect, to the astonishment of everyone. Eventually, of course, all is revealed. Lloyd would use this scene in discussing how much of the secret of a gag the audience should be allowed to know in advance. The film was previewed with both alternatives – knowledge or ignorance – and ignorance was chosen. The film also has a sequence resembling Buster Keaton's *The Navigator,* in which two characters hunt for each other around an empty ship, missing contact by inches. Though regarded by many as his best film, *The Kid Brother* has always been among the less widely screened. A contemporary critic rated it well below *The Freshman* and just below *Grandma's Boy* and *Safety Last.* As I remember at the time the last two were considerably more popular.

For Clara Bow, without any doubt, 1927 was IT year, when the sobriquet bestowed on her by novelist Elinor Glyn was perpetuated in celluloid. In actual fact, it is the boss of the department store in which she and her friends work in the film, who is credited by them with

Clara Bow, the IT girl and, though not without her rivals, the most famous exponent of the Jazz Age and all that it signified. The rarity of colour in those days meant that the flaming red of her hair was usually left to the imagination.

IT quality. For the final fade-out the ITs come together – on a ship's anchor. The film *It* was directed by Clarence Badger. Clara Bow is at her most vivacious and, needless to say, does everything her audiences expect of her. Antonio Moreno is suitable handsome and charming, though it is William Austin as his silly-ass friend whom we remember. The film flooded the box-office despite a mixed press. One British critic fulminated against it as 'abysmal, sufficiently inane to be beneath contempt were it not for the fact that it will probably exercise the worst possible effect on our million surplus flappers.' Whether such forebodings were fulfilled has never been revealed – nor what, exactly, was a 'surplus' flapper.

Colleen Moore was regarded in some ways as a sort of sister star to Clara Bow, though their screen personalities were very different. Her reputation as the epitome of the flapper was not really justified. In the only film in which the word appears in the title she is only pretending to be one (*The Perfect Flapper,* 1924), and in *Flaming Youth* (1923) her flaming is of the mildest kind. (The word 'flapper', incidentally, was much older than the 'twenties to which it is so often applied: it was common in America by 1910 and was known in England as early as the 1890s. It originally referred to the coy flapping of long hair, according to the most likely of several suggested derivations.) More frequently Colleen Moore was the plain or neglected nice girl determined to blossom out, as in this year's *Orchids and Ermine* (directed by Alfred Santell), while in *Naughty But Nice* (directed by Millard Webb) her naughtiness is innocent and her niceness genuine. In the former film she is partnered by Jack Mulhall, reminding one at moments in this particular instance of Harold Lloyd. Mulhall was a slightly-built, pleasant-looking and competent leading man in dozens of mainly light films of the 'twenties without making very much of a mark. Later he was to be seen gallantly but rather sadly battling on in minor

The pert, contemptuous prettiness of flirtatious Alice White arouses the indignation of the more staid Mary Astor and Kate Price in *The Sea Tiger*. It was the first film of the ex-scriptgirl who was set up as a rival to Clara Bow.

supporting roles, sometimes merely as an attendant hovering in the background. He died in 1979 at the good age of 91, but had not made a film for some twenty years previously. In his early years he enjoyed considerable popularity, and is reputed to have been the first male actor to earn $1,000 a week.

In *Naughty But Nice* Colleen Moore starts off as plain and bespectacled until a finishing school takes her in hand, enabling her ultimately to win the somewhat plodding Donald Reed. Claude Gillingwater, as Judge John R. Altwold, is a delight, as always.

Much closer to Clara Bow than Colleen Moore was Alice White, who was in fact deliberately schooled as a possible rival. Previously a typist, then a script girl, she first appeared in *The Sea Tiger* (directed by John Francis Dillon), a Milton Sills feature, in which she played a minor part as a fiery Spanish girl – though in fact hailing from Paterson, New Jersey. Petite, pert, with large brown eyes and wearing, in this instance, a fetching costume of 'rolled stockings' and scanty skirt, she quickly won the approbation of the susceptible. She made quite a number of films during the remaining silent years, and after the arrival of sound appeared in several small-scale musicals, having by this time turned blonde. Though lively and attractive, and for a time with quite a large following, she was no rival to Clara in acting ability, nor indeed in flamboyant personality. She retired around the end of the 'forties and, after two marriages and two divorces, died in 1983, aged 76.

Josef von Sternberg directed *Underworld*, a dark, compelling crime picture with a strong, tense story and three fine performances from George Bancroft, Clive Brook (almost unrecognizable in the opening scenes as a shabby down-and-out) and a splendidly sultry Evelyn Brent, known as 'Feathers' on account of her predilection for wearing them. Though bearing hallmarks of Sternberg's work in his use of shadowy settings, dramatic lighting and camera work, it is also the forerunner of all the gangster films of the 'thirties, as gripping to us at the time in silence as the screeching cars and clattering machine-guns would be to a later generation in sound.

Ernst Lubitsch's *The Student Prince in Old Heidelberg* (generally known as *The Student Prince*) is based on an old German play of 1902 and also on Sigmund Romberg's famous musical, but as a silent film it is derived mainly from the former. If, except for a few brief touches such as the universal raising of top hats to royalty, the behaviour of the small dog during the lovers' walk through the arches, the contrasting appearances of a 'mossy bank' used as symbols, it is not really typical Lubitsch, he nevertheless invests the old story of love *versus* duty among highborn Ruritanians (in this case Karlsburgians) with gentle sentiment never tipping over into sentimentality, and laced with equally gentle humour. He draws from his cast, Ramon Novarro, Norma Shearer and above all Jean Hersholt as the kindly tutor, performances that equal their best in any film. Gustav von Seyffertitz, Otis Harlan and Edgar Norton (soon to give a memorable performance as Dr Jekyll's devoted manservant in the 1932 *Dr Jekyll and Mr Hyde*) are equally strong in support.

Hotel Imperial (directed by Mauritz Stiller) finds Pola Negri in somewhat unexpected guise as a Galician chambermaid in a hotel situated between the Russian and Austrian lines during the First World War. However, she soon manages to get out of her servant's uniform and into the Parisian finery we would expect of her, as she befriends an Austrian officer (James Hall) and consents to the advances of a Russian general (George Siegmann) in order to save the former. Espionage also has its part in the story. It is minor Negri, but enjoyable, and enables her to reveal a pleasant sense of comedy. A permanent set of eight rooms was built for the production so that the camera could move around without loss of continuity.

Other American films included *Love*, based on Tolstoy's *Anna Karenina* (directed by Edmund Goulding): undoubtedly 'LOVE, WITH GRETA GARBO AND JOHN GILBERT' looked better in lights than the name *Anna Karenina*, and Tolstoy was dead and buried and unable to voice his opinion of what MGM were doing to his great novel. You could even have a happy ending if you wanted to. The two great G's do their best – which admittedly is pretty good – but one had to be a fairly ardent Garbo or Gilbert devotee to suffer some of the *longueurs*. Fortunately the costumes and settings are some compensation, and there is a good supporting cast with George Fawcett, Brandon Hurst and Emily Fitzroy.

In *The Fighting Eagle* (directed by Donald Crisp) Rod la Rocque makes a surprisingly effective Brigadier Gerard in a lively version of Conan Doyle's stories about the boastful, dashingly exuberant Napoleonic officer – rated by quite a number of people as a greater creation than Sherlock Holmes. Sam de Grasse is a credible Talleyrand and Max Barwyn will pass as Napoleon, but it is la Rocque's opportunity and he grabs it with both hands. The title of the film has been altered somewhat confusingly. In England it was shown as and referred to as *Brigadier Gerard*, in America it was generally known as *The Fighting Eagle* but also, for some strange reason, as *Brigadier General*.

The Patent Leather Kid (directed by Alfred Santell), a mixture of boxing and the First

World War, features a rather embarrassing finale in which the once anti-war hero's paralysed arm miraculously rises in slow salute as his country's flag unfurls, but is redeemed by one of Richard Barthelmess's most sympathetic performances and the magnificent battle scenes, photographed by Arthur Edeson, who was later cameraman on *All Quiet on the Western Front*.

The Monkey Talks (directed by Raoul Walsh) was an unusual and interesting circus film, adapted from the French, in which, as part of an act, a man is disguised as a monkey that can talk. The plot has the old triangle basis, but the treatment and trimmings are strikingly original; it might well have become

That JOHN GILBERT AND GRETA GARBO IN LOVE looked more effective on a cinema marquee than LEO TOLSTOY'S ANNA KARENINA seems proven by this photograph of the waiting multitude, so who can blame the studio for its change of title?

a 'cult' film had such a term existed in those days. Jacques Lerner, in what appears to have been his only film, gives a bravura performance in the title role, a part he played also on the stage in both Britain and the USA. The girl at the apex of the triangle is played by Olive Borden, who decorated a number of films during the period, first as a Sennett bathing beauty, then as a leading lady in the films of Tom Mix, John Ford, Howard Hawks and other big names. She was yet another victim to the coming of sound and died, sadly, in a home for destitute women at the age of 40.

The Blood Ship (directed by George B. Seitz), was a 'rattling good yarn' of courage, violence and mutiny on board a schooner, the success of which did a lot to put the recently launched Columbia Pictures on the cinema map. It also offered a fine acting opportunity to Hobart Bosworth, who ran away to sea as a boy. A real pioneer in pictures, he started his career in 1909 and worked as actor, director, producer and screenwriter until 1942, dying the following year aged 75. Suitably vigorous in his support in *Blood Ship* were Richard Arlen and Jacqueline Logan (Mary Magdalene of *The King of Kings*). Watching it in a small Nottingham cinema on a hot summer afternoon, we could almost smell the tar and feel the salt spray on our perspiring faces.

Wolf's Clothing (directed by Roy del Ruth) was an unusually bright and amusing comedy-mystery about a subway guard who is knocked unconscious by a car driver who is escaping from an insane asylum, and the wild imaginings that occur while he is 'out'. The director keeps the fantastical events moving with entertaining verve and humour, aided by splendidly off-beat performances from Monte Blue as the guard and in particular John Miljan as the crazy driver. Miljan, one of the busiest actors of the late 'twenties, seizes with obvious relish the chance to escape from the suave villains he was frequently called upon to portray. Tall, dark and handsome, he survived the change to sound with ease, being possessed also of an excellent voice. One of his last, brief appearances was as the blind man in *The Ten Commandments* in 1956. He died four years later, aged 68.

In *Annie Laurie* (directed by John S. Robertson), one of Lillian Gish's few failures, the American cast struggles bravely to feel at home in kilts against painted backgrounds while enacting a tediously phony story. Miss Gish, however, looked more fetching than ever as a prettily tam-o'shantered Annie.

After Midnight (directed by Monta Bell) opens with Norma Shearer on her way home from her job as a nightclub cigarette girl. As she walks along the deserted road she is approached by a young man who asks, with intended menace though it is obvious he is no hardened criminal, that she buy the length of lead piping he is holding. Wisely, she does so, then runs after him and bangs him on the head with it, laying him out. From this unconventional meeting develops love for Miss Shearer, and for us a compelling picture

Opposite: a scene from Monte Blue's unconscious imaginings in *Wolf's Clothing*, in which he and a girl (Patsy Ruth Miller), who turns out to be a nurse in the hospital to which he has been taken, are miniaturized by gigantic sets and furniture.

Below: John Miljan (right) and Monte Blue (left) in the same wildly fantastical and entertaining film.

of two sisters, a flighty one (Gwen Lee) and a thrifty one (Norma Shearer), struggling to make a life for themselves in the Big City. Directed and played with great skill and sympathy, the film retains its hold on the watcher's interest and emotions throughout, ending with one of the most original and gently moving sequences of any film of its time.

Soft Cushions (directed by Edward F. Cline) was an entertaining Arabian Nights fantasy with Douglas MacLean – an undeservedly forgotten light comedian – as a Fairbanks-type thief, and Sue Carol (in time to become both Alan Ladd's wife and his formidable manager) entirely enchanting as a slave girl.

Delightful Sue Carol, who enlivened many a light comedy in films with such titles as *Soft Cushions*, *Win That Girl*, *Girls Gone Wild*, *Why Leave Home?* and *The Exalted Flapper* before eventually becoming both Alan Ladd's wife and his business manager.

The Wizard (directed by Richard Rosson) starred Gustav von Seyffertitz at the top of his form as a doctor whose some has been executed for murder and who trains an ape to carry out various nefarious deeds in revenge. The somewhat improbable story, with Edgar Allan Poe undertones, was in fact taken from one entitled *Balaoo* by Gaston Leroux, author of *The Phantom of the Opera*.

Rolled Stockings (directed by Richard Rosson), a lightweight but entertaining college/jazz-age commentary, has James Hall winning the boat race after various misadventures, and Louise Brooks popularizing an ephemeral fashion of rolled stockings and bare knees.

The Jazz Singer (directed by Alan Crosland), sometimes inaccurately referred to as the first sound picture, was in reality a pretty worthless piece of hokum which, had it not been for a few songs and an unexpected line from Al Jolson, would have been quickly and deservedly forgotten. The unfortunate Warner Oland and May McAvoy struggle against their material but are ultimately swamped by the sickly sentimentality and bottomless bathos of the script. It is either regrettable or symbolic that the 'death of the silent film' should have been heralded by so tawdry a specimen of cinema.

Three films of 1927 long regarded as 'lost', but which in recent years have been rediscovered, deserve mention: *The Enemy* (directed by Fred Niblo), a powerful dramatization of Channing Pollock's anti-war play, with Lillian Gish and Ralph Forbes; *The Show* (directed by Tod Browning), with John Gilbert as a bouncy and dishonest sideshow barker who also performs in the 'show' as, of all people, John the Baptist, with Renée Adorée as Salome; and *The Garden of Allah* (directed by Rex Ingram), starring his wife Alice Terry and Ivan Petrovich in Robert Hitchens' famous love-or-duty melodrama, later remade with Marlene Dietrich and Charles Boyer.

A fourth film, still sadly lost, less prestigious

than the above but remembered by contemporary filmgoers with pleasure, is *Taxi! Taxi!* (directed by Melville W. Brown), a modest but enjoyable comedy from a *Saturday Evening Post* story, enlivened by an excellent and well-knit cast of such silent stalwarts as Edward Everett Horton, Marian Nixon, Lucien Littlefield and Burr McIntosh, all of whom survived into sound.

In the field of short films the year marked the first comedy (*Putting Pants on Philip*) in which Laurel and Hardy played together as a team; and the opening episodes of the long-running and very popular series *The Collegians*.

Alfred Hitchcock helped to fill out another thin British year with three productions: *Downhill* (in America, *When Boys Leave Home*), *Easy Virtue* and *The Ring*. The first two were derived from stage plays, the former play by Ivor Novello and Constance Collier, the second by Noël Coward. Both are minor Hitchcock, though touches of his experimental direction are evident in each, particularly some dream sequences in *Downhill*.

The Ring, his first production for BIP, is a more important step in his development, and is from a script he wrote with Eliot Stannard. A young boxer, played by the Danish actor Carl Brisson, marries a cashier, loses her to a champion fighter, fights the latter at the Royal Albert Hall, appears to be losing, is encouraged by his wife, and wins. Hitchcock makes this not startlingly original material into an interesting film by ingenious symbols and visual narrative points that at the time aroused sharply contrasting opinions. 'It is treated visually, but there the merit ends,' said one. 'He has invested his picture with an element of continual surprise – a triumph for British films and for Hitchcock in particular,' eulogized another. The film's title refers not only to the boxing-ring but to a 'serpent' bracelet given to the wife, of which symbolic use is made. Other typical touches include a glass of champagne the bubbles of which go

flat during a party in which the young boxer becomes aware of his wife's infidelity, and a clean '2' display card outside the boxing booth at a fair contrasted with the well-worn '1', indicating that the fight in progress is the first time a challenger has lasted more than one round against the resident boxer. The art direction involves an early use of the Schuftan process, whereby time and money are saved in set-building by an ingenious combination of backgrounds and mirrors.

Eliot Stannard was also responsible for the script of *Blighty* (directed by Adrian Brunel), from a story by Ivor Montagu. It was the director's first film for Gainsborough and a popular success. The somewhat sentimental story of a titled lady's son and her chauffeur enlisting together, the son marrying a French girl, and the chauffeur bringing her child back to England after the son's death and eventually marrying the widow, caught the curious mood of nostalgia already evident in *Mademoiselle from Armentières* the previous year. Actual shots of the fighting in France and the Armistice celebrations which were inserted to inject reality into the story (and to save money) merely make its artificiality more obvious. However, both the events and the class distinctions were found acceptable at the time, and a capable performance from Jameson Thomas – reliable and popular star of the period – helps matters along. The French girl is played by Nadia Sibirskaia, star of *Menilmontant*, a much-discussed *avant-garde* film from France in 1924.

More First World War memories are revived in *Roses of Picardy* (directed by Maurice Elvey), this time taken from one of the most distinguished of all WWI novels, R. H. Mottram's trilogy entitled *The Spanish Farm*. The film inevitably condenses the long book, but manages to convey something of the spirit of the original. Jameson Thomas is again outstanding in a generally excellent cast that includes John Stuart, Lilian Hall-Davis and Humberston Wright. The change of title to that of the popular song may have helped the box-office but does the film no other service.

In the main, original scripts were conspicuous by their absence this year. Ivor Novello appeared in Noël Coward's play *The Vortex* (directed by Adrian Brunel); Henry Edwards in Frederick Lonsdale's play *The Fake* (directed by George Jakoby); Lili Damita in Noël Coward's play *The Queen was in the Parlour* (directed by Graham Cutts); Guy Newall in Arnold Ridley's play *The Ghost Train* (directed by Geza M. Bolvary); Norman McKinnel in *Hindle Wakes* from Stanley Houghton's play (directed by Maurice Elvey). About the latter a contemporary critic rhapsodized, 'It is indeed pleasant to be able to give unqualified praise to a British film, not only because it is British but on account of its intrinsic merit.'

Dorothy Gish and Will Rogers were in London from the USA to make *Tiptoes* for Herbert Wilcox. It may seem an odd undertaking nowadays to make a silent picture of a musical comedy (George Gershwin) and with a star, Will Rogers, whose forte was a combination of rope-handling and chat; but such drawbacks did not worry us much in those days because we knew no better – and were quite satisfied with visual wit, particularly with Dorothy Gish at her most delightful. She followed it with *Madame Pompadour,* also directed by Herbert Wilcox, with Antonio Moreno opposite her.

Of the two main foreign-language films that came our way during the year, one was from Germany (*The Love of Jeanne Ney,* directed by G. W. Pabst) and the other from France (*The Italian Straw Hat,* directed by René Clair): the latter has been generally available since, the former is less well-known.

The Love of Jeanne Ney was taken from a long novel by the Russian writer Ilya Ehrenburg. Much of the action takes place in Paris. It concerns a French bourgeois girl in love with a young Russian Communist despite the fact that his political associates have killed her father for ideological reasons. Opposing them is an anti-Communist agent, who murders her uncle and abandons his blind daughter after promising to marry her. It seems to have been rather dangerous to be a relative of Miss Ney. The story was considerably modified in the film, and a happy ending was tacked on, against the wishes of the director, in place of the tragic one in the original. The murderous agent is played by the brilliantly menacing Fritz Rasp (the Actor with the Flat Back to his Head), later to become widely known for his role in *Emil and the Detectives*; and the blind girl by Brigitte Helm, unforgettable as both the real and the manufactured Maria in Fritz Lang's *Metropolis.*

The social satire of *The Italian Straw Hat,* from a famous farce by Eugène Labiche, is never allowed to swamp the joyous comedy that springs from the misadventures of a man who, on his way to his wedding, has the misfortune of his horse eating the hat of an army officer's mistress. Sparklingly directed by Clair at the top of his form (together with *Le Million,* it is widely regarded as his masterpiece), and with a wonderful series of running gags, such as the gentleman with the recalcitrant bow tie, it can be thoroughly enjoyed without any awareness of underlying sociological significance.

1927

The World at Large

'Black Friday' in Germany as economic system collapses

Britain breaks off diplomatic relations with the USSR

Leon Trotsky is expelled from the Communist Party

Programme of the NSDAP (Hitler's Nazi Party) is published

Sacco and Vanzetti are executed in Massachusetts

Charles Lindbergh flies solo from New York to Paris

Nan Britton claims she bore President Harding a daughter in 1917

Ruth Snyder/Judd Gray murder trial in USA

Death of Lizzie Borden, who was tried for the murder of her parents in 1893 but was acquitted

Cinema

British International Pictures takes over British National Studios at Elstree

Herbert Wilcox opens new studios, also at Elstree

Roxy Cinema, New York, opens (6214 seats)

Wampas Baby Stars: Patricia Avery, Ruth Carewe, Helene Costello, Barbara Kent, Natalie Kingston, Gladys McConnell, Sally Phipps, Sally Rand, Martha Sleeper, Adamae Vaughn, Iris Stuart, Mary McAlister, Gwen Lee

Births: Janet Leigh, Gina Lollobrigida, Ken Russell, George C. Scott, Robert Shaw

Theatre

Robert Sherwood, *The Road to Rome*
Somerset Maugham, *The Letter*
Miles Malleson, *The Fanatics*
Hamilton Deane/Bram Stoker, *Dracula* (first London production)

George Gershwin, *Funny Face*
Jerome Kern/Oscar Hammerstein, *Show Boat*
Harry Tierney, *Rio Rita*
Vincent Youmans, *Hit the Deck*
Kurt Weill, *The Rise and Fall of the City of Mahagonny*

Fiction

Virginia Woolf, *To the Lighthouse*
Sinclair Lewis, *Elmer Gantry*
B. Traven, *The Treasure of the Sierra Madre*
Thornton Wilder, *The Bridge of San Luis Rey*
Willa Cather, *Death Comes for the Archbishop*
J. B. Priestley, *Benighted* (filmed as *The Old Dark House*)
A. Conan Doyle, *The Casebook of Sherlock Holmes*
Francis Brett Young, *Portrait of Clare*
Henry Williamson, *Tarka the Otter*

Music

Shostakovich, Symphony no. 2
Stravinsky, *Oedipus Rex*
Aaron Copland, Concerto for piano and orchestra
Vaughan Williams, *Riders to the Sea* (opera)
Ernst Krenek, *Jonny Strikes Up* (first jazz opera)

Popular Songs

'Old Man River'
'My Heart Stood Still'
'My Blue Heaven'
'Blue Skies'
'Rio Rita'

Fashion Note

Skirts often 'clipped' at the back or sides, particularly for evening wear

1928

Though many cinema-owners, with apprehension in their hearts and their hands deep in their pockets, were installing sound equipment during the year there were still many more silents than talkies to be seen by the average filmgoer. For anyone travelling from town to town across Britain, as I was, a part-talkie was still a curiosity, and an all-talkie, let alone an all-talking-all-singing-all-dancing talkie, rarer still. In general we did not feel in any way deprived. We had a highly developed art form available to us (even if it did not often achieve sublimity), and though we looked forward to hearing the voices of a favourite player there were plenty of voiceless movies around, either from former years or from the current output. Josef von Sternberg's *The Last Command,* for instance, stands comparison with anything of the period, with Emil Jannings at his powerful best as an arrogant general in the Imperial Russian Army who slashes an agitator across the face and is forced to pay for the act later. When the Revolution breaks out he is attacked by the mob, humiliated, and saved from death only by the intervention of a beautiful spy (Evelyn Brent) whom he has befriended.

The scene just before the powerful climax of von Sternberg's *The Last Command,* with Emil Jannings, as a former Russian general now a film extra in Hollywood, and William Powell, as a former political agitator now a famous film director.

When she herself is killed in a train which plunges into a river he is distraught, and starts shaking with the palsy. The film opens ten years after these events, when, enfeebled and derelict, he has drifted to America and picks up an occasional job as a film extra. The story is told in a long flashback as he sits with other extras before a mirror, trying to put on his make-up with trembling hands. By the one questionable coincidence in the script it turns out that the director of the film for which he is engaged is the former agitator whom he whipped, and who has never forgotten it. He recognizes the ex-officer and assigns him to the small part of a Russian general facing rebellious troops. The old man tries to rise to the occasion, loses control as terrible memories surface, and collapses in death. Sternberg, who states that he wrote the scenario from an idea given him by Ernst Lubitsch, directs with great power, resulting in a haunting and moving film more memorable than the romantic improbabilities of his later American sound films with Marlene Dietrich.

Sternberg's other big production of the year was *The Docks of New York,* a comparatively straightforward, simple, sordid story of waterfront life – theft, murder, suicide and all – made noteworthy by his flair for creating atmosphere, and embellished with much effective photography (Harold Rosson). His reputation as a tough, autocratic and arrogant director may be justified, but he drew fine performances from George Bancroft, Betty Compson and the flamboyantly handsome Russian actress Olga Baclanova, eventually to be turned into a chicken in Tod Browning's *Freaks*.

An underworld film which had occasional hints of Sternberg's hand but was in fact directed by Victor Schertzinger was *Forgotten Faces*, starring familiar Sternberg players – Clive Brook, William Powell, Olga Baclanova. Brook plays Heliotrope Harry, a sort of serious New York Raffles who, when

Olga Baclanova, the Russian dramatic actress, as the distraught unfaithful wife of 'Heliotrope Harry' (Clive Brook), who has been deliberately and subtly terrifying her – for a laudable purpose – in *Forgotten Faces*.

he finds his wife with another man, shoots him. He then takes his baby daughter away, leaves her on the doorstep of a rich couple and surrenders to the police. Years later he reads of the girl's engagement to an eligible society man but his venomous wife visits him in prison and torments him by declaring that she will now claim her daughter. When, very conveniently, he saves the life of a prison warder and is released on parole, he tracks the woman down. Deliberately, by subtle suggestion – making use of 'the whiff of heliotrope' (the title of the original story, and the perfume by which he knows she will recognize him) – he terrifies her into mortally wounding him. She is now in her turn imprisoned and Heliotrope Harry dies happy in the knowledge that his daughter's future is secured. The tense climax, strongly directed and splendidly played, held the audience firmly in its seats until the National Anthem — then, and for long afterwards, a statutory event at the close of each day's screening.

In a busy year Emil Jannings made three further films. In the first, *Sins of the Fathers* (directed by Ludwig Berger), he plays a German-American restaurateur who goes through numerous traumas and afflictions after falling victim to the wiles of an adventuress, played by Ruth Chatterton, a distinguished recruit from the theatre. After losing his long-suffering wife (who dies from a broken heart), becoming a bootlegger, seeing his own son go blind through drinking poisonous spirits, losing his money and serving a prison sentence, he decides enough is enough and becomes — rather unwisely, one might think – a waiter in a beer garden. However, by the time the film fades out he has found his son, no longer blind, and they end up happily reunited. It all seems rather to add up to a contrived catalogue of Janningsonian sufferings. In *The Street of Sin* (directed by Mauritz Stiller) he appears as Basher Bill, once a boxer, now a criminal who pretends to reform by going to a Salvation Army hostel (the film is set, not too convincingly, in London), becomes genuinely converted, and when trouble comes sacrifices his life not only for the Salvation Army but also, perhaps more understandably, for Fay Wray. Part-author of this rather tall story was none other than Josef von Sternberg, with whom Stiller had some differences of opinion. He left before the film was finally completed, and it seems that Lothar Mendes did some final directorial work on it. Mauritz Stiller himself, broken down in health – and some say in heart – returned to Sweden and, after directing a production of the American crime play *Broadway*, died there this same year.

Jannings' other film, however, was a very different matter from the above two *Sins*. *The Patriot* (directed by Ernst Lubitsch) is one of the 'lost' films one fervently hopes may be recovered. Taken from the English stage adaptation of the novel by Alfred Neumann, and brilliantly directed by Lubitsch in one of his 'serious' moods, it tells of the mad Czar Paul of Russia and his death at the hands of his trusted Count Pahlen (the 'patriot' of the title) for the good of Russia, after which Pahlen himself prepares for his own death by suicide. Jannings' part is a fairly short one, but it is his presence that is felt throughout the film, despite the fine and dignified performance by Lewis Stone. Florence Vidor is equally impressive – and stunningly beautiful – as Pahlen's devious mistress. With *every* excuse to indulge himself in the wild grimacings of which he was sometimes over-fond, Jannings here uses them only as necessary for his portrayal of the insane ruler. A critic's opinion that 'Emil Jannings' portrayal in *The Patriot* is one of the greatest in the history of stage or screen and definitely places him as an outstanding actor in any current form of dramatic art' may seem a little fulsome, but remembering the immediate effect the film had on the audience, it is understandable.

Von Sternberg's *The Dragnet* (sometimes spelt *Drag Net*), also listed as 'lost', is a minor work, a gangster melodrama of hi-jackers *versus* tough detective (George Bancroft). Other familiar Sternberg names in the cast are Evelyn Brent and William Powell.

The Trail of '98 (directed by Clarence Brown) is one of the last great silent spectaculars, possibly the very last. Work started on the production in 1927 and continued well into 1928; it opened in London during September for a run at our old friend the Tivoli. Based on the 1910 best-seller by Robert W. Service, it tells a panoramic story of the Klondike Gold Rush in 1897, and of the sufferings, the few triumphs and the many

Emil Jannings gives another fine performance as the mad Czar Paul in Lubitsch's superb film *The Patriot*. With him is Florence Vidor, equally impressive and stunningly beautiful as the devious mistress of the 'patriot', Count Pahlen, played by Lewis Stone.

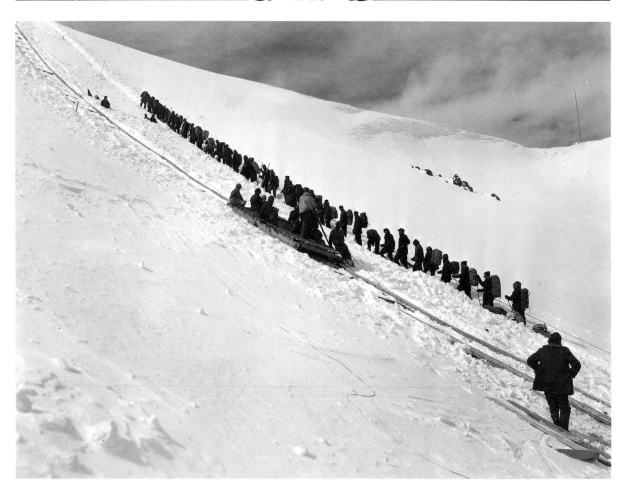

An interesting production still, showing the dark line of people tracked by the camera as they trudge through the snow, heading for Alaska in search of gold, in *The Trail of '98.*

disasters that befell the adventurers who braved the terrible Chilkoot Pass in their search for fortune. The first sight of the long, long trail up the snow-covered slope – well caught in a superb still – is unforgettable, as are the great set pieces: the avalanche under which many of the gold-seekers are buried, the White Horse rapids, the burning of Dawson City. Clarence Brown, better known for his work in the warmer atmosphere of Garbo films, tackled the rigours of the deep-frozen North with a sure touch, seeing to it that the puny lives of the individual characters were not altogether swamped by the grimly magnificent spectacle, and he had a fine cast in Dolores Del Rio, Ralph Forbes, Tully Marshall, Harry Carey and others to make us care for what happens to them. Many of the gold-rush scenes were shot near Denver in temperatures as low as 60 degrees below zero. Several extras reportedly lost their lives during the shooting: doubtless they regarded the risks as part of the job, much as a racing driver, a deep-sea diver, a steeplejack might – but it was perhaps as well for the audience's enjoyment that they did not know this at the Tivoli that evening.

D. W. Griffith's two productions were lesser ones, to put it kindly. *Drums of Love* is a version – or travesty – of the famous Paolo and Francesca tragedy moved up a century or two and from Italy to Portuguese South America for no discernible reason. Mary Philbin is insipid, Don Alvorado dull. Lionel Barrymore, padded to the neck as the hunchbacked husband, does his best, but on the whole, despite one or two effective Griffith set pieces, it is a sad effort. *The Battle of the Sexes* is a remake of his much earlier film of the same title (made in 1914 with Lillian Gish and Owen Moore). Updated to a trite tale of a family man (Jean Hersholt) led astray by a gold-digger, its only redeeming feature is the presence of the lively Phyllis Haver, who could, one would imagine, have found gold in much more profitable and attractive fields.

In *Laugh, Clown, Laugh* (directed by Herbert Brenon) Lon Chaney plays the age-old *pagliaccio* – the clown who loves and loses. Variations on the theme are that the girl is his adopted daughter; that she learns of his love and out of kindness and gratitude tells him that she returns his love; and that his not wholly unexpected death – leaving her free to marry a wealthy nobleman – is accidental. Brenon directs with a sensitivity, lightened with gentle humour, that makes a potentially mawkish subject tender and true. It was Chaney's own favourite among all his films, and the sentimental but apposite theme song specially composed for it (though it was a silent film) was played at his funeral. Loretta Young, totally charming as the girl, Simonetta, secured the part in a slightly roundabout way. She is the youngest of three sisters, all of whom appeared in films when small children – on one occasion as waifs in Valentino's *The Sheik*, spot them if you can. In 1927 the director Millard Webb telephoned the boarding-house run by their mother to engage the eldest daughter, Polly Ann Young (born 1908), for a small part in a Colleen Moore film, *Naughty But Nice*. She was not available, but Gretchen (as Loretta Young was then called) put her own name forward. She was accepted, and this led to the important role with Lon Chaney, her name being changed to Loretta. She was only fourteen at the time, and rumour has it that small pieces of padding were necessary in later parts of the film to suggest the requisite state of maturity. Padded or not, she was an

The second of Lon Chaney's famous clown characterizations, from his own favourite of all his films, *Laugh, Clown, Laugh*. With him is the teenaged Loretta Young as his ward, with whom he later falls in love only to lose her in the end.

immediate success, and thereby started an illustrious career. That of her elder sister was much briefer. She is to be found in the cast lists of a few films during the late 'twenties and the 'thirties (Victor Seastrom's *Masks of the Devil*, Monta Bell's *The Bellamy Trial*, Edward Griffith's *Rich People*, etc.) but after 1941 there seems to be no trace of her. The middle Young sister, Elizabeth Jane, known professionally as Sally Blane, after making her entry in a small part in the series *The Collegians*, appeared in a number of silent and early sound features before retiring on her marriage in 1937 to the actor and director Norman Foster. As an actress she was both pretty and competent. It was, incidentally, in the Young family home that David Niven stayed on first arriving in Hollywood.

Chaney's other two films, *While the City Sleeps* (directed by Jack Conway) and *The Big City* (directed by Tod Browning), are efficient but fairly routine crime pictures. In

A maturer and less athletic Douglas Fairbanks sizes up the vivacious young Lupe Velez (later to become known as the Mexican Spitfire) in *The Gaucho*, her first feature film.

the first he appears as a tough detective, in the second as a tough crook: with only slight changes of make-up he nevertheless presents totally contrasting characterizations. In *The Big City* he is reunited with Betty Compson, his partner in the film that brought them both fame in 1919, *The Miracle Man*.

Douglas Fairbanks is not at his best in *The Gaucho* (directed by F. Richard Jones), 'an unfortunate blend of religion and acrobatics', according to one critic. Despite a reasonable amount of the latter (a little less athletic than hitherto – he was, after all, over 40 years old), good support from some staunch

characters led by Gustav von Seyffertitz, and above all the introduction of the Mexican spitfire Lupe Velez, whose previous appearance had been in a Laurel and Hardy short, the whole film seems to hang fire. It is difficult to arouse much anxiety about the outcome of the jealousy of the Mountain Girl (Miss Velez) who loves the Cowboy from the American pampas (Fairbanks), who in his turn misunderstands the purity of the intentions of a 'miracle girl' or Girl of the Shrine (Ceraine Greear) towards him. Even a brief glimpse of an ethereally lit Mary Pickford as Our Lady of the Shrine fails to spark off a lot of excitement. However, it filled a dull evening for us in one of those provincial towns philanthropic enough to have started Sunday cinema openings – as yet by no means general.

A very different aspect of religion is treated in Gloria Swanson's *Sadie Thompson* (directed by Raoul Walsh), from Somerset

Gloria Swanson in one of her best roles, Sadie Thompson, being admonished by Lionel Barrymore (as Alfred Atkinson) to mend her ways, in a film based on Somerset Maugham's *Rain*.

Maugham's famous story *Rain*. Comment was made that the change of title shifted the emphasis from the plot to the star, but in actual fact the story itself was originally called *Miss Thompson*. Where the film was weakened was by making the man who seduces her (then commits suicide) a religious reformer rather than a minister of the Church. Apart from that it is a powerful movie, with Gloria Swanson at her best, and Lionel Barrymore conveying with effective restraint his desperate fight against and final submission to the sins of the flesh. For its time it was quite a daring production, announced

on the front of the Capitol, Haymarket with a fine flourish: 'SHOULD THE CENSOR HAVE PASSED THIS FILM?? SEE GLORIA SWANSON AS A SUPER-SLUT!'

After such a challenge, who could resist handing over the admission price?

King Vidor's *The Crowd* is one of those films, familiar to many today, whose reputation has grown steadily with the years; indeed, it is now looked on by many as a 'silent classic'. The simple story of two young people trying to find happiness, build a home and raise a family in the densely populated and unheeding city perhaps strikes a more sympathetic note in later, more disillusioned years than it did for us in the pre-Crash 'twenties.

Critically it was awarded high praise, but though we felt we knew and understood the rather cocky, inadequate clerk and his non-glamorous wife (most beautifully played by Eleanor Boardman) and appreciated the skill

Louise Brooks as the Girl in France ('the lady in black tights') and Victor McLaglen as the roistering sailor, getting together in Howard Hawks' *A Girl in Every Port*.

with which their predicaments had been presented, I do not recall that waiting queues of cinemagoers were at that time encircling the blocks. It seems that no fewer than seven different endings were made (later reduced to two), which appears to indicate some uncertainty of purpose in the script, even allowing for possible interference imposed by the 'front office' for box-office reasons. The fade-out most generally seen, that of the little family laughing heartily (with a hint perhaps of rather desperate hysteria) at a cinema cartoon, is probably the best in its disturbing ambiguity. James Murray, who as

the clerk leapt deservedly to stardom and could have had a lasting career, proved incapable of handling sudden success, became unmanageable in the studio, took to drink, and after appearing in a number of increasingly unimportant pictures was found drowned in the Hudson River in 1936 – whether from accident or suicide remains uncertain. He was 35 years old.

Louise Brooks, an often caustic critic of Hollywood in later years, had been forced to waste her magnetic personality and striking looks on a number of conventional, though quite entertaining, jazz-age stories. On the verge of the sound period, however, she landed two superior films. The first, *A Girl in Every Port* (directed by Howard Hawks), stars Victor McLaglen as a typically roistering sailor. Louise Brooks is only one of a series of girls he encounters on his maritime wanderings – others being Natalie Kingston (ex-*Tarzan* serial heroine) as the Girl in the South Sea Islands, Sally Rand (famous fan dancer) as the Girl in Bombay, Caryl Lincoln as the Girl in Liverpool and Myrna Loy as the Girl in the Orient – but Louise Brooks, as the Girl in France, is the special one who threatens to disrupt his friendship with a fellow sailor. It moves at a cracking pace, and with the verve and vigour Hawks was to display in later years with greater films. Brooks' second film, *Beggars of Life* (directed by William A. Wellman), was equally well received and is probably the best of her silent pictures. It tells of life among the wandering hoboes who used to hop the freight trains. Nancy (Louise Brooks) is helped to escape from the police – after killing her violent foster-father in a moment of panic – by young Jim (Richard Arlen), who takes her to a hobo camp ruled by two tough rivals (Wallace Beery and Robert Perry). For much of the film she is disguised as a boy, in old clothes and cloth cap, a situation she carries off with aplomb. The film was made both as a silent and as a part-talkie with music and sound effects.

White Shadows in the South Seas was originally to have been directed by Robert S. Flaherty, noted maker of such documentaries as *Moana* and *Louisiana Story*, but after arriving on location in the Marquesas Islands he found himself unable to cope with studio rules and politics, and W. S. van Dyke took over. The film, which might today be described as a dramatized documentary, deals with the exploitation of the Marquesan natives by greedy and dishonest white traders. Apart from the local extras it has a cast of only three – Monte Blue, Robert Anderson and Raquel Torres, an exotic beauty from Mexico whose first film this was. She worked on some foreign-language films for MGM but made only a few further pictures – the best being *The Bridge of San Luis Rey* in 1929, and the least expected being the Marx Brothers' *Duck Soup* in 1933; she followed this with one British film, *Red Wagon,* in 1934, before retiring in order to get married.

A noteworthy film in John Ford's 'Irish' output – other early examples were *The Shamrock Handicap* (1926) and *Mother Machree* (1928) – was *Hangman's House,* from a novel by Donn Byrne. The story is a simple one: an Irish girl, to please her dying father, marries a drunken wastrel, but after the latter's death in a duel with a man whose sister he has wronged is left free to go to the childhood sweetheart she really loves. This is one of those occasional films that, for no reason that can easily be explained, stick in the memory – in this case mainly through Ford's skilful creation of atmosphere and through a remarkable performance by Earle Foxe as the wastrel. Foxe was yet another of the thoroughly efficient, and occasionally outstanding, supporting players of the period whose names are too little known; though he lived until 1973 he appears to have made no film after 1940, and references to him in print are few. Staunch old pioneer Hobart Bosworth appears as the old father on the brink of death, and June Collyer is pretty, if a bit colourless, as the dutiful daughter with the odd forename of 'Connaught'.

An equally unforgettable, though rarely mentioned, film of this year was James Cruze's *The Red Mark*. The setting, a French penal colony in New Caledonia during the last century, is a grim one, and the story – by John Russell, author of *Where the Pavement Ends* – seems headed for a tragic outcome, though a happy ending is contrived by an admittedly extreme coincidence. The island's executioner is about to hang for manslaughter a young pickpocket whom he regards as a rival for the girl he himself desires, when at the last moment he discovers the boy is his own son. The case collapses as the prisoner is proved innocent. Related in cold blood, it seems a somewhat improbable resolution. So cunningly, however, had Cruze worked up an atmosphere of tension and overhanging menace and involved us in the fate of the characters that by this time we were ready to accept anything that would let the two young

From left to right: Rose Dione, Gaston Glass, Gustav von Seyffertitz, Nena Quartaro and Luke Cosgrave in James Cruze's little-known but strangely haunting study of overshadowing menace in a French penal colony, *The Red Mark.*

lovers (almost literally) off the hook. He was aided by excellent performances from Gaston Glass as the young man, Nena Quartaro as the girl, and above all, dominating everything and everyone as the intimidating executioner, our old friend Gustav von Seyffertitz. At the small cinema in Windsor, Berks., where I first saw it the modest orchestra played an exceptionally well-chosen accompaniment, which may well have considerably increased its effect on the audience. A contemporary critic wrote of the film that 'It is remarkable for its forceful appeal and the excellence of the various artists.' He then refers to 'newcomer Lena Quartarie', thus misspelling both her names, but otherwise I can only agree with him entirely.

Apart from *The Trail of '98,* spectacle was scarce this year as the reign of silence drew to its end. The only other large-scale movie I recollect was *Noah's Ark* (directed by Michael Curtiz). It followed the DeMille formula of using the past to provide a parallel with or a warning about the present – in this case the First World War and the Flood. Dolores Costello, George O'Brien and various featured players appeared in tenuously parallel roles past and present, with name changes such as Mary/Miriam, Travis/Japhet and Al/Ham – with Myrna Loy transformed from show dancer to slave girl. It was described at the time (and has appeared in similar lists since) as among 'the worst movies ever made', and the modern sequences are certainly notably unmemorable. However, benumbed by the thundering advance publicity at the time, we were waiting expectantly for the climactic scenes of the Flood inself, which were as spectacular as anything during the period, with thousands of gallons of water released from huge tanks swamping both the immense sets and the crowds of extras milling around in them. Later, when it was revealed that several extras had in fact been injured, and one reported drowned, an outcry was raised (not for the first time) at the risks taken by some directors in order to obtain sensational shots.

The titles of Greta Garbo's films were becoming a little monotonous: *The Divine Woman, The Mysterious Lady, A Woman of Affairs* . . . To be frank, the films were getting rather monotonous too. *The Divine Woman* had Victor Seastrom as director and two excellent actors, Lars Hanson and Lowell Sherman, in support, but the script, derived from a play based on the life of Sarah Bernhardt, preferred melodramatics to truth and was dull even on its own terms. In *The Mysterious Lady* (directed by Fred Niblo) Garbo was mysterious as a spy as well as a lady. Being less pretentious the film was more enjoyable than *The Divine Woman,* but totally predictable, without even the surprise of an unhappy ending. In the third film, *A Woman of Affairs* (directed by Clarence Brown), the unhappy ending duly occurred, but as practically everyone had been reading Michael Arlen's runaway bestseller *The Green Hat,* castigating modern morals and manners, on which it was based, there was no surprise here either. As entertainment it was the best of the three, in its slightly ridiculous way.

Comedy had another good year, with *The Circus* from Chaplin, *Speedy* from Lloyd, *Steamboat Bill, Jr.* and *The Cameraman* from Keaton.

The Circus was made during a period of great personal stress in Chaplin's life and he spoke and wrote little of it afterwards. We of course knew nothing of this at the time — what we went to the New Gallery Cinema in Regent Street to see was just 'A NEW

Gustav von Seyffertitz menacing again. This time he threatens Greta Garbo, a spy in his employ, in *The Mysterious Lady*.

CHAPLIN'. Much discussion was going on then as to whether a comedian should introduce pathos into his films, and if so, how much. It was generally Chaplin who was mentioned. One contemporary critic concluded, 'As long as this trait [pathos] never obtrudes itself to the exclusion of the humour I cannot see that anyone is entitled to complain' — thus separating the two emotions firmly into separate compartments. *The Circus* itself was regarded as definitely Chaplin's masterpiece, funnier than *The Kid* and more coherent than *The Gold Rush* – so funny in fact that no one should cavil at the inevitable pathetic ending. So far as I recollect, none of us did, as we watched the slowly departing caravans behind the motionless figure, and the final typical back kick with which he went away from the already disintegrating 'ring'. The same review referred to the 'usually decorous' New Gallery audiences shouting with unrestrained laughter — an interesting if questionable suggestion that,

Left to right: Julanne Johnston, Colleen Moore, the inimitable Claude Gillingwater at his most outraged, and Lawrence Gray in *Oh, Kay!*, an entertaining trifle that shows the silent screen could successfully adapt even a musical comedy when directed (in this case by Mervyn LeRoy) with the right touch.

even apart from the art houses, particular cinemas in those days attracted particular audiences whatever films they were showing. Merna Kennedy, who played the bareback rider whom the tramp loved and lost, was suggested for the part by Lita Grey Chaplin, his wife at the time, who had been her childhood friend. Later she would accuse her, apparently without evidence, of adultery with her husband. Formerly a dancer, Merna Kennedy married director Busby Berkeley in 1934 but they were divorced the following year. She died of a heart attack in 1944, aged 35.

The title of Harold Lloyd's last silent film, *Speedy* (directed by Ted Wilde), was also the name given to him by his father, and it indicates the type of character he plays in it – 'an irresponsible, flip, scatter-brained, baseball-crazy youth of a kind the city breeds by the thousand'. The change of girlfriend from gentle, ringleted Jobyna Ralston to lively, bobbed-haired, short-skirted Ann Christie also indicates a change of style. A brisk, action-filled movie, much of it was shot on location in New York, sometimes with hidden cameras, and its story was about the fight to save a horse-car franchise against a gang of thugs employed by railroad businessmen. It was very successful, and one commentator went so far as to advise Buster Keaton to follow Lloyd's example and make but one film a year – in which case his (Keaton's) pictures would have time to be clever!

In truth, Keaton's *Steamboat Bill, Jr.* (directed by Charles F. Reisner) is surely 'clever' enough to satisfy the most captious

Buster Keaton rescues Marion Byron (one of the most delightful of all his long-suffering heroines) in the brilliantly inventive and hilarious *Steamboat Bill, Jr.*

critic. It contains sequences such as that in which, taken to a haberdasher by his despairing father to find suitable headwear, he tries on a widely varied series of hats before a mirror, including – and hastily relinquishing – one that is familiar to all Keaton devotees; and the superbly staged cyclone which culminates in an entire house-front falling to the ground and framing him neatly in a window as it does so. Such scenes will stand up to any comparisons, which are in any case irrelevant as well as odious. Marion Byron as Keaton's girl is delightful, and must rank next to Marion Mack of *The General*, while Ernest Torrence is marvellously despairing as the rough river-boat father of an effete college-boy son. *The*

Cameraman is less widely known – the only Keaton feature I missed at the time and have never caught up with. It is the first he made under his new and ultimately disastrous contract with MGM, but it appears to have retained some of the spirit of his earlier masterpieces; he plays a struggling newsreel photographer (old type) with an unfortunate habit of forgetting to insert film into his camera.

Two of Marion Davies' pleasant comedies made their appearance in 1928. In *The Patsy* (alternatively titled, for the ignorant, *The Politic Flapper*) she and her sister (Jane Winton) are rivals for various boyfriends, and one in particular (Orville Caldwell). Eventually, not unexpectedly but against considerable odds, Marion gets him. The director, King Vidor, wisely allowed her considerable freedom in putting over some wickedly brilliant impersonations of such Hollywood notables as Pola Negri and Lillian Gish, and the result was a popular success. The plot of

Marion Davies and her father (Dell Henderson) framed in the doorway of the studio casting office when she arrives in Hollywood as a young hopeful, in King Vidor's *Show People.*

Show People (also directed by King Vidor) is the oldie about the girl who wants to become a film actress and becomes spoilt and arrogant when successful. Marion Davies gives one of her most sparkling performances, including a hilarious parody of Mae Murray and her 'bee-stung lips'. John Gilbert, Chaplin, Elinor Glyn and others make brief personal appearances, and King Vidor himself steps in front of the camera as director of the 'film within a film' at the climax. Film buffs may enjoy spotting how many familiar faces they can name as the camera pans slowly round the VIPs' circular lunch-table in the MGM studio.

In a publicity shot taken during the making of *Gentlemen Prefer Blondes,* Ruth Taylor (Lorelei) and Alice White (Dorothy) try to make out what director Malcolm St Clair wants them to do.

The silent version of *Gentlemen Prefer Blondes* (directed by Malcolm St Clair) is a modest production but much truer to the spirit of the original book by Anita Loos than the overblown and flaccid updated version of 1963. It also has the advantage of an excellently well-suited cast. Ruth Taylor as Lorelei and Alice White as Dorothy transform themselves into the book's characters, whereas Jane Russell and Marilyn Monroe, encumbered with some not very memorable songs, merely 'did their own things' and were unrecognizable as the originals. Heavily flirtatious Mack Swain and ramrod-stiff Emily Fitzroy give somewhat exaggerated but acceptable portrayals of the Beekmans, Holmes Herbert is the perfect self-appointed inspector of immoral American tourists, and Ford Sterling, former leader of the Keystone Kops, is ideally coarse-grained as the Chicago button manufacturer. The span of 25 years to the musical and a further 25 to the present day may have dulled the impact of Anita Loos' two gold-diggers but, even allowing for the loss of the verbal wit of the book, Ruth Taylor and Alice White will always represent the true Lorelei and Dorothy to many who saw them at the time. Alice White, who was chosen by Anita Loos herself to play Dorothy, made no fewer than ten further films at about this time; on the other hand Ruth Taylor's career, which started so promisingly, seems to have been brief. She appeared in a few Mack Sennett comedies before *Gentlemen Prefer Blondes,* in a few features and shorts afterwards, then seems to have disappeared

Two popular silent stars, both of whom were to transfer successfully to sound: Nancy Carroll and Richard Dix in *Easy Come, Easy Go*, a light-hearted crook comedy directed by Frank Tuttle.

Clara Bow and William Austin in *Red Hair*, a typical star vehicle for the IT girl, who appears as a gold-digging manicurist.

from public view until her death in 1984 – a year after her co-star – aged 76.

The basic story of *The Wind* (directed by Victor Seastrom) is that of a young girl destroyed by the elements – the dreadful, relentless sand-laden wind of the western prairies – and by the resentful people among whom she has been forced to come to live. After marrying, in desperation, a well-meaning but rough-living rancher she is driven, during his absence, to murder a would-be rapist, attempts to bury the body in the blowing sand and wanders off into the storm, her mind gone – that is, according to the original version which followed the book written by Dorothy Scarborough. In fact, a happy ending to the film was forced on the director by 'those above': in other words, the front office. Together with a few enthusiasts who would go anywhere to see a Lillian Gish film, I saw *The Wind* soon after its release in a small provincial theatre with a piano accompaniment throughout. We were impressed and held – but not overwhelmed. Comparing this with the shattering impression made on a packed audience at the Dominion Theatre in London in 1983 when the film, in a Movietone print (music and effects) found by Kevin Brownlow and David Gill, presented by Thames Television and accompanied by a superb score from Carl Davis, almost literally brought the house down, provides a useful example of the way in which presentation can affect judgement. Even the obligatory false ending so deplored by Lillian Gish and others could not wipe out the effect of what had gone before, with its thunderous climax of the storm and the symbolic wild horse striding the sky.

Other American films (silent or with silent version) included *The Cossacks* (directed by George Hill), reuniting John Gilbert and Renée Adorée in an action-filled but not too successful adaptation of the Tolstoy story about a young man who shrinks from joining his comrades in killing Turks, but later redeems himself.

Sojin and Anna May Wong together again, joined by Myrna Loy who, as a Chinese girl, is once more to lose the man she loves (a British aristocrat played by John Miljan), in *The Crimson City*.

Our Dancing Daughters (directed by Harry Beaumont) stars Joan Crawford exemplifying the Jazz Age in company with John Mack Brown, Nils Asther, Dorothy Sebastian and Anita Page. Sue Carol does much the same in *Walking Back* (directed by Rupert Julian), in company with Ivan Lebedeff and Richard Walling.

Red Hair (directed by Clarence Badger) is another Elinor Glyn story (updated from 1905), about a gold-digging manicurist, with a famous scene in which the heroine, played by Clara Bow, runs across a garden half-naked (but discreetly hidden by convenient shrubbery) and leaps into a pool. William Austin (from *It*) and Lane Chandler appear in support, with the latter winning Clara after the pool episode.

The Crimson City (directed by Archie Mayo) is an exciting, slickly directed thriller, set mainly in China, in which a young British aristocrat is falsely accused of embezzlement and flees there to prove his innocence. The film is interesting in that (a) John Miljan has an unusual chance to act the hero and (b) Myrna Loy has the equally unusual one to play a Chinese girl, which she does very creditably even when set against Anna May Wong. Sojin is well in evidence, up to his usual villainies, as is another regular villain, Matthew Betz. Needless to say, this being the 1920s, Myrna Loy does not get John Miljan, but Leila Hyams does.

State Street Sadie (directed by Archie Mayo) stars Myrna Loy again, and with the

Conrad Veidt gives a remarkable performance in the title role of *The Man Who Laughs,* the most original of Paul Leni's sadly few American films.

same director, but in a very different role, that of a murdered policeman's daughter who poses as S.S.S., a girl no better than she should be – although we see little of how she goes about it. Her true purpose, of course, is to avenge the death of her father. In this estimable work she is joined by a young man out to avenge the murder of his brother. Both objects are ultimately achieved and all ends happily in marriage. The young man is played by Conrad Nagel, a handsome romantic star of both stage and screen whose pleasant speaking voice enabled him to overcome the sound hurdle with ease. In his spare time he was for a time President of the Academy of Motion Picture Arts and Sciences, played an important part in the formation of the Academy Awards (Oscars), and was later

and until his death in 1970 President of the Associated Actors and Artists of America.

Turn Back the Hours (directed by Howard Bretherton) brought yet another change of nationality for Myrna Loy, as the daughter of a Spanish colonel (Josef Swickard) who nurses a discharged naval lieutenant back to health and is then let down by him when she and her father need defending from bandits. However, he redeems himself in time for the fade-out. The part is played by Walter Pidgeon in one of his few silent films at the start of a long and illustrious career; he died in 1984 at the age of 87. In the current year Myrna Loy made no fewer than eight of these small-scale but by no means unentertaining movies and was, it seems, getting a little tired of them – though this never shows in her always eminently watchable (and memorable) performances. One theory put forward for her rather slow rise to stardom was that her slightly slanting eyes rendered her particularly effective for exotic roles, of which there were plenty to be filled in the Warner Bros.' studios at that time, though always of minor importance.

Fazil (directed by Howard Hawks) is a moderately spectacular melodrama set in Arabia, Venice and Paris and dealing with the familiar problem of East/West marriages. Though the melodramatics completely obliterate any serious discussion of the subject (with flighty French girl marrying Arab chieftain, becoming disillusioned and leaving him, turning jealous when he establishes a harem, etc.), the film moves fast and often excitingly, and at least has the courage of a logically 'unhappy' ending. It also affords the Swedish actress Greta Nissen a chance to look stunningly beautiful: formerly a ballet dancer, she made a number of silent films and one or two talkies, but her accent doomed her soon after the coming of sound. She made one or two pictures in Britain, including the circus film *Red Wagon* in which Raquel Torres also appeared, before disappearing from the screen.

Elegant Rod la Rocque and dainty Sue Carol form a good couple in *Captain Swagger*, a cheerful lightweight crook melodrama directed by Edward H. Griffith. The film was also released with sound effects and an inessential theme song.

Street Angel (directed by Frank Borzage) saw Janet Gaynor and Charles Farrell together again, and with their *Seventh Heaven* director, but for some reason their trials and tribulations as poor Neapolitans, though touching, seemed to lack the immediacy they had when they were poor Parisians. She is a circus performer, he is a painter who asks her to pose as a Madonna he is working on for a church. The ending slips dangerously towards the sentimentality which the former film on the whole managed to avoid. However, it must be said that Janet Gaynor's performance was linked with that of the earlier film for her Academy Award.

The Man Who Laughs, the third of Paul Leni's American films, is taken from the Victor Hugo novel about a boy whose face is distorted into a permanent horrible grin on the order of King James II because of the political activities of his father, who is himself tortured to death. The boy grows up to become a famous clown, travelling in a circus with a blind girl with whom he finds romance. Later he inherits a peerage and they are parted, but after many complicated adventures are finally reunited. The film, made in America from a French novel and directed by a German, has a little difficulty in presenting the England of the late Stuarts but is enjoyable as a semi-horror story, beautifully photographed and excellently played by Conrad Veidt. Sam de Grasse does not really resemble King James very closely, but Josephine Crowell passes fairly easily from Griffith's Catherine de Medici, through Harold Lloyd's mother-in-law, to Queen Anne.

Two Lovers (directed by Fred Niblo), with Ronald Colman and Vilma Banky, is interest-

Gary Cooper and Colleen Moore find themselves in the not unfamiliar situation of billeted airman and French farm girl falling in love: one of the quieter moments from the action-packed and highly regarded First World War drama *Lilac Time*.

ing if nostalgic as the last film together of one of the best-known of all pairs of lovers in the silent cinema. Unhappily, this costume romance of the time of William of Orange (William the Silent), from a novel by Baroness 'Scarlet Pimpernel' Orczy, never achieved the popularity of the earlier films, despite Miss Banky's brave climactic ride to Ghent.

Lilac Time (directed by George Fitzmaurice) has Colleen Moore and Gary Cooper co-starred in a First World War romantic drama which some contemporary opinions placed higher even than *Wings*. A young British airman in France falls in love with the daughter of the farmer on whom he is billeted. He is sent on a dangerous mission, crashes and is taken to a military hospital. She searches for him, finds the hospital, but is falsely informed that he has died. Sadly, she asks that a bunch of lilacs be sent to him as a memorial and wanders away. Cooper sees her from the window of his room and yells after her, but his voice is drowned by the 'sound' of passing artillery teams. Finally she turns, sees him, and rushes back to the hospital to be reunited with him in a finely directed sequence. The director delicately avoids the mawkish in this potentially embarrassing novelette, and the charming playing of both stars enables disbelief to remain suspended.

Ramona (directed by Edwin Carewe) touches on the question of race relations before they were known as such, when a half-breed girl defies the wealthy Spanish farmer who adopted her and elopes with a North American Indian chieftain – played by true-American Ohio-born Warner Baxter. The outcome is tragic: he is accused of stealing horses and killed by a settler. Dolores del Rio proves she is capable of some fine emotional acting, and the story, from the late nineteenth-century novel by Helen Hunt Jackson, is told with dignity and integrity. The film gave rise to the enormously popular song of the same title, which in turn was used to promote it.

Chicago (directed by Frank Urson) is a stimulatingly cynical look at the law, publicity stunts and general moral standards in the urban life of the period, with a splendidly brash and hard-boiled performance from ex-Sennett bathing beauty Phyllis Haver. The film was remade with Ginger Rogers in the 'forties as *Roxie Hart*. The satire in the later film may be sharper, but by no means serves to obliterate memories of Miss Haver.

The Fleet's In (directed by Malcolm St Clair) and *Ladies of the Mob* (directed by William Wellman) provided two nicely contrasting roles for Clara Bow. The first, a rip-roaring tale of sailors ashore, dance-hall girls and brawls, features the Clara we all know. The second, however, a dramatic story of a girl brought up as a crook to avenge her father's death in the electric chair and her struggle to save her lover (Richard Arlen) and herself from the inevitable consequences, gave her a chance to extend her range beyond the Jazz Age hoyden – and very capably she does so – in much the same way as Diana Dors was to do many years later in *Yield to the Night.*

Harold Teen (directed by Mervyn LeRoy) is worthy of mention because this bright comedy of high-school fun and games (based on a comic-strip character), while unlikely to be on any serious critic's list of the Ten Best, has its small part in social history as a light-hearted record of young American life and activities in, or close to, the Age of Innocence. Teen is played by the likeable Arthur Lake, later to become more widely known in another comic-strip series as Dagwood in *Blondie,* episodes from which are still televised from time to time. A lively supporting cast includes Mary Brian, Alice White, Lucien Littlefield (as Dad), Jack Duffy, a youngish man who made capital out of his loss of teeth by appearing as mumbling old men in countless silent comedies (as Grandad), and future columnist Hedda Hopper.

The British scene held more of interest this year, led by two outstanding films directed by Anthony Asquith. Although he is listed only as 'Assistant' on *Shooting Stars,* after A. V. Bramble, his influence on the film is strongly evident throughout, and it is always looked upon as an Asquith work. The story is simple and not particularly original, but the direction shows a virtuosity and subtlety which places the result high among the decade's best from any source. A film actor discovers his actress wife's infidelity with a Mack Sennett-type comedian and threatens to divorce her. Knowing that the scandal would ruin her career she plans to kill him by substituting a real bullet for a blank in a gun to be used in one of his scenes. By chance a blank is fired after all; the gun is taken to an adjoining set – with the real bullet now in place – fired at the comedian during some knockabout action, and kills him. The irony of the plot is cleverly reflected in the ironical view of studio drudgery: Sennett high jinks on a dreary grey

seashore; small-scale western villainy in the enormous, cold studio. The same irony permeates three memorable scenes: the comedian's transformation from jolly clown to sad, mean little man as he removes his make-up, his death while swinging on a chandelier during a sequence intended to rouse audiences to uproarious laughter, and the wife genuinely praying in a large church setting while it is dismantled around her. The film closes on a famous shot in which, informed by her husband (now a well-known director who does not even recognize her) that he has no work to offer, the woman slowly crosses the enormous empty wastes of the studio floor and disappears through a tiny door in the distance. The small, excellent cast includes Annette Benson, Brian Aherne, and above all Donald Calthrop, unrivalled portrayer of mean little nasties.

Asquith's second film, *Underground,* for which he received full credit as director and scriptwriter, was shot mainly on location in the London Underground and adjacent streets – providing today an interesting

A knock-about comedian (Donald Calthrop), handsome male star (Brian Aherne) and the latter's unfaithful actress wife (Annette Benson) form the eternal triangle in the aptly titled and imaginatively directed *Shooting Stars.*

historical record of the 'Tube' as it was. It deals with the love-hate relationships of a porter, a power-station electrician, a shop girl and the electrician's drab little ex-mistress. Some contemporary criticism found fault with Asquith for overloading a straightforward love-quartet story with heavy German Symbolic lighting effects, but audiences of the time enjoyed it as a skilfully told tale of ordinary working people, building up considerable tension and concluding with a highly exciting chase. Once again a small cast is admirable: Brian Aherne (soon to leave for America where a successful career and marriage to Joan Fontaine awaited him) as the porter, Cyril McLaglen (one of Victor's

Sybil Thorndike gives a performance of great dignity and compassion in *Dawn* as Nurse Edith Cavell, based on the life of the British nurse who worked in a British Red Cross Hospital in Brussels and was executed by the Germans in 1915 for helping Allied soldiers to escape to Britain.

five acting brothers) as the menacing electrician, Norah Baring (adept at the pathetic) as his ex-girl, and the strikingly attractive Elissa Landi, perhaps somewhat too aristocratic (she was born Elisabeth-Marie-Christine Kühnelt, reputed granddaughter of Elisabeth of Austria), as the shopgirl. It was her first film apart from a brief appearance in Herbert Wilcox's *London* (from a story by Thomas Burke) in 1926.

If not altogether convincing as a shop girl in *Underground*, Elissa Landi is radiantly right in *Bolibar* (directed by Walter Summers), an unusual and apparently little-remembered film which, despite some melodramatic extravagance, deserves a better fate than total oblivion. Set in the time of the Peninsular War, with the town of Bolibar in the hands of Napoleonic troops and the garrison besieged by Spanish guerillas, it deals with various attempted strategies to break the deadlock – and also with rather too many romantic interludes among the Napoleonic staff. It seems to have completely vanished, having arrived at a luckless time – with sound just around the corner – for anything at all original; but it remains in the memory as a visually beautiful film, flamboyantly acted by a cast of Hessian soldiers obviously enjoying themselves, and illuminated by Elissa Landi's beauty in 1808 period style.

Dawn marked a change in Herbert Wilcox's output from costume spectacular to quicker-moving, smaller-scale productions. It is a straightforward and mainly unbiased account of events that were still very much alive in the memories of most audiences of the time – the execution by the Germans in 1915 of Nurse Edith Cavell, a British nurse working as matron in a Brussels Red Cross hospital, for helping over 200 British, French and Belgian soldiers to escape from the invading armies. The whole film is dominated by Sybil Thorndike's nobly moving and unmannered performance: a renowned British stage actress in the grand manner (remembered in particular for her creation of *St Joan* in

Bernard Shaw's chronicle play of 1924), she appeared in a fairly modest number of films, but left her mark on each of them. *Dawn* encountered a good deal of opposition, often from people who had never seen the film and even refused to do so on the grounds that bygones should be bygones and that it would be bound to affront the former enemy by misrepresenting them. The result was, of course, much useful publicity for all concerned.

The Constant Nymph (directed by Adrian Brunel) was Basil Dean's first professional engagement with filmmaking. He both produced it and, together with Brunel, Alma Reville (Hitchcock's wife) and Margaret Kennedy (writer of the best-selling novel), wrote the script, having previously adapted and directed it for the stage. Mabel Poulton is a winsome nymph and Ivor Novello at his best as the conventionally tempestuous composer. His big moment is when (after careful coaching) he conducts a full-scale symphony orchestra at the Queen's Hall in a totally inaudible symphony. According to Basil Dean the members of the orchestra were not quite so inaudible during the interminable repetitions necessitated by Novello's errors and various technical mishaps. Though criticized for sticking too closely to the play, the film has some fine location work in the Austrian Tyrol, and the pace – unlike that of many such transfers – is never slow. Prominent in a strong cast are Frances Doble, Mary Clare and Benita Hume. Elsa Lanchester, later to become Mrs Charles Laughton, appears as a 'lady'. The film opened at the Marble Arch Pavilion and was voted by filmgoers the Best British Picture of the Year.

Tesha (directed by Victor Saville) tackles the then tricky subject of a woman – a former ballerina in the Russian Imperial Ballet – who marries a man who longs for a son to inherit his business, but whose war disabilities (presented as shellshock) make this impossible. Later she has a brief affair with a handsome stranger and discovers – by a thunderbolt of a coincidence – that he is her husband's best friend. The not unexpected happens: a child is conceived. The final solution, so obvious today, was more questionable sixty years ago, but in the event the husband happily accepts both situation and son. Adapted from a work of romantic fiction by Countess Barcynska (also known as Oliver Sandys), the film was handled, in the words of a contemporary critic, 'with commendable artistry and restraint', though he wondered whether it was worth handling at all – the answer being presumably yes, if it brings the customers to the box-office. The part of Tesha was played by Maria Corda, first wife of Sir Alexander Korda, and that of the eventually contented husband by Jameson Thomas.

Matheson Lang, primarily a stage actor, had one of his biggest successes in *The Triumph of the Scarlet Pimpernel*, directed on a spectacular scale by the American T. Hayes Hunter and known to Americans (who were presumably judged in those days to be ignorant of Baroness Orczy) as *The Scarlet Devil*. Lang gives a powerfully dominating performance, appearing as a shabby revolutionary in a disguise of which Lon Chaney himself might have been proud. The crowd-and-tumbril effects thrilled audiences as much as the very successful casting of famous comedian and revue artist Nelson Keys surprised them. According to a story current at the time, during the making of the film the publicity manager of British Dominion – makers of the picture – agreed to 'sit in' for a missing aristocrat being driven to the scaffold in the usual manner, and was pelted with refuse and vegetables by the infuriated rabble of 300 or so extras until his face was bruised and his eyes blackened; it must have taken a heroic effort for him to resist the natural instincts of his job and keep the incident out of the news.

From Germany, Fritz Lang's *The Spy* contains an amount of overt violence unusual for this director at the time. The story of a master criminal aiming to produce a state of anarchy in order to attain world power, hiding his identity under the guise of chief of a large bank, running an organization with powers to gain control of vitally important documents, and ruthlessly destroying any obstacles, human or otherwise, that stand in his way – all this has the makings of a super Hollywood gangster melodrama of the 1930s, but Lang invests the whole film with a dark atmosphere of brooding menace that almost lifts it into one of his more ambitious studies of human destiny. The various set pieces of violence – train smash, bomb outrage, the committing of hara-kiri, the massive destruction of the bank – are all made to symbolize a greater, unimaginable evil that threatens to be let loose over the world. The final, abrupt climax, when the grotesque takes over (a clown performing in a theatre puts an apparently fake gun to his own head but actually uses a real one, and kills himself), is brilliantly contrived to close the film on a note of deep unease far removed from the ending of an ordinary thriller.

One of the great performances of the silent cinema – suffering personified in the wonderful face of the French actress Falconetti, known for one film only, Carl Dreyer's unforgettable *The Passion of Joan of Arc*.

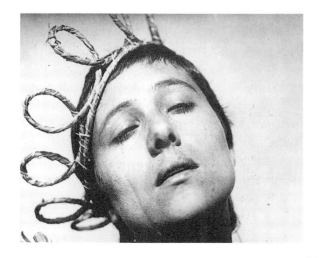

The Danish director Carl Dreyer's *The Passion of Joan of Arc* – most famous of all the films on the subject – originated in a proposal from the Société Générale des Films to the director that he should choose the story of one of three famous women on which to base a major production: Catherine de Medici, Marie Antoinette or Joan of Arc. *Joan of Arc* cost about £50,000 and opened in Copenhagen in April of 1928. All the action takes place within the precincts of a set built to represent the castle at Rouen. It was constructed as one large unit, painted pink so as to appear grey against the sky. The great proportion of the film is shot in close-ups, often huge, of the participants in the trial – judges, guards, officials, monks – none of whom wore make-up. It is probable that never before, and not often since, has the human face, in all its revealing and concealing mobility, been so relentlessly studied. For minute after minute we are shown the tragedy, pity, compassion, corruption, nobility, understanding and stupidity of those two hours (Joan's trial in fact took 1½ years, here compressed into about two hours), revealed through the expressions of those taking part. The costumes are cunningly contrived to look correct without dropping an alienating veil of 'mediaevalism' between the events depicted and our involvement in them. The Earl of Warwick, for instance, looks not unlike a member of the National Fire Service during the Second World War, yet remains entirely in period. Falconetti's Joan is one of the great performances of the silent cinema, 'inspired' in the true sense of that much abused word. Both the human weakness and the spiritual strength of the girl receive their full emphasis – neither being stressed to the detriment of the other. Consequently her two main crises – her confession of heresy and her recantation when, crouching alone in her cell, she sees a guard sweeping up the crown of reeds which is the symbol of her Passion – are both wholly convincing. The closing sequence of Joan's death, with its bustle, its clattering preparations as the soldiers prepare to meet possible trouble, its billowing smoke and grotesque, weeping crowds, its sense of business-like, solemn urgency, its long agony and final catastrophe – all these induce in the watcher an emptiness, a draining of emotion such as may be experienced at the close of a fine production of Shakespearean or Greek tragedy. It achieves, in fact, that rarity – a true catharsis.

To many who first saw it in the version so brilliantly restored in the late 1970s by Kevin Brownlow and David Gill, with the full triptych finale and orchestral accompaniment by Carl Davis, Abel Gance's *Napoléon* must with some justification have appeared to be the apotheosis of the silent film. The full story of that great labour of love, indeed the whole history, personal and technical, of the making of the film – which covers Napoléon's life from boyhood to the campaign to liberate Italy from the Austrian occupation – is fully told in Kevin Brownlow's detailed and lavishly illustrated book, *Napoléon – Abel Gance's Classic Film*, which reads as excitingly as any detective thriller. Thanks to such efforts, the film's reputation is probably safe for many years to come. On its first showing, at the Paris Opera House (with a young and unknown Charles de Gaulle in the audience) in a version lasting about 3½ hours, to music specially composed by Honegger and complete with the 'triptych' – when side curtains silently parted, enlarging the screen to forty feet, the extra width being used both as a simple panoramic picture and for aesthetic and dramatic effects with each panel showing different images – the reception was rapturous.

This was, however, by no means the case everywhere in the period covered here. In France generally the film could to some extent be accounted a qualified success, with receptions that varied from high praise to cool dismissal. As Brownlow himself reports, 'I have pored over the reviews, trying to find

A beautiful still featuring Vladimir Roudenko as the young *Napoléon* in the opening sequence of Abel Gance's great epic, in which he is seen commanding a snow fortress and fighting a snowball battle with twenty comrades against sixty – a foreshadowing of the great events to come.

a perceptive critic who expresses unqualified enthusiasm, and I was unable to find one.' In America on the whole it met with, at best, indifference. In England a special edition, known as the 'English version', was a *débâcle*. In both cases the disgracefully poor quality of presentation was at least partly responsible. The film's opening at the Tivoli in London (often, as is clear from this book, so successful in launching new films) in June 1928 is described in terms of outraged horror by Gance's secretary, who was sent over to view it. Apart from insensitive cuts, he reported, as quoted by Brownlow, 'When the time came to project the triptych scenes, a green curtain was lowered several metres in front of the ordinary screen. This made a disagreeable interruption to the film – about two minutes on June 28th. The screen was not three times the size of an ordinary screen, but was merely a panorama seen on a screen half the height so the effect of visual enlargement was lost.' Critical reaction was predictable. 'Overmuch stress,' said one, 'is laid on the power of the hypnotic eye. Mobs, troops, generals, revolutionary leaders and ladies of easy virtue – one and all wilted beneath the fixed, but expressionless, gaze of Napoleon, whose general appearance and make-up suggested nothing so much as a depressed water-spaniel. Continuity is conspicuous by its total absence . . . restless and meaningless devices were employed throughout the film . . . the chief impression I retain is a vast,

whirling phantasmagoria of the Convention mob, engulfed by waves, tri-colour sails, pet eagles, more waves, Napoleon's face, Josephine's face . . . and a final seething ocean in full spate.' After a good deal more in the same vein, he rather oddly concludes: 'It made one wish that technique had never been invented, and that, for once in a way, it might be found possible to direct a straight-forward story in a straightforward manner.' The British trade paper, *Bioscope,* also had reservations: '. . . cannot be graded as convincing either in historical accuracy or as a study of character . . . love affairs entirely lacking in impact . . . far too much use of camera trickery.' The writer however allowed 'much fine imagination and many impressive scenes' and considered that 'drastic cutting might result in greatly enhanced interest'.

Few cinemas in any case would have been able to screen the triptych, perhaps the crowning glory of the film, and it might be truly said that no one had ever really seen Abel Gance's masterpiece until that overwhelming and unforgettable presentation (preserved in a fine photograph in Brownlow's book) at the Empire Theatre, Leicester Square, London, on 30 November 1980.

Two examples of the triptych, used with shattering effect when the screen opens out to three times its width at the climax of *Napoléon.*

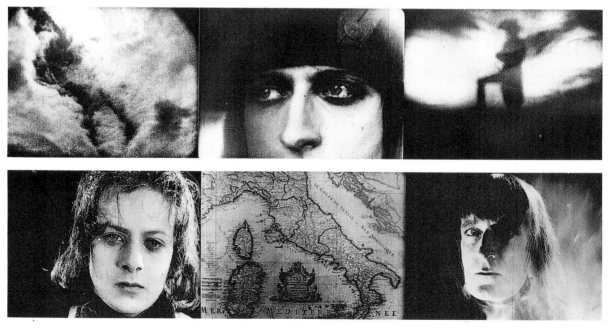

1928

The World at Large

Herbert Hoover elected President of the USA

Age of women's suffrage in Britain reduced from 30 to 21

First Five Year Plan inaugurated in the USSR

Kellogg-Briand Pact signed, outlawing war

Italy signs twenty-year treaty of friendship with Ethiopia

Graf Zeppelin flies from Germany to New Jersey in 4 days 15½ hours

Amelia Earheart becomes first woman to fly the Atlantic (in 1932 she became the first woman to fly it solo)

Mary Nutter, last of the 'Lancashire witches', dies

Deaths of Thomas Hardy and Mauritz Stiller

Cinema

RKO (Radio-Keith-Orpheum) founded

Associated British Cinemas circuit registered

British Instructional Films opens new studios at Welwyn, Herts.

Gaumont Studios at Lime Grove, Shepherd's Bush, London, becomes home of Gainsborough Pictures

Art deco style appears in film design, e.g. Cedric Gibbons' work in *Our Dancing Daughters*

Regal, Marble Arch, London (later Odeon) opens with Al Jolson tear-jerker *The Singing Fool*

Carlton, Haymarket, originally a 'live' theatre, turns to films with *Wings*

Empire Cinema, Leicester Square, opens with *Trelawney of the Wells*

MGM lion roars audibly

Mary Pickford finally, with full publicity, has her curls cut off

Wampas Baby Stars: Lina Basquette, Sue Carol, June Collyer, Alice Day, Dorothy Gulliver, Molly O'Day, Flora Bramley, Ann Christy, Sally Eilers, Audrey Ferris, Gwen Lee, Ruth Taylor, Lupe Velez

Births: Laurence Harvey, Grace Kelly, Stanley Kubrick, Roddy MacDowell, Roger Moore, Jeanne Moreau, Alan Pakula, Tony Richardson

Theatre

Eugene O'Neill, *Strange Interlude*

Philip Barry, *Holiday*

Hecht and MacArthur, *The Front Page*

Sean O'Casey, *The Silver Tassie*

John van Druten, *Young Woodley*

Sigmund Romberg, *The Student Prince*

Franz Lehar, *Frederika*

Kurt Weill, *The Threepenny Opera*

Fiction

Aldous Huxley, *Point Counter Point*

D. H. Lawrence, *Lady Chatterley's Lover*

Evelyn Waugh, *Decline and Fall*

Francis Brett Young, *My Brother Jonathan*

Somerset Maugham, *Ashendon*

Christopher Isherwood, *All the Conspirators*

Michael Arlen, *Lily Christine*

Radclyffe Hall, *The Well of Loneliness*

Music

Alban Berg, *Lulu* (opera)

Maurice Ravel, *Boléro*

Honegger, *Rugby* (tone poem)

Stravinsky, *Apollon Musagète* (ballet)

Gershwin, *An American in Paris*

Popular Music

'Am I Blue?'

'Crazy Rhythm'

'Makin' Whoopee'

'You're the Cream in my Coffee'

'Button Up Your Overcoat'

'Make-Believe'

Fashion Note

Dress designers start to lengthen skirts

An impressive representation of the great Bridge of San Luis Rey, the collapse of which, in the film of this title, caused the death of five people and led to the local villagers calling upon their priest to explain the apparent arbitrary callousness of God.

Opposite: two of those who were crossing the Bridge: Emily Fitzroy (right) as the ageing and lonely Marquesa, giving a deeply moving performance far removed from her more usual domineering characterizations, and Raquel Torres (left) equally affecting as her young ward.

1929

This year has often been referred to as marking the final flickers of the silent film. As regards production this is undoubtedly true, but in terms of movies available and cinemas showing them the silent era had some life in it yet. Many of the films discussed in previous pages could be seen for some time after their date of completion or release, particularly in the smaller and more remote picture houses. In addition there were numerous hybrid productions, with music and sound effects and often rather dreadful and intrusive 'talking sequences' which seemed only to achieve the worst of both worlds. Fortunately these were generally provided with alternative silent versions.

One of the most memorable films of the year, sound or silent, is *The Bridge of San Luis Rey* (directed by Charles Brabin), based on the prize-winning novel by Thornton Wilder. The bridge, built by the Incas across a ravine near Lima, is regarded as sacred by the villagers and as a symbol of their communication with God. When one day in 1714 it collapses, hurtling five people to their death, the villagers call on their priest, Father Juniper, to explain the apparently arbitrary callousness of the Almighty, and to reassure them that the collapse is not a forewarning of their own doom. After the priest has investigated their lives he is able to explain how each happened to be there and how in each case God's blessed purpose was evident. Brabin handles a potentially embarrassing subject with the utmost delicacy and restraint, and a complete absence of both sentimentality and religiosity. Henry B. Walthall (the famous 'little colonel' in Griffith's *Birth of a Nation*) is impressive and kindly in a comparatively small part, and Emily Fitzroy once again stands out as an ageing and lonely marquesa. With no big names in the cast, and – apart from the name of the author – no great drawing-power in the subject of the book, the audience in the small and not particularly comfortable old picture house where I saw it was held in complete silence, as if in a spell – foot-shufflers, title-whisperers, sweetpaper-

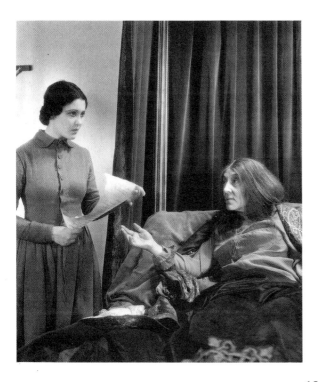

A fantastic climax to a fantastic mystery-thriller, *Seven Footprints to Satan*, with the seven illuminated steps leading to the black-hooded figure on the throne, and the invited audience anxiously awaiting developments.

cracklers and all. In its modest way it was as good an affirmation as any that the silent picture's claim to be – just occasionally – a true art form was a valid one.

For his last film, *Lady of the Pavements*, D. W. Griffith turned to a romantic drama set in the Paris of Napoleon III. A French countess, piqued because her fiancé, a German military attaché, is – not unnaturally – angry when he suspects she is unfaithful to him, declaring he would rather marry a woman of the streets, decides to provide him with the opportunity. She discovers a low-class café singer, trains her in the high arts of being a lady, and lets

her loose on him. As the girl she chooses is Lupe Velez it is not surprising that he falls for her and, after finding out the truth, forgives her and takes her away from the cabaret to which she has returned after being discovered for what she is. Jetta Goudal is commandingly beautiful as the Countess and William (Hopalong Cassidy) Boyd is an adequate attaché. The film, though by no means first-rate Griffith, was not too dismal a farewell to his great silent-screen days. Critical reception, however, was in general unfriendly and even condescending, with more attention paid to Miss Velez than to the director. For the audience, however, the film was quite enjoyable as bright and handsome entertainment, not to be taken seriously – but not much the worse for that.

The later, sound version of *The Four Feathers* is so well-known through revivals that the earlier silent one (directed by Merian

C. Cooper, Ernest B. Schoedsack and Lothar Mendes) is apt to be forgotten. It is, however, a very creditable and exciting dramatization, with Richard Arlen, Clive Brook, Theodore von Eltz and William Powell as the four friends and a pre-*King Kong* Fay Wray charming in the small part of the oddly named Miss Ethne Eustace (and, of course, if one is lucky enough to choose the silent version, no American accents for the British to worry about). Most of the film was shot in Africa and the Egyptian Sudan, hence the presence as co-directors of Cooper and Schoedsack, makers of the famous animal film *Chang* (1927), though in that case elephants and apes took the place of the herd of hippopotami that features here.

Two particularly ingenious mystery-thrillers came from European directors working in America. *Seven Footprints to Satan* (directed by Benjamin Christensen), taken from a story by Abraham Merrit, is a wild and woolly tale of a priceless gem that disappears in unusually strange circumstances during a reception at a young woman's home. In their hunt to recover it she and her fiancé become involved in increasingly fantastic adventures with one of the weirdest collections of people ever gathered together on one screen (including Satan's mistress), until they begin to wonder if they are losing their senses, as indeed do we. Finally it all turns out to be a hoax planned by the hero's uncle to prove that his mild and ineffectual nephew is not of the calibre to succeed in an expedition to the African jungle that he is unwisely contemplating: a wildly improbable climax, but so amusingly done and so completely in accord with the improbabilities that have already occurred that none of us felt let down.

Christensen, maker of the famous *Haxan*, or *Witchcraft Through the Ages*, may well have been attracted by the demonological aspects of the story and directs it all with great high spirits, having assembled a fine collection of experts in the sinister and odd, including Sheldon Lewis, William V. Mong – evil genius

of many a silent – and Sojin, as himself. Creighton Hale, well-known serial star of earlier years, appears here as the mystified hero, and the girl is played by Thelma Todd, who was to die in mysterious and never fully explained circumstances six years later.

The Last Warning, dealing with mystery and mayhem in an empty theatre, was the sadly apt title of Paul Leni's last film. It was taken from a play by Thomas F. Fallon and had a fairly cool critical reception, partly owing to the poor technical quality of the sound version; the silent one is far more effective, but it was not a time for leaving well alone. The mechanics of neither film nor play bear much looking into, being full of unexplained and potentially lethal mishaps (falling scenery, heavy sandbags crashing from the flies, sudden blackouts, even a ghost), while the story concerns an adventurous producer who decides to reopen the theatre with a play during a performance of which a man has been murdered, and starts

Left to right: John Boles, Laura la Plante, Roy D'Arcy and Margaret Livingstone are suitably puzzled by strange happenings in an empty theatre. The surprised elderly lady in the armchair is probably Carrie Daumery.

Glen Tryon and the young Canadian actress Barbara Kent in the simple and quite charming *Lonesome,* a film far better in its original silent version than in its later form when banal and unnecessary dialogue sequences were added.

rehearsals. Leni, however, employs camera tricks and lighting effects with evident and infectious enjoyment, and a strong cast includes Laura la Plante, Montagu Love,

Roy D'Arcy, Margaret Livingstone, John Boles and comedy stalwarts Mack Swain, Slim Summerville and Bert Roach.

The year's third film from a Continental director was of a very different kind. *Lonesome* (by Paul Fejos, from Hungary) follows the events of a single typical day – yet finally an important one – in the lives of two lonely young people, named simply Mary and John, who both work at humble jobs in the same factory. They meet by chance on Coney Island, are instantly attracted to each other, become separated, undergo various adventures and mishaps before giving each other up as lost, and return home despondent, to find they are neighbours. On this fragile frame Fejos constructs a touching little story which at moments seems to echo – amid the din and bustle of the day – the 'still, sad music of humanity'. It is a notable achievement and he is well served by his two young people, Barbara Kent and Glenn Tryon. The film has been compared to Vidor's *The Crowd* and even (a little ambitiously) to Murnau's *Sunrise*. Certainly there are resemblances to the former, if only superficial ones, but it stands very well on its own, if only as a convincing portrait of contemporary everyday existence. These comments, by the way, apply only to the silent version: dialogue sequences were later added, apparently of so appallingly banal a quality as to destroy totally the delicate texture so carefully created.

F. W. Murnau's *Four Devils*, regrettably, appears to have joined the legion of the 'lost'. It is a circus film, divided into two parts. In the first an old clown takes charge of four children who are being maltreated by the circus owner and brings them up himself; in the second all four are grown acrobats working together, and a not very original story is woven round their personal lives, which focus on a love affair threatened by a vamp, a near-tragedy and a happy ending. The names of directors certainly meant something to the audiences of this time, but not so much as in later years and they were not so disposed dutifully to admire any particular film because of the name on the credit titles. Despite *Four Devils* being the work of a director of such stature as Murnau, I do not recollect that we thought a great deal about it, or remembered many details, except that J. Farrell MacDonald – a familiar comedy character actor throughout the decade – was a suitably kindly clown and that Janet Gaynor, Nancy Drexel, Barry

Norton and Charles Morton looked very impressive in their acrobatic gear. The vamp is played by Mary Duncan, recently arrived from the theatre.

A definitely 'lost' film – also greatly to be regretted – is *The Case of Lena Smith*. Directed by Josef von Sternberg, it featured what I have always remembered as Esther Ralston's greatest performance as the young Hungarian working-girl who resorts to desperate attempts to keep the child fathered on her by a young officer, watching him grow up only to march off in the end to the battlefields of the First World War. She mentions the film but briefly in her autobiography, but it is interesting to read her appreciation of von Sternberg's 'patience and understanding' while directing her in her first dramatic role, in view of his reputation as a ruthless martinet. A strong supporting cast includes James Hall, Emily Fitzroy, Gustav von Seyffertitz, Lawrence Grant and Leone Lane. Perhaps one day a sufficiently undamaged print will be found that can be restored.

Emily Fitzroy domineering again, with Esther Ralston in *The Case of Lena Smith* – a lost film in which Miss Ralston gave a memorable performance.

Corinne Griffiths as a somewhat unlikely but forgivably beautiful Emma Hamilton with an equally glamorous Nelson (Victor Varconi) in *The Divine Lady*.

If beauty had been the sole criterion Corinne Griffith's name would assuredly have appeared many times in these pages, for she played in well over thirty films during the 'twenties. Truth to tell, however, few of them were memorable. Her best performance was probably in *The Garden of Eden* (directed by Lewis Milestone, 1928), but it was a dull film from a dull play. More interesting is her gallant attempt at Lady Emma Hamilton in *The Divine Lady* (directed by Frank Lloyd) and, though perhaps the unlikeliest cook's daughter ever to have come out of the kitchen, she looked so ravishing in the clothes of the period that we were ready to

accept anything. Victor Varconi is a passable if rather heavy Nelson, H. B. Warner as reliable as ever in a character well suited to him as Sir William Hamilton – and Marie Dressler makes a brief appearance while awaiting her success in *Anna Christie*. Historical fact was no more distorted than in most 'true-life' pictures of the day (and since), and the film, even apart from Miss Griffith, was generally good to look at.

Colleen Moore continued her portrayals of ebullient youth in *Synthetic Sin* (directed by William A. Seiter) as a pretty, stage-struck girl who gets involved with gangsters, and *Why Be Good?* (also directed by Seiter; it was originally entitled *That's a Bad Girl*, but the change was not much of an improvement) as a pretty – but prim – sales clerk who gets involved with a disreputable roadhouse. Alice White does much the same in *Show Girl* (directed by Alfred Santell) with sugar-daddies and nightclubs, and Joan Crawford

in *Our Modern Maidens* (directed by Jack Conway) with the Jazz Age in general. All were modest but bright and quite entertaining little movies of interest as representing a style and outlook soon to disappear, seemingly forever, as the shadows of Depression and later war and fear-ridden disillusion gathered.

The year 1929 also saw the last Buster Keaton silent, *Spite Marriage* (directed by Edward Sedgwick), and the first Harold Lloyd talkie, *Welcome, Danger* (directed by Clyde Bruckman). More than any other, it was the world of comedy that was to be changed for us by the arrival of sound. The Harold Lloyd of *Welcome, Danger* was a less likeable character than the Lloyd of the earlier silents, and the gags lost something of their spirit when accompanied by muttered grunts, gasps and 'Oh dears'. Lloyd was to make several more films that were successful and generally well received, but it is by his pre-sound masterpieces that he is most affectionately

South Sea islander Ramon Novarro cradles Dorothy Janis in his gentle arm in *The Pagan*, a minor but high-spirited and enjoyable film, with optional musical and singing sequences which revealed that Novarro had a very pleasant tenor voice.

remembered. Keaton's *Spite Marriage,* the second he made for MGM and in which he no longer had absolute artistic control, is probably the least familiar of any of his films. It has its hilarious moments, and Dorothy Sebastian is an excellent partner, but that odd, indefinable Keaton magic was fading, soon to be extinguished under the stress of professional and private worries.

The Pagan (directed by W. S. van Dyke), though a hybrid, with 'singing sequences' and Movietone musical score, was among the most enjoyable movies of the year, thanks largely to a joyous performance by Ramon Novarro as a happy-go-lucky South

Sea islander who rescues a girl from a vicious trader (Donald Crisp, well up to form), loses her and rescues her again, this time for keeps. With these gossamer threads director and cast spin a web of visual beauty and infectious high spirits that made it one of Novarro's most delightful – if modest – films. For once the partial break into sound is a pleasure, as Novarro proves that he has a very pleasant singing voice. The girl is played by Dorothy Janis, one of those actresses who flits prettily across the screen for a few pictures then

disappears. The cast was completed by Renée Adorée, making a perfect foursome.

Finally, Greta Garbo had three more silent films released during 1929 (four, if one includes *A Man's Man*, a behind-the-scenes-in-Hollywood comedy-drama in which she appears briefly as herself): *The Kiss* (directed by Jacques Feyder), with Conrad Nagel, Lew Ayres and Holmes Herbert; *The Single Standard* (directed by John S. Robertson), with Nils Asther and John Mack Brown; and *Wild Orchids* (directed by Sidney Franklin), with Nils Asther and Lewis Stone. All are recognizable and fairly disposable Garbo fare, designated 'romantic dramas'. *Wild Orchids*, set mainly in Java, is the best-looking and easiest to remember. In *The Single Standard* she is burdened with the Christian name 'Arden' – but Nils Asther

Anna May Wong suffering at the hands of King Ho-Chang in the uneven but interestingly photographed and designed *Piccadilly*, written by Arnold Bennett.

fares even worse, having to cope with being called 'Packy', which makes it just as well that the film is silent. It seems that as much Garbo as possible was being rushed on to the screen while the going was good – no one being in a position to foresee her triumph in her first sound film, *Anna Christie.*

Among the few remaining silent films to be made in Britain was *Piccadilly* (directed by E. A. Dupont, noted German director of *Variété,* or *Vaudeville*), a mystery-thriller about a nightclub proprietor with a mistress of whom he is tiring and a young Chinese girl who is promoted from work in the kitchen to replace the mistress in her dance act – as a result of which the girl is done to death. The script is written by the renowned novelist Arnold Bennett, and at the time of its release it was described by one critic (perhaps influenced by the appearance of so illustrious a name in the credit titles) as the best film to have been made by British International Pictures. Unremarkable in general, and lacking any particular connection with its topographical title, it is nevertheless interesting for its sets and camera work, and for a brief glimpse of Charles Laughton as a disgruntled diner. The dancer is played by the Polish-born actress Gilda Gray (of 'shimmy' fame), and the Chinese girl by the redoubtable Anna May Wong.

If Britain had a silent comedian who could justifiably be placed beside the American Big Four, it would undoubtedly be Walter Forde. After a childhood of stage training in tumbling, juggling and dancing, and a later spell as a music-hall pianist, he made his film début in a series of shorts in 1921, and soon became known for his hallmark, a be-ribboned straw hat, and for his character of a normal, well-meaning young man who lands himself in endless difficulties. He may have been influenced by Harold Lloyd, but his style is distinctive. In the latter years of the 1920s he appeared in several feature-length comedies: *Would You Believe It!,* which he

Most notable of British comedians – and later well-known director – Walter Forde finds wrapping up a sausage balloon a task requiring considerable ingenuity in *Would You Believe It!*

directed, is both the widest-known and the best of these, and it enjoyed a record run of 22 weeks at the Tivoli Cinema in London. Forde plays a mild young man who invents a wireless-controlled army tank, an achievement that gets him involved with foreign spies. He directs it with great liveliness and some of the sequences, such as when he is serving in a toy shop and has to wrap up a sausage-shaped balloon for a horrible young customer, are as hilarious as those from many American comedies of the period. Unfortunately they appeared on the very threshold of sound, and are not widely known today. He himself went on to a successful career as a director through the 'thirties and 'forties.

Alfred Hitchcock had a poor opinion of his last silent picture, *The Manxman* (from Hall Caine's best-selling novel), describing it to François Truffaut as 'banal'. Even so, the handling of the story of love, self-sacrifice, the return of a lover presumed dead, an illegitimate child, an attempted suicide and other melodramatic ingredients showed his increasing skill in creating and sustaining

Louise Brooks' memories of silent Hollywood were not, it seems, of the happiest, but in silent Germany, under the direction of G. W. Pabst, she certainly fulfilled herself, and thrilled us, in two strongly atmospheric, unusual and disturbing films – *Pandora's Box* and *Diary of a Lost Girl*.

suspense. The location photography in the Isle of Man is impressive, and there are numerous 'Hitchcock touches' to help things along. He had no reason to be ashamed of it.

Ivor Novello revived his apache for *The Return of the Rat* (directed by Graham Cutts), but two sequels proved too many, despite the presence this time of Mabel Poulton, and the Rat would have done better to have stayed away. Otherwise most of the British output seemed once again to rely on unadventurous adaptations of popular plays – *Young Woodley*, *White Cargo*, *When Knights Were Bold*, etc.

＊

From Germany this year came the two great Pabst/Louise Brooks collaborations. In the first and best-known, *Pandora's Box*, taken from two plays by Franz Wedekind (the source also of Alban Berg's opera *Lulu*), Louise Brooks draws a strongly erotic portrait of a sensual girl bearing in herself the seeds of her own destruction as in turn, almost unconsciously, she destroys the men with whom she associates. In the end she meets – indeed welcomes – her own fate at the hands of a totally fictional Jack the Ripper, a character who has no connection whatever with the 'real' murderer. The reception of this remarkable film was by no means universally favourable, one complaint being that the absence of dialogue destroys the essential contrast between her appearance and the words she speaks. This may well be true up to a point, but the ambivalence of her character is clearly indicated in Louise Brooks' sensitive performance and the subtlety of Pabst's direction.

In the second film, *Diary of a Lost Girl*, she plays a somewhat similar character, though the theme in this case is more like a variation on the old downfall-of-innocence plot of melodrama. A chemist's daughter is seduced by his assistant (Fritz Rasp), which leads to her incarceration in a horrifying reform school where the cruel treatment of the inmates can be seen, with hindsight, as a shadow of the evil soon to overshadow Germany. When she and a friend manage to escape, it is to a brothel.

After these two fine productions in Germany Louise Brooks played in one admired but apparently little-seen French film, *Prix de Beauté* (directed by Auguste Genina), returned to Hollywood, found it little to her liking, and led a more or less reclusive existence until some years later, when she wrote a number of fairly caustic articles about the film colony, published a brief but fascinating book of memoirs and gave a number of television interviews. She died in 1985.

1929

The World at Large

Labour government in Britain
First female British Cabinet Minister (Margaret Bondfield)
Aristide Briand becomes President of France
Heinrich Himmler appointed Reichsführer SS
Construction of Maginot Line fortifications starts
'Black Friday' on New York Stock Exchange (28 October) as prices collapse
The term 'apartheid' first used in South Africa
St Valentine's Day Massacre in Chicago
Museum of Modern Art opened in New York
Death of Lily Langtry, the 'Jersey Lily'

Cinema

British and Dominions (Herbert Wilcox) equips sound studio at Boreham Wood, Hertfordshire
John Grierson founds the Empire Marketing Board Film Unit to make documentaries
Ealing Studios, future home of Ealing comedies, opens
Kodak company introduces 16mm colour film
Warner Bros. acquires all First National assets
Academy Cinema, Oxford Street, London, opens as an 'art house'
Brixton Astoria and Hammersmith Commodore, two major 'atmospheric' cinemas, open in London
In a fire at the Glen Cinema, Paisley, Scotland, on New Year's Eve, some 70 children in an audience of 500 are killed as panic breaks out
The first Academy of Motion Picture Arts and Sciences Awards (Oscars) ceremony is held on 19 May. Winners: Best Picture, *Wings*; Best Actor, Emil Jannings (*The Last Command, The Way of All Flesh*); Best Actress, Janet Gaynor (*Seventh Heaven, Street Angel, Sunrise*); Best Director, Frank Borzage (*Seventh Heaven*)
Wampas Baby Stars: Jean Arthur, Ethlyn Clair, Doris Dawson, Helen Foster, Caryl Lincoln, Mona Rico, Betty Boyd, Sally Blane, Josephine Dunn, Doris Hill, Anita Page, Helen Twelvetrees, Loretta Young
Births: John Cassavetes, Audrey Hepburn, Jean Simmons, Peter Yates

Theatre

R. C. Sherriff, *Journey's End*
Elmer Rice, *Street Scene*
Bernard Shaw, *The Apple Cart*
Patrick Hamilton, *Rope*
Noël Coward, *Bitter Sweet*
Ralph Benatzky, *White Horse Inn*
George Gershwin, *Show Girl*
Franz Lehar, *The Land of Smiles*

Fiction

Ernest Hemingway, *A Farewell to Arms*
Sinclair Lewis, *Dodsworth*
J. B. Priestley, *The Good Companions*
Erich Maria Remarque, *All Quiet on the Western Front*
William Faulkner, *The Sound and the Fury*
Richard Aldington, *Death of a Hero*
Edna Ferber, *Cimarron*
Richard Hughes, *A High Wind in Jamaica*
Vicki Baum, *Grand Hotel*
W. R. Burnett, *Little Caesar*
Ellery Queen, *The Roman Hat Mystery*

Music

Constant Lambert, *The Rio Grande*
Darius Milhaud, Concerto for percussion and small orchestra
Roy Harris, *American Portraits for Orchestra*
Samuel Barber, Serenade for String Orchestra

Popular Songs

'Tiptoe through the Tulips'
'Singin' in the Rain'
'If I Had a Talking Picture of You'
'Stardust'
'I'm a Dreamer, Aren't We All?'
'Sunny Side Up'
'Pagan Love Song'
'You're the Cream in my Coffee'

Fashion Note

Skirts continue to lengthen
Multiple bangles become fashionable
Double-breasted jackets and waistcoats popular for men

Fade-out?

Despite the appearance in the 1930s of one or two silent masterpieces such as *Modern Times, City Lights, Tabu* and *The Silent Enemy*, it cannot be denied that the world of the silent cinema seemed to end, as the 1920s came to a close, with a whimper rather than a bang, its bright flame puffed out by the blast of sound. This was an obvious and inevitable development, and regret for the loss of its unique qualities may seem pointless. But during the few years when it shone at its brightest it brought excitement and enjoyment, a widening of horizons and experience, and pleasure (and of course profit) to very many people: I consider myself fortunate to have witnessed it in its greatest period.

Today, however carefully the settings, costumes and so on are reconstructed, a *theatrical* play from the silent period (or indeed any other period) will inevitably be adapted – subtly, even unconsciously – to the modern conception of that period. Equally inevitably the reader of a novel written in the past envisages the events described through the eyes of the present. A silent film, however, if perfectly projected, will be seen exactly as it originally was, presenting the past to the present without any compensating adjustments in taste or outlook. It therefore makes a considerably greater demand on us as a modern audience, with our so-called sophistication, increased knowledge of the world, our different moral standards, our exposure to the relentless bombardment of images and sound from radio, film, television and video. Even so, a gentle willingness to meet the silent picture half-way, to appreciate that, as L. P. Hartley puts it, 'the past is a foreign country; they do things differently there', can often bring rich rewards.

The recent remarkable revival of interest, made possible by devoted work on the recovery and restoration of the old films, proves that the magic of the silent era still retains its power: the final fade-out is yet to come.

Index